Towards Drug Policy Justice

Taking the shifting global drug policy terrain as a starting point, this collection moves beyond debates about whether to reform drug policies to a focus on delivering 'drug policy justice' – repairing the damage caused by the war on drugs as a component of reform efforts and safeguarding against future harms in legal markets.

This book brings together some of the leading international thinkers and advocates on harm reduction and drug policy to introduce key questions in contemporary drug policy. Across five themes, and with contributions from different regions and disciplines, it explores ethical, legal, empirical and historical perspectives on delivering 'drug policy justice' from supply through to use. Essays cover a wide range of issues, from the effects of COVID on drug policy to securing economic and environmental justice, and from human rights in Asian drug policy to questions of race and equity in cannabis reforms, providing diverse insights on both prominent and overlooked drug policy challenges.

Towards Drug Policy Justice is a benchmark text for scholars, students, advocates and policymakers as the book explores new models of global drug policy reform.

Damon Barrett is a senior lecturer in human rights at the School of Global Studies, University of Gothenburg, Sweden. He is Co-Director of the International Centre on Human Rights and Drug Policy, based at the Human Rights Centre, University of Essex. His work has focused on what it means to adopt a human rights-based approach to drugs, with a particular focus on the rights of the child.

Rick Lines is Professor of Criminology in the Faculty of Social Sciences at Swansea University in Wales, where he is Co-Director of Global Drug Policy Observatory. He has been called 'a key figure in the emerging field of human rights and drug policy' and is Chair of the International Centre of Human Rights and Drug Policy at the University of Essex and author of *Drug Control and Human Rights in International Law*. In 2022, he joined Public Health Wales where he leads national policy, programming and research on drug use and harm reduction.

Drugs, Crime and Society
Series Editors: Jack Spicer and Mark Monaghan

This new series will be a natural home for research on the topic of drugs and crime, bringing together original, innovative and topical books that, broadly conceived, address the role and impact of drugs and drugs policy on crime, criminality, the criminal justice system and its agents. Aiming to showcase cutting edge theory and research in the area, it will serve as a focal point around which the field can continue to develop and flourish. Welcoming both research monographs and edited volumes, the series will serve as an outlet for exceptional early career researchers, established scholars and productive collaborations between those working in the field, across the globe.

The Cannabis Social Club
Mafalda Pardal

Cannabis Criminology
Johannes Wheeldon and Jon Heidt

Disneyization of Drug Use
Understanding Atypical Intoxication in Party Zones
Tim Turner

Mexico's Drug-Related Violence
Omar Camarillo

Towards Drug Policy Justice
Harm Reduction, Human Rights and Changing Drug Policy Contexts
Edited by Damon Barrett and Rick Lines

For more information about this series, please visit: www.routledge.com/Drugs-Crime-and-Society/book-series/DCS

Towards Drug Policy Justice

Harm Reduction, Human Rights and Changing Drug Policy Contexts

Edited by Damon Barrett and Rick Lines

Routledge
Taylor & Francis Group
LONDON AND NEW YORK

First published 2024
by Routledge
4 Park Square, Milton Park, Abingdon, Oxon OX14 4RN

and by Routledge
605 Third Avenue, New York, NY 10158

Routledge is an imprint of the Taylor & Francis Group, an informa business

British Library Cataloguing-in-Publication Data
A catalogue record for this book is available from the British Library

ISBN: 978-0-367-77095-2 (hbk)
ISBN: 978-0-367-77096-9 (pbk)
ISBN: 978-1-003-16976-5 (ebk)

DOI: 10.4324/9781003169765

Typeset in Times New Roman
by Newgen Publishing UK

Dedicated to our friends, Pat O'Hare and Joanne Csete. Warriors for drug policy justice.

Contents

Illustrations

Figures

Maps

Contributors

Naomi Burke-Shyne is the Executive Director of Harm Reduction International (HRI). She is an expert with two decades of experience at the intersection of law, HIV, human rights and public health. Prior to joining HRI, Naomi worked at the Open Society Foundations on harm reduction, health and law in Eastern Africa, Eastern and Central Asia, and Asia and with the International Development Law Organization on access to justice projects with criminalised groups in Asia and the Pacific. Naomi spent the first five years of her career practising law in Australia, has a Bachelor of Laws from the University of Queensland and a Masters in International and Community Development from Deakin University.

Scott Burris is Professor of Law and Public Health and Director of the Center for Public Health Law Research at Temple University. His work focuses on how law influences public health. He is an editor of *Legal Epidemiology: Theory and Methods* (2023) and author of *The New Public Health Law: A Transdisciplinary Approach to Practice and Advocacy* (2022). Burris received the APHA Law Section Lifetime Achievement Award and the ASLME Jay Healey Health Law Teachers Award. He is a graduate of Washington University in St. Louis (A.B.) and Yale Law School (J.D.).

John Collins is Director of Academic Engagement, The Global Initiative against Transnational Organized Crime, Vienna. John was Founding Executive Director of the International Drug Policy Unit at the London School of Economics, a fellow of the LSE US Centre and a distinguished visiting fellow of the Yale Centre for the Study of Globalization. He is Editor-in-Chief of the *Journal of Illicit Economies and Development* and a board member of the International Society for the Study of Drug Policy.

Luis Felipe Cruz-Olivera is a lawyer and sociologist from Universidad Nacional de Colombia. He has studied the quality of life in coca-growing territories, and the impact of drug policies on access to social rights in coca-growing populations. He is currently a researcher in the drug policy area at Dejusticia.

Corey S. Davis is Director of the Harm Reduction Legal Project at the Network for Public Health Law. He was previously a senior attorney at the National Health

Law Program, where he helped advance access to quality health care for low-income and underserved individuals. Davis is a recipient of the International AIDS Society's Young Investigator Award and has published extensively in the lay and academic press. He is a graduate of the Indiana University of Pennsylvania (B.S.), the University of North Carolina at Chapel Hill (M.S.P.H.) and Temple University (J.D.).

Niamh Eastwood is Executive Director of Release, the UK's centre of expertise on drugs and drugs law. Niamh has co-authored a number of Release's policy papers including 'A Quite Revolution: Drug Decriminalisation across the Globe' and 'The Colour of Injustice: "Race", drugs and law enforcement in England and Wales'. She is an associate member of the Drug and Alcohol Research Centre, Middlesex University, a member of the Expert Reference Group for the London Commission on Drugs, the Research Advisory Panel for Universities UK's Drugs Taskforce and a committee member of DrugScience. She has been a technical advisor to the Global Commission on Drug Policy. Niamh is regularly asked to comment in the national media on drug policy.

Laura Garius is a Senior Lecturer in Criminology at Kingston University London. Her research focuses on reducing alcohol and drug-related harm and she received her PhD in November 2015. Laura has previously worked as a policy lead for Release – the UK's centre of expertise on drugs and drugs law – and has co-authored a number of national policy papers and policy responses evidencing the need for drug policy reform in the United Kingdom.

Imani Mason Jordan (they/them) is an interdisciplinary artist and writer. They are co-director of the Drug Policy and Racial Justice short course at Birkbeck College, University of London and the former Communications Strategist and editor of TalkingDrugs for Release, the UK's centre for expertise on drugs and drugs law, where they now serve on the Board of Trustees. Imani has published on the impacts of global drug policy on women and on decolonising drug policy, as well as having spoken at numerous national and international drug policy conferences. Alongside Camille Barton, Imani was co-producer of RE:GENERATE in 2018, a black-led arts festival that focused on the intersections of drug policy, harm reduction and racial justice.

Kojo Koram is a writer and an academic, teaching at the School of Law at Birkbeck College, University of London. Born in Accra, Ghana and raised on Merseyside, he is now based in London. He was called to the Bar of England and Wales in November 2011 and received his PhD in September 2017. In 2018, the Association for the Study of Law, Culture and the Humanities awarded his PhD the prestigious Julien Mezey Award. In addition to his academic writing, he has written for the *New Statesman*, the *Guardian*, *Dissent*, *The Nation* and *The Washington Post* and has appeared on *CNN* and *Sky News*. He is the editor of *The War on Drugs and the Global Colour Line* (2019) and author of *Uncommon Wealth: Britain and the Aftermath of Empire* (2022).

Eliza Kurcevič is Program Manager for the Eurasian Harm Reduction Association in Vilnius, Lithuania. She has extensive knowledge on drug policy, human rights, community mobilization and capacity building in the Central and Eastern Europe and Central Asia region. Currently, Eliza is working on issues related to new psychoactive substances, advocacy for the innovative harm reduction services, peer involvement in harm reduction programmes and young people who use drugs. Eliza holds a Bachelor's degree in Law and Master's degree in International Law. She is a research associate at the Global Drug Policy Observatory at Swansea University, United Kingdom.

Gloria Lai is the Regional Director: Asia for the International Drug Policy Consortium, a global network of civil society organisations advocating for drug policies that promote human rights and social justice. She has worked for the Consortium since 2011. She previously worked as a senior policy advisor in the Illicit Drugs Section, Australian Government Attorney-General's Department and the Law Enforcement Strategy Division, Australian Customs and Border Protection Service.

Ajeng Larasati is a human rights and public health specialist and works as the Human Rights Lead at Harm Reduction International (HRI). Prior to joining HRI, she worked for Lembaga Bantuan Hukum Masyarakat (LBHM) in Jakarta, Indonesia, where she spearheaded the organisations' advocacy work on human rights, HIV and drug policy. Ajeng coordinates the Lawyering on the Margins Network and sits on the Steering Committee of the HIV Justice Network. She holds an LLM degree in Economic, Social and Cultural Rights from the University of Essex and a Bachelor of Laws from the University of Indonesia.

Diederik Lohman is a health and human rights advocate who has worked as a consultant with, among others, Open Society Foundations, the Global Fund to Fight AIDS, TB and Malaria and the Office of the UN High Commissioner for Human Rights. He has also served as a senior advisor in the Public Health Program of the Open Society Foundations, director of Human Rights Watch's Health and Human Rights Division and director of Human Rights Watch's Moscow office. Lohman holds an MSPH from the London School of Hygiene and Tropical Medicine and an MA from the University of Leiden.

Kasia Malinowska-Sempruch is the Director of Drug Policy at Global Programs, within Open Society Foundations. The Drug Policy team promotes drug policies rooted in human rights, social justice and public health. She previously led the Open Society's International Harm Reduction Development program. Before joining the Open Society Foundations, she worked for the United Nations Development Program in New York and Warsaw, leading capacity building and drug and HIV policy reform in Central and Eastern Europe and the former Soviet Union. Malinowska serves as an adjunct faculty at The New School and Montclair State University and holds an MSW from the University of Pennsylvania and a DrPH from Columbia University.

Michelle Miao is an associate professor at the Faculty of Law, the Chinese University of Hong Kong. Her research expertise covers criminal justice, socio-legal studies and comparative law. She is an awardee of the American Society of Comparative Law's Hessel Yntema Prize for most outstanding scholarship by a scholar under 40. Professor Miao has published extensively in her field and has conducted research as a New York University Global Fellow, University of Oxford's Howard League Fellow and the British Academy's prestigious Postdoc Research Fellow.

Ediomo-Ubong E. Nelson is the Africa project lead for the Global Drug Policy Observatory, Swansea University, United Kingdom. He is also a research associate with the Centre for Research and Information on Substance Abuse, Nigeria. His research explores the criminal justice and public health aspects of drug control policies. He has published extensively on drug policy, street-level policing, harm reduction for people who inject drugs and the impact of drug control on essential medicine for pain management in Nigeria and Africa.

Isidore S. Obot is the Executive Director of the Centre for Research and Information on Substance Abuse, Nigeria, and Editor-in-Chief of the *African Journal of Drug and Alcohol Studies*. He worked for many years as a professor of psychology and public health and continues to consult on substance abuse issues in Africa. Professor Obot has published widely on the epidemiology of substance use and on drug and alcohol policy.

Isabel Pereira-Arana is the Senior Coordinator for drug policy at Dejusticia, where she focuses on the impact of drug policies on rural development, the right to health and women. Previously, Isabel worked professionally in international cooperation projects for development in conflict zones in Colombia and as an advisor to the national government in multilateral negotiations. She holds a political science degree from Universidad de Los Andes and Masters in Development Studies from The Graduate Institute, Geneva.

Elizabeth Platt is the Director of Research and Operations at the Center for Public Health Law Research at the Temple University Beasley School of Law. She leads several rigorous projects using policy surveillance, including the Prescription Drug Abuse Policy System (PDAPS), a source of legal policy data tracking key state drug laws, and CityHealth, an assessment of the largest US cities across different policy domains impacting people's everyday wellness. She is a graduate of Clemson University (B.A.) and Syracuse University's College of Law (J.D.) and Maxwell School of Citizenship and Public Affairs (M.A. in International Relations).

Alejandro Rodríguez-Llach is an economist whose work focuses on analysing the relationship between fiscal policy and human rights. He was a senior researcher on Tax Justice in Dejusticia and now is Head of Advocacy at Independent Commission for the Reform of International Corporate Taxation.

He holds an MA in Applied Economics with a specialisation in Public Policy from Universidad de los Andes, Bogota.

Shaun Shelly is Policy, Advocacy and Human Rights Manager for People Who Use Drugs at TB/HIV Care in Cape Town. He holds a research post at the University of Pretoria, Department of Family Medicine, where a team is implementing a community oriented primary care approach to address drug use in the City of Tshwane. Shaun is a founding member and the Chair of the South African Network of People Who Use Drugs (SANPUD) and former deputy secretary of the United Nations Vienna NGO Committee on Narcotic Drugs.

Zara Snapp has a Masters in Public Policy from the University of Harvard and a degree in Political Science from the University of Colorado at Denver. She is the Director of Instituto RIA in Mexico, advisor to Acción Técnica Social in Colombia and author of the book *Diccionario de Drogas*, along with numerous book chapters and articles.

Jorge Herrera Valderrábano holds a BA in International Relations and Social Work, is a member of Ágora México and is a regional coordinator at the United Network of Young Peacebuilders.

María Alejandra Vélez is Director of the Center for Studies on Security and Drugs (CESED) and a full professor at the Faculty of Economics, Universidad de los Andes, Bogota, Colombia. She is an economist from Universidad de los Andes and holds a PhD in Resources Economics from the University of Massachusetts, Amherst.

Luis Daniel Santiago Vidargas is a communications consultant, data analyst and writer, with a BA in Communications and a Specialty in data mining and visualisation. He has over eight years of experience in developing communications strategies for political campaigns, in-office governments and NGOs in Mexico, Guatemala, Honduras, Panama, Ecuador, Colombia and Spain.

Foreword by Ernesto Zedillo Ponce de León

The protection of human rights must have supremacy in international and national laws, simply because they are essential to the dignity, freedom and well-being of all individuals. Human rights principles – as expressed in the Universal Declaration of Human Rights – are intended to be generally recognised and embraced. Governments are legally obligated to uphold the human rights of all persons within their jurisdiction based on many treaties developed since that landmark Declaration was adopted. These principles seek to ensure that human rights abuses are not tolerated and that those responsible for such abuses are held accountable. And yet they are often violated with total impunity for the perpetrators, including in drug control.

For too long and with few exceptions, drug policies throughout the world have essentially relied on prohibition and law enforcement. This approach is totally inconsistent with our best knowledge from life sciences, sound public health research and economic analyses. From the latter's perspective, prohibition of the production and consumption of any merchandise for which some demand exists under any circumstance would lead invariably to the creation of a black market by individuals and organisations willing to violate the law. By decreeing the illegality of the demand and supply of a substance, the State, rather than assuming its responsibility to regulate the market to protect people's health, actually lays the foundations of business to be developed and managed by the worst elements in societies, those willing to violate the law and preserve and expand their market power by means of crime, violence, intimidation and corruption.

Despite the robustness of this basic proposition and of many others from other disciplines, prohibition with criminalisation is what most countries use to deal with the problem of production, distribution and consumption of narcotics. This approach corresponds with the Single Convention on Narcotic Drugs of 1961 (as amended by the 1972 Protocol), the Convention on Psychotropic Substances of 1971 and the United Nations Convention against Illicit Traffic in Narcotic Drugs and Psychotropic Substances of 1988. Together, these legal instruments along with a set of United Nations entities, constitute the UN's international drug control regime. In fact, this framework provides international legal cover to the so-called global 'war on drugs' that has been going on for over a century, although in its contemporary form for a bit longer than 50 years.

The evidence is overwhelming. The global war on drugs, based on prohibition with criminalisation, has failed, with devastating consequences for individuals and societies around the world.[1] By any pertinent indicator, none of the objectives of the international drug control regime have been achieved. It is not only that it has failed to control production and consumption of drugs but that it has also had other tragic consequences for public health and human rights. By now there should not be any doubt that the international regime on drugs control works against the protection of the universal human rights principles. The global data confirming the failure of prohibition is sound and clear. But the disaster can be better manifested by looking at the experience of individual countries. Sadly, a most paradigmatic case happens to be the one of my own country, Mexico, which has modelled its drug policies after the UN conventions and its collaboration with other countries, most significantly the United States.

Despite incurring an incredibly large economic and human cost, Mexico has failed to control the production and traffic of drugs. Rather, the problem has worsened and dramatically so since, in response to the violence fuelled by organised crime, the country's war on drugs was escalated in 2006. A few years ago, I worked with some Mexican scholars to assess the war on drugs since such escalation started. Our findings were shocking: Between 2006 and 2017, a quarter of a million homicides occurred, around 230,000 people were internally displaced and over 35,000 people were disappeared. In turn, the evidence for having controlled the drug traffic problem was nowhere to be found. By all accounts, it has gotten worse not better.[2]

What we did find was that the country's drug policies exist in violation of important rights well defined in our Constitution for the Mexican people and other residents of the country. Subsequently, the unconstitutionality of prohibition and criminalisation has been further studied, not only confirming our earlier conclusion but extending and deepening it. By virtue of a 2011 reform, the Mexican Constitution protects all human rights included in it, as well as those contained in treaties ratified by Mexico. Therefore, the human rights included in ratified treaties now enjoy constitutional status. Additionally, the Mexican Supreme Court interpreted the new constitutional provisions in a series of rulings issued between 2011 and 2015. In those rulings, the Court emphasised that only treaties containing human rights norms enjoy constitutional status. Consequently, there should be no doubt that human rights do have constitutional supremacy in the Mexican legal system.

With this principle in mind, the analysis of the laws that mandate prohibition and its enforcement delivers solid arguments to conclude that Mexico's drug policies violate the rights to health, development of personality and to equality, as well as the rights to life, personal integrity, personal freedom and security, due process, professional freedom, a healthy environment, as well as the rights of indigenous communities. Furthermore, those policies also collide with the constitutional provisions (called non-rights violations) on market integrity and State management of the economy, federalism and the principle of legality and other standards associated to the preservation of the rule of law.[3]

In short, Mexico's prohibitionist drug policy violates constitutional rights, prevents individuals from pursuing legitimate life plans, permanently creates inequality and generates severe and massive damage to the life and health of individuals. Prohibition goes against the health of the Mexican people and disrupts the operation of the Mexican State, and clearly is compromising the most structural aspects of democracy and the rule of law in Mexico. The legal scholars submitting this opinion, which I fully share, hold that the country's drug policy is a 'systemic constitutional underminer'.[4] This legal perspective arrives at the same conclusion proposed by the Global Commission on Drug Policy,[5] that governments should deal with the drug problem by decriminalising consumption and regulating the supply of drugs with legal and institutional frameworks that abide by the universal principles of human rights and actively pursue ambitious public health objectives.

This reasonable proposition is also supported by a proper interpretation of international law. Where there is a clash between international drug control laws and human rights, international human rights law should prevail. One of the fundamental purposes of the UN is the promotion and protection of human rights. This is not so for drug prohibition. To conform to this conception, and in light of the systemic threat to human rights it poses, it follows that the current international regime on drug control should be reformed to protect the human rights and health of all individuals. As an intermediate step, the international drug conventions that now justify prohibition should be rejected, preferably multilaterally but, if not, then unilaterally by countries themselves. This is the right way to resolve the existing and unacceptable tension between the drugs control regime and the pursuit of universal human rights.

Removing barriers to reform and the realisation of human rights must go hand in hand with thinking about policy alternatives, something that it is done lucidly in the essays in this collection. They represent the kinds of analyses and discussions we need in this challenging drug policy landscape. These discussions are much needed to keep proving the failure of the war on drugs, persuading the public of the urgency to change course and changing the legal and institutional framework to deal with the demand and supply of drugs without relying on prohibition and criminalisation. All of this can be accomplished if the protection of the human rights, health and safety of the people becomes the focus of public policy.

Ernesto Zedillo Ponce de León
Yale University, Former President of Mexico

Notes

1 See Global Commission on Drug Policy, 'Taking Control: Pathways to Drug Policies that Work' (Global Commission on Drug Policy, 2014).; Global Commission on Drug Policy, 'Time to End Prohibition' (Global Commission on Drug Policy, 2021).

2 Ernesto Zedillo, Catalina Pérez-Correa, Alejandro Madrazo & Fernanda Alonso, 'Drug Policy in Mexico: The Cause of a National Tragedy—A Radical but Indispensable Proposal to Fix It' (2019) 41 *University of Pennsylvania Journal of International Law* 107.

3 Ibid.
4 Francisca Pou Giménez and Catalina Pérez Correa, 'Prohibitionist Drug Policy in Mexico: A Systemic Constitutional Underminer' (2021) 31 *Washington International Law Journal* 58.
5 See Global Commission on Drug Policy (n 1).

Foreword by the Series Editors

The idea for this book series emerged in 2019. Our aim, in creating this series, is to bring together original, innovative and topical books from scholars of all career stages. The series aims to be methodologically diverse, theoretically sophisticated, and international in its outlook. With drug policy reform gathering traction, yet many drug harms intensifying, now more than ever such learning is required.

The range of books published in the series so far attests to this ambition. Mafalda Pardal's edited collection on Cannabis Social Clubs provided important insight into the form and function of these intriguing drug spaces as they exist across various countries. Tim Turner put forward a theoretically sophisticated thesis of the 'Disneyisation of Drug Use', grounded in fieldwork conducted among Ibiza revellers. Returning to perhaps the most popular illicit drug, Wheeldon and Heidt's put forward an ambitious sweep of the current cannabis landscape, proposing the sub-discipline of 'Cannabis Criminology' as a way of capturing the significance of the remarkable policy reforms undertaken internationally in this area, while not losing sight of the important lessons that can be learnt from the significant body of work published on this area over the last few decades. Finally, Omar Camarillo's recent book adds further diversity, with its critical analysis of the violence stemming from the drug trade in Mexico.

If all the books in the series so far reflect the shifting, messy and often unstable nature of contemporary drug policy, it is this terrain that Barrett and Lines attempt to tackle head on in this next addition. The twin pillars of human rights and harm reduction act as guiding principles throughout the text, helping to orient the variety of contributions provided in this edited collection. Readers with an interest in drug policy will welcome the range of areas covered in the chapters, which cover a significant number of vital topics through various disciplinary lenses. This includes environmental issues, the continued role of racialisation in drug control, drug policy reform in Asia and what a post-drug war world could and should look like. These are all areas that people interested in drug policy must not just be aware of, but be able to have critical, informed discussions on. It is one of this book's achievements that it provides the necessary resources required for these discussions.

Perhaps above all, the value of this wide-ranging eclectic collection is its rigorous dedication to 'drug policy justice'. Whether it be from the chapters based on empirical data, those that propose a theoretical argument, the contributions focused on particular policy dimensions or the chapters that stress the importance of not ignoring the lessons of the past, all demonstrate a fundamental commitment to ensuring that what happens next in the long running saga of drug policy places has justice at its heart. As the reform movement continues to gather pace, advocates, opponents, and decision makers will need to keep all of this in mind if the harms of the past are to be suitably repaired and this moment of change successfully utilised for the future.

Towards Drug Policy Justice provides a welcome addition to the Drugs, Crime and Society series and an important contribution to the drug policy literature more broadly. A timely and essential read, it challenges us to think differently about high-profile drug policy issues and give more attention to those that we may overlook.

Jack Spicer – University of Bath, UK
Mark Monaghan – Loughborough University, UK

Acknowledgements

Putting together an edited collection such as this is, by definition, a team effort, and one into which many people make contributions to bring it to publication. In that spirit, there are many people we'd like to thank who supported us in the preparation of this book.

First and foremost, we'd like to thank all the authors who contributed chapters. Some are people we've known and worked alongside for years. Others are new relationships we have made through the process of doing the book. We are grateful to all of them for taking the time and energy to share their research and ideas for this book, as it would not exist without them.

We would like to thank Ernesto Zedillo *Ponce de León* for agreeing to contribute the Foreword, as well as for his leadership on international drug policy reform.

We'd like to thank Swansea University, who granted Rick study leave in 2022 that was crucial to finishing the manuscript.

We'd like to thank Routledge for their enthusiasm when we proposed the book idea, and Lydia De Cruz, Medha Malaviya and Sujeesh Krishna who helped support us through the process.

We'd like to thank our friend and colleague, Joanne Csete, whose speech at the Harm Reduction International Conference in 2011 inspired the title of the book. Joanne's work and clarity of thought have always been an inspiration to us, and her early support for our efforts to engage human rights law as a tool to progress harm reduction and drug policy reform (at a time when many were sceptical) convinced us we were not wasting our time.

Introduction

Towards Drug Policy Justice

Damon Barrett and Rick Lines

In March 2009, the two of us were walking through the 'Rotunda' at the UN headquarters in Vienna. This is the home of the UN Commission on Narcotic Drugs and the other institutions of global drug control. It was a time when the words 'harm reduction' were nervously whispered by diplomats and human rights issues were regularly vetoed from Commission resolutions. The Rotunda is where governments hold their public exhibitions, providing free samples of products from 'alternative development' projects, handing out printed copies of their drug strategies or presenting some new treatment initiative.

As we walked through, we both paused at the same exhibition, struck by the image of a man, hands shackled behind his back, surrounded by uniformed police, with a bag over his head. It was an image we both instantly associated with the infamous images from Abu Ghraib prison: a prisoner, wired up, standing on a box, with a bag over his head. However, rather than an anti-torture exhibition, this was promotion for a cross-border enforcement co-operation project along the border of China, and proudly bore the logo of the United Nations Office on Drugs and Crime, the project's sponsor.[1]

Two years earlier, we had, with other colleagues, established the first human rights programme within an international harm reduction NGO and set about the challenge of using international human rights law and mechanisms as tools to promote harm reduction and the rights of people who use drugs. As part of that programme, we set up the first project monitoring the death penalty for drug offences worldwide, a project that continues producing important work to this day.[2] So images of a suspected drug trafficker being extradited from Laos to China were particularly salient to us, and we found out later after some digging that by the time we were viewing the image the man in the photo was already dead, having been executed on 26 June the previous year as part of the Chinese government's commemoration of the International Day against Drug Abuse and Illicit Trafficking.[3] The day – known these days as 'World Drug Day' – falls on the same date each year as the International Day in Support of Victims of Torture, and both are commemorated within the UN system.

The date of the execution, 26 June 2008, came just three months after the first ever human rights resolution at the Commission on Narcotic Drugs had been

DOI: 10.4324/9781003169765-1

adopted, a process in which we were both involved. That resolution could only be agreed by Member States after any mention of the death penalty was specifically removed from the draft text during informal meetings between delegations, along with removing any reference to indigenous rights or even specific aspects of the UN human rights system. Mention of human rights within the UN drug control system was so controversial at the time that it was only possible to agree the most stripped-down version of the resolution during the year in which the rest of the UN system was celebrating the 60th anniversary of the adoption of the 1948 Universal Declaration of Human Rights. Such was the disconnect between drug policy and human rights within UN institutions at that time.

Since then, human rights have become more and more prominent in drug policy debates, with the death penalty being by far the apex issue, seen as a prime example of the excesses of punitive prohibition. Indeed, the drug policy environment is in some ways unrecognisable from what it was only two decades ago. There is now a wide recognition that the international system of drug control is not fit for purpose. Decriminalisation at the demand side and cannabis legalisation (both medicinal and recreational) have come to prominence. Harm reduction is mainstream to the extent that previously antagonistic countries, such as Sweden, have opened up to harm reduction services. Safe consumption sites (or overdose prevention centres) have proliferated. More and more UN bodies are engaging in international drug policy debates, bringing much needed attention not only to health issues but also to development, indigenous rights, prisons and detention, racism, gender and other key issues.[4] *International Guidelines on Human Rights and Drug Policy* have been drafted and supported by a range of UN agencies and recognised by the UN Human Rights Council.[5]

These developments are remarkable, but for many people little has changed. In too many places, we see the ongoing tragedy of preventable overdose deaths, poor and even reduced funding for basic services, overcrowded prisons and the same punitive and violent responses at the production and supply side. At the time of writing in May 2023, despite all that progress on raising human rights issues, Singapore has just executed a man for a minor, inchoate drug offence, in the face of widespread appeals for mercy.[6] There has been change, and no change at all.

Observers of drug policy understand that the same issues and controversies have been recycled over the decades. These issues will continue to recur, but questions of human rights and solidarity have opened spaces for perspectives that are either relatively new to drug policy (even if they are long standing in wider social movements) or have struggled for a place in drug policy reform discussions for a very long time, crowded out by public health or other paradigms. These perspectives are especially timely in a context in which there are real reform processes under way, as well as realistic possibilities for change on the horizon. In this evolving discourse, prohibitionist drug policies appear ever more rigid and brittle in response to ethical and empirical challenges. Harm reduction and human rights, in contrast, are dynamic and fluid, more open and responsive to the new questions that arise. What does racial justice mean in the context of drug policy reform? What role is there for harm reduction if prohibition ends? How do we protect the rural poor from the reach of big capital in new cannabis markets?

This book hopes to contribute to that dynamism as the drug policy landscape shifts, including where it exposes blind spots in human rights or harm reduction advocacy, draws our attention to long overlooked injustices, questions prevailing theories or practices or warns us about potential future risks. The title is inspired by our friend and colleague Joanne Csete's keynote address at the opening of the Harm Reduction International Conference in Beirut in 2011. In that speech, Csete challenged conventional thinking in drug policy advocacy, arguing that we needed to stop talking in the narrow language of regulatory reform and instead focus on processes of delivering 'drug policy justice'. She emphasised that drug laws do not exist in isolation from other systems of discrimination, coercion and control. On the contrary, they may be instrumental in maintaining them.

The concept of 'drug policy justice' suggests a move from a focus on policy reform in isolation and instead to the 'intersection of the war on drugs with poverty and other forms of marginalisation', in which drug policies are not merely a technical regulatory problem but 'instruments of poverty, racism and the subordination of women'.[7] Drug policy justice understands that drug law reform alone is not sufficient unless it addresses the past injustices of prohibition that endure to the present day. It ensures that the risk of future harms are minimised as corporate interests seek to dominate newly legalised drug environments. The possible negative consequences of any reforms, after all, are also a question of accountability, and ultimately, justice. It also acknowledges that drug policy reform alone is not sufficient to redress the broader social, economic and racial injustices that punitive drugs laws have for so long been a useful tool to enforce.

This book is a contribution to the development of these ideas. It consists of 13 chapters across five themes, addressing key aspects of the changing landscape for drug policy.

Part I: The Evolving Drug Policy Space addresses important questions of global drug policy reform, including growing questions of social justice, advocacy post-COVID and regional contexts. Garius, Mason Jordan and Eastwood highlight the increasing social justice consciousness within which reform discussions are now taking place, challenging siloed approaches to drugs that neglect historical injustices and current patterns of contemporary oppression. Malinowska-Sempruch and Lohman take stock of challenges and opportunities presented by external shocks, in this case the COVID-19 pandemic. 'By upending normality' the authors say, 'COVID-19 has shone a new light on society, allowing us to see it from a different perspective, evaluate whether policies, systems and institutions do what they should, and recreate a better world'. Miao and Lai, meanwhile, look to regional space, and the need for contextually nuanced reform work that avoids stereotypes and generalisations, including that human rights do not fit in an Asian context.

Part II: Tracking Progress looks to lessons learned from other commodities and existing drug policy reforms, as well as methods through which responsibility can be taken for tracking developments from legislative change. Various countries have now moved forward with cannabis reforms, most notably Canada as the first G8 country to do so at national level, as well as multiple US states. Snapp, Valderrábano and Santiago Vidargas reflect on lessons from cannabis reforms to date, with a focus on the Americas, and social justice and human rights questions. Nelson and Obot continue with an analysis of lessons for currently illicit drugs from alcohol control policy in Africa, in particular the need to place public health over profit in new cannabis markets and the vulnerability of less powerful States to corporate influence. Burris, Davis and Platt zoom out by considering a vital question for any reform efforts relying on legal change: How can we know if the law produces the desired effects, or can be linked to unintended consequences? These methodological questions, after all, were not asked at the birth of prohibitionist frameworks. But responsible reform efforts must include them now. The authors present 'legal epidemiology' as an empirical approach to law's effects.

In Part III: Harm Reduction in the Changing Landscape attention is turned to a key paradigm that has posed some of the most searching empirical and theoretical challenges to prohibition. Burke-Shyne and Larasati reflect on the role of harm reduction within post-prohibition scenarios. Is the raison d'être of harm reduction lost in post-prohibition frameworks, or does it find new, more flexible spaces in which to function? Do new forms of potential harm arise through ending prohibition? Kurcevič turns her attention both to online and geographical space through the use of online forums to reduce harm in the 'real world' context of some of the strictest drugs regimes in the world – countries with little likelihood of the kinds of reforms seen elsewhere, especially with regard to the types of drugs that are of the most importance for harm reduction in the region. Shelly challenges the construction of people who use drugs in drug policy reform. The author takes aim at a long-standing harm reduction trope, that of the 'patient' versus the 'criminal'. For Shelly, harm reduction and human rights are emancipatory projects, which are not well served either by criminal justice frameworks or medical pathologising of people who use drugs.

Part IV: Emerging Rights Issues at the Supply Side consists of two chapters focused on Colombia. While supply-side human rights issues have not been exactly invisible in drug policy reform, they have been overshadowed by dominant demand-side and harm reduction discussions. Reforms for growers of illicit crops have been far slower, within an international legal framework in which flexibilities at this end of the drug policy spectrum are far more limited. Production side issues raise distinct human rights concerns, closely linked to development and global equity. Rodríguez, Pereira and Cruz critically analyse the key issue of economic justice for rural peasants in relation to cannabis reforms, for whom a corporate model of reform may make little difference to the harms they have experienced. Vélez, meanwhile, presents an empirical assessment of coca production and deforestation in one of the most biodiverse regions of the world, speaking to environmental justice as a long overlooked and now unavoidable drug policy issue.

Part V: Reckoning with the Past takes two very different perspectives on what we can learn from history in terms of our current drug policy condition, and future directions for international diplomacy. Collins looks at the tensions between consensus and fragmentation in the international drug control regime over time and asks if past State adaptations to challenges to the drug control system might predict future behaviour in the light of national reforms. In a fitting final chapter to the book, Koram focuses on the United Kingdom to 'illustrate how drug policy can reflect shifting material and political interests rather than the purely moralistic or scientific language it is often couched within'. Through the lens of a country that has been central to global drug control since its inception, Koram's chapter invites readers to reflect on what lies behind where we have found ourselves, and to better pinpoint those interests that move governments forward or hold them still.

In the end, we hope this collection offers more questions than it answers and opens more conversations than it closes. For many decades, widespread 'consensus' was the bedrock of the global drug control system and the national laws that developed from it. That consensus is now broken, and the drug policy landscape is changing through both bottom-up and top-down debates and reforms. In place of the certainties of the past must come educated doubts about the future, from which more ethically and empirically informed rights-based responses can develop in pursuit of drug policy justice.

Notes

1 See Rick Lines, Damon Barrett & Patrick Gallahue, 'Complicity or Abolition: The Death Penalty and International Support for Drug Enforcement' (Harm Reduction International, 2010) 21.

2 See, for example, Giada Girelli and Ajeng Larasati, 'The Death Penalty for Drug Offence: Global Overview 2021' (Harm Reduction International, 2022).

3 'Authorities Execute at Least Six Offenders on UN Anti-Drug Day, *South China Morning Post* (27 June 2008).

4 On human rights, see Julie Hannah and Rick Lines, 'Drug Control and Human Rights: Parallel Universes, Universal Parallels' in Chris Hallam, David R Bewley-Taylor & Khalid Tinasti (eds.), *Research Handbook on International Drug Policy* (Edward Elgar, 2020).

5 *International Guidelines on Human Rights and Drug Policy* <www.humanrights-drugpolicy.org> accessed 1 May 2023.

6 'Singapore Executes Man for Trafficking Two Pounds of Cannabis' CNN (26 April 2023). The headline is misleading. Tangaraju Suppiah was hanged for conspiracy, as he had been in phone contact with those who were trafficking just over a kilo of cannabis.

7 Joanne Csete quoted in 'Drug Policy Justice "Must Be Central to Harm Reduction"', *Harm Reduction 2011 Daily Conference Update* (4 April 2011) 1.

Part I

The Evolving Drug Policy Space

1 Towards Transformative Drug Policy Reform

Laura Garius, Imani Mason Jordan and Niamh Eastwood

Introduction

Drug use is ubiquitous across society, regardless of economic status or ethnicity. The 2020 United Kingdom Home Office review carried out by Dame Carol Black shows that use of cocaine and ecstasy is higher among 'professionals' than any other group, and that cannabis use is only slightly higher in groups considered the 'least deprived' compared to more affluent sections of society.[1] In the United Kingdom, we only need to look at candidates for the leadership of the Conservative Party in 2019 to see that among the ruling elite, drug use is rife.[2] Yet, the enforcement of the drug laws and the attendant impact on an individual's circumstances, across a range of economic and social factors, disproportionately impacts on Black and ethnic minority communities and those living in deprivation.[3] The harms of drug law enforcement are not limited to those who use or supply drugs but are also felt by those communities who are over-policed and over-surveilled.

In the United Kingdom, Black people are nine times more likely to be searched by police, despite using drugs at a lower rate than White people.[4] When caught in possession of cannabis (and it is important to note that Black people are less likely to be caught in possession subsequent to a police stop),[5] Black people are 12 times more likely to be prosecuted.[6] Research has also shown that over-policing of communities occurs in the poorest parts of our towns and cities.[7] In the United States, a similar story plays out, although one that is compounded by the shame of mass incarceration and its devastating impact on communities.[8] In Brazil, Black people in the favelas are much more likely to be victims of police violence through extra-judicial killings.[9] Across the globe, we can see that the war on drugs is racialised, targeting the poor and disenfranchised. As scholars such as Dr Kojo Koram have demonstrated, the profound and multifaceted impacts of colonialism play out in and as prohibitionist rhetoric through racialised and socio-economic means.[10] Punitive drug policy is not, and has never been, about the drugs.

Drug policy reform, and working towards a post-prohibitionist society, is fundamental to achieving societal change. But how that is done matters. Though reform of the drug control framework may go some way to relieving the risks and harms created by the criminal justice system, it will not necessarily address economic, social or racial injustices for the most marginalised and vulnerable. In order to

DOI: 10.4324/9781003169765-3

work towards transformative change, we must ally ourselves with movements working in those arenas and ensure that the reforms we are demanding bring about greater possibility for a just and fair society, and do not replicate or further exacerbate the harms of prohibition.

The Oppressive Roots of Drug Control

If we look at the genesis of the modern drug law framework in the US context, and to some degree in the UK as well, it was driven by the economic threat of migrant labour and, as is the case today, the control of racialised and impoverished communities.[11] Stereotypes about racialised groups, rather than scientific evidence about substances themselves, often led to direct policy and legislative changes, as well as widespread cultural assumptions that persist, as racial discrimination, classism and other such injustices do.[12]

In the late 1800s, Chinese immigrants to the United States were blamed for low wages and scapegoated as the cause of a negative economic environment. They were also linked to opium consumption and seen as a threat to the socially constructed virtue of White women, who would be 'corrupted' by Chinese men in opium dens.[13] The US Federal Government's Chinese Exclusion Act of 1892 allowed for the arrest and deportation of Chinese immigrants considered 'opium addicts'.[14] Similarly, cocaine was used to further demonise African Americans, who purportedly suffered different effects from this drug than their White counterparts. Sensationalist reports from law enforcement, politicians and the media actively spread misinformation about African Americans, thought to use the substance to make themselves stronger, more aggressive and resilient to pain, and thus better equipped to be able to carry out crimes.[15] This led to a number of US states limiting the availability of cocaine. The non-medical use and supply of cocaine, opium and a number of other opiates became illegal under the 1914 Harrison Act.[16] In 1937, possession and supply of cannabis in the United States without the relevant registration and license were prohibited through the Marihuana Tax Act.[17] The use of cannabis was largely associated with the Hispanic community who, like the Chinese before them, were seen as an economic threat to labour, and like African Americans, they were allegedly more likely to commit crime and become violent under the influence of the drug.[18]

In the United Kingdom, as well as in the United States, similar narratives have played out. Domestic prohibition of opium was driven by press hysteria, the anti-opium movement and, to a lesser extent, the link to Chinese shop owners in the East End of London and the existence of opium dens.[19] Drug prohibition's historical beginnings, linked to racial injustice, social control and economic protectionism, persist even today, with disastrous consequences.

Drug policy does not exist in a silo. Rather it is driven by, and used to further exacerbate, the carceral-colonial architectures of contemporary State violence. As advocates for a truly liberatory post-prohibition society, we cannot address the myriad of intersectional harms that the war on drugs perpetuates if we seek to reform drug policies only as if they exist in a silo, as if they are a means to an end in and of themselves. Without sufficient attention placed on the colonial origins of drug prohibition and its relationship to contemporary carceral systems and practices, we are ill-equipped to address the harms of the war on drugs.

Drug policy reform alone does not have the ability to end the racial and social injustices suffered at the hands of the State. Thus, understanding the short and long-term impacts of the reforms we advocate is critical. For example, will police diversion schemes improve the lives of young Black kids in London as intended? Will it reduce the prevalence of stop and search and the harms that law enforcement causes to communities who for too long have been subject to high levels of State control and surveillance? If decriminalisation still requires a sanction, how can we advocate against the discriminatory application of police discretion, which will simply continue the harassment and violence meted out to racialised communities and people living in poverty, notwithstanding those who are dependent on drugs?[20] Is legalisation that recategorises the drug market from an illicit one (often providing significant income for some of the most deprived communities within our contemporary economic system) to a legal one (which creates profit for corporations at the expense of those very same communities) an acceptable goal?

Examining Contemporary Approaches to Drug Policy 'Reform'

If we aspire to sustainable, transformative change, we must resist the easy temptation of believing that *any* drug reform is a step in the right direction, because 'reform for reform's sake' risks creating further and differing harms. As other jurisdictions around the world move to liberalise drug policies, we are able to observe real-world examples of reform done well, and reforms left wanting, where the harms of prohibition are still able to prosper. As such, due diligence, strategically minded collaboration, organising and critical reflection are required by drug reform advocates.

On the question of *decriminalising* drug possession for personal use, three specific alternatives are most evident globally: depenalisation (a reduction in the use of criminal sanctions); diversion (often police-led initiatives that direct people away from criminal sanctions towards educative, therapeutic or social services); and decriminalisation *de jure* (the removal, in law, of criminal sanctions for the possession of drugs for personal use). In relation to *legislation* – speaking specifically here of cannabis – there is a rapidly growing number of jurisdictions across the world, including within Europe, that are establishing legal, retail markets for adult recreational use,[21] although it is important to note that legalisation is not necessarily happening in tandem with depenalisation, diversion or decriminalisation *de jure*.

While such reforms are poised to remove *one* tool of control, namely, criminal enforcement of the drug possession laws, true and equitable progress is dependent on *how* policy is reformed. In many countries that have implemented some form of decriminalisation, reform has been driven primarily by the financial costs of enforcing possession laws on police, court and prison resources,[22] rather than recognition of the expanse of harms caused by punitive drug policies to whole communities, or with an awareness of how the harms of prohibition are able to continue unless actively addressed.

Police-Led Reform: Is It Just a Diversion?

Drug offence diversion schemes

> usually apply to the possession of illegal drugs for personal use, or sometimes to minor supply or cultivation offences... [whereby] Police offer to divert people to an assessment, and/or targeted support such as drug education, harm reduction or treatment, as an alternative to arresting, prosecuting or formally cautioning them.[23]

Diversion schemes can occur either pre-arrest (at street level) or post-arrest, with the key aim(s) being the provision of opportunities to engage with support and services, and an avoidance of declarable criminal records. There are a growing number of police diversion schemes in England and Wales, including schemes run by police forces in Avon & Somerset, Bedfordshire, Cleveland, Devon and Cornwall, Durham, Dyfed-Powys, Hampshire, Hertfordshire, Kent, Leicestershire, North Wales, Thames Valley and the West Midlands.[24]

While there is potential for reductions in disproportionality under new diversion schemes, particularly pre-arrest schemes,[25] existing research indicates that Black young adults are *less* likely to be given diversionary routes compared to White young adults.[26] Such programmes increase officers' discretion to divert offenders to community resources,[27] with room for officer discretion presenting a major flaw in police-led schemes. Evidence from the US pre-arrest diversion scheme, the Seattle Law Enforcement Assisted Diversion (LEAD) programme, which has been replicated in communities across the United States, indicates that 'programme success relies heavily on the receptiveness of police officers and criminal justice agencies that traditionally have been resistant to progressive reforms'.[28] Given resistance to progressive reforms often documented among police, it is important to consider how officers' operational styles influence receptiveness to such reforms.[29] Where the impact of policing styles on officers' willingness to make referrals into pre-arrest diversion initiatives has been studied, it is found that 'officers with a legalistic policing style are less likely to make a referral, while officers who are more service-oriented are more likely to make a referral'.[30] In both Seattle and Albany, police officers were recorded as being reluctant to divert offenders through LEAD programmes owing to their view that this constituted an 'enabling of addiction'.[31]

If there is room for police discretion in offering diversion, history dictates that this will allow for racial disparities and the overrepresentation of people from deprived communities to continue.[32] It may also potentially result in bringing *more* people into contact with the criminal justice system (net-widening) and imposing *more* control on them (net-deepening) than if the alternative did not exist.[33] A notable example is the 280% increase in people being processed by the courts after the introduction of the cannabis expiation scheme in South Australia.[34] Net-widening is determined to be more likely 'if the primary gatekeepers [police] detect and refer more drug users than they would have if diversion programs were not provided'.[35] This is a concern in the context of referrals to diversion schemes, which are considerably *faster* to process than other disposals, with the Avon and Somerset diversion scheme evaluation revealing that a diversion referral took less than 30 minutes compared to previous disposal methods taking two to four hours.[36]

In addition to concerns around net-widening/deepening, diversion schemes are framed as offering 'a route to support without unnecessary, and often counterproductive, criminalisation'.[37] A question, however, remains around whether support is actually *required* by the majority of individuals found in possession of drugs, given that the vast majority of people who use drugs do so without experiencing problematic use (nine in ten according to United Nations estimates).[38]

Transformative reform should bring us closer to a drug policy framework that is independent of the criminal justice system. However, police-led reforms instead require new forms of collaboration with the very systems we are trying to eradicate from drug legislation.

Collaboration with the criminal justice system will not result in eradicating harms or bringing us closer to our vision of a post-prohibitionist society. Such reforms have been described as 'wholly inadequate for all' and 'immediately dangerous for some'.[39] It is an approach described by Ruth Wilson Gilmore and others as 'carceral or police humanitarianism', which seeks to 'identify and attend to the (relatively) innocent victims of too much policing and prison', rather than advocate for a more *radical* rejection of carcerality and punishment itself.[40] These approaches may also further entrench the idea that police are necessary in maintaining public safety in the context of drugs and result in more resources being allocated towards law enforcement. Instead, decriminalisation should result in defunding police and reallocation of enforcement funding into other areas, such as communities or independent bodies, rather than creating a rationale for *re*-funding police-led alternatives.

Decriminalisation

Decriminalisation is described as 'the de jure removal of criminal sanctions for the possession of drugs for personal use'.[41] In jurisdictions adopting decriminalisation *de jure* (in law), criminal sanctions can either be 'replaced by civil penalties (for example, fines for "infractions", as in the Czech Republic and some US states), by measures that compel people towards health or social support (as in Portugal), or by no sanction at all'.[42]

Decriminalisation is supported by all 31 United Nations agencies[43] and acknowledged by the World Health Organization as a 'critical enabler' of drug service access.[44] Drug decriminalisation, when done well, can improve health outcomes, reduce drug-related deaths, reduce offending and recidivism, and reduce the burden on public spending related to social costs.[45] Additionally, there is evidence that policy liberalisation is *not* associated with increases in drug consumption in countries that have reformed their laws.[46]

However, the efficacy of a decriminalisation model is dependent on a number of factors. Some research shows that some jurisdictions have 'failed woefully' in implementation, and in some cases have created much greater harms for people who use drugs.[47] Russia, which moved towards decriminalisation in the early 2000s, is one such example. The extremely low thresholds (the quantity which defines the amount possessed as being for personal use) make the system in Russia unworkable, with those caught in possession of very small quantities of drugs facing imprisonment. This, coupled with the lack of health and harm reduction services available to people who use drugs in the country, creates a particularly dire situation, with human rights abuses widespread.[48] Other countries implement unnecessary punitive systems within a civil law response, with coercive and punitive regimes founded in the civil law responses able to cause as much damage as criminalisation.[49]

In Portugal, the most studied jurisdiction adopting decriminalisation, individuals found in possession for personal use, subject to threshold amounts, do risk drug confiscation and possible administrative penalties. However, the vast majority of cases are simply suspended by the Dissuasion Commissions (the panels responsible for implementing the decriminalisation model in Portugal).[50]

The 'gold standard' for decriminalisation involves no punitive sanctions of any kind (civil or criminal).[51] The 'no punishment' model is the approach taken by Spain, the Netherlands and Uruguay.[52] It is also the approach we currently have in the United Kingdom in relation to the psychoactive substances, which fall under the Psychoactive Substances Act, 2016,[53] as opposed to those falling under the Misuse of Drugs Act, 1971.[54]

Legalisation and Regulation

Decriminalisation, when done correctly, is an effective way to end the criminalisation of people who use drugs. There has, however, been little progress to date under decriminalisation models in addressing the historic harms of prohibition, for example, expunging criminal records for those convicted of drug possession offences. Attempts to unravel the damage of criminalisation are happening in some of the cannabis reform models emerging in some US states, based on principles of social equity. This is not the case though in all North American jurisdictions, where, in some circumstances the creation of a legal cannabis market has displaced drugs policing, and the new retail industry has shut out the very people who suffered the most in the name of the drug laws.

With over a third of US states legalising cannabis for recreational use, and with our European neighbours including Malta, Germany, Luxembourg and Switzerland[55] racing to be among the first European legal cannabis jurisdictions,[56] the prospect of a legal retail cannabis market in many countries is inching closer. With cannabis as the most widely used illicit drug in the world,[57] and the drug that brings the most people into contact with the criminal justice system,[58] change is both inevitable and long overdue.

Cannabis reform is not only about ensuring that the war on cannabis is finally ended but is also a vital opportunity to 'direct the legislature and justice system to assist those previously convicted'.[59] Social equity models of cannabis reform, which embed social and racial justice in the regulatory framework, are being developed, with notable examples found in New York and Massachusetts. Such models include the introduction of social equity programmes, which concentrate on increasing participation of ethnic minority and historically disadvantaged groups in the legal cannabis market and providing opportunities for affected individuals both within and outside of the legal cannabis industry, including in some cases, opportunities that extend to the family members of those previously convicted.[60]

Ultimately, cannabis reform does not represent real progress if the harms of cannabis prohibition continue for some. As we can see in other jurisdictions, when these principles are not front and centre in the process of reform, people will continue to be punished for cannabis use. The community harms caused by cannabis-focused law enforcement will not be rectified and social and racial exclusion will continue to prosper. Even within regulated markets, opportunities still exist for punishment, especially racially disparate punishment, if they are not designed out. For example, we can see the outcomes when cannabis decriminalisation does not accompany legalisation and regulation. In Canada, people who access cannabis for personal use through the unregulated ('legacy') market – often due to reduced availability[61] or higher pricing of regulated retail cannabis[62] – continue to be at risk of severe punishment.

Though all US states with a legal cannabis market have (to date) also decriminalised personal cannabis possession,[63] we see a different, equally concerning trend of racial disparity in the policing of public cannabis consumption[64] and under-age[65] cannabis use post-legalisation. We see an absence of clear routes into industry for people living in deprivation, who may depend on the drug trade as their primary source of income.[66] In some states, we see the active *exclusion* of people with previous drug convictions from the legal cannabis industry.[67] Such restrictions are undeniably hypocritical in practice, but also exacerbate racial disparities in dispensary ownership by excluding a higher percentage of Black and other ethnic minority individuals as they have been, and continue to be, disproportionately searched, arrested, prosecuted and imprisoned for drug offences. Indeed, within established legal cannabis markets, racial diversity is lacking, particularly in ownership and executive positions.[68] These issues, among others, reserve the legal cannabis industry to the White and the wealthy, who experienced relative impunity throughout prohibition while scores of people from minority ethnic and lower-income communities have been criminalised.

There are a growing number of reports on the importance of, and guides to, embedding social equity principles and programmes into regulatory models,[69] with a recent report from Release outlining 14 key principles for equitable cannabis reform in the United Kingdom.[70]

Some key principles include:

- Decriminalisation alongside regulation by ending criminal sanctions for use or possession of cannabis, *regardless* of its origin, and including *public* use.
- Automatic release from prison where the offence is cannabis-related only and the automatic expungement of prior cannabis-related convictions with the minimum possible input from those previously convicted.
- Tax revenue to be reinvested in communities that have been over-criminalised and to support harm-reduction interventions and wider drug treatment initiatives.
- The establishment of social equity programmes designed to award a set percentage of licences to minority groups disproportionately affected by the war on drugs.
- Meaningful consultation with people from over-policed communities and those with lived experience of cannabis policing.
- Schemes in place to support the integration of people who have been criminalised for cannabis-related activities into the legal industry, and transition those currently operating in the illicit market into the licit market.
- Cooperative models (such as social clubs) for the distribution of cannabis to be incorporated into any new regulatory system, along with protections for *non-commercial* domestic cannabis cultivation.

The depth and scale of the injustice of the war on drugs should be reason enough to reform UK drug policy.[71] However, even the staunchest oppositionist to cannabis reform may be influenced by the estimated £1 billion to £3.5 billion in tax revenue that legalising cannabis is predicted to generate annually in the United Kingdom.[72] It is the present authors' contention that when the legalisation and regulation of cannabis do occur, industry interests should not be at the forefront of the approach. We must resist what will be, by design, an exploitative and extractive retail market, and instead prioritise measures that address the harm: past, present and future.

Conclusion

If we are to use the experiences of those most harmed by the war on drugs as a lens to view the havoc that has been caused, our solutions must be ones that remedy those harms, not only through drug policy reform itself but also by allying ourselves with movements committed to addressing broader structural inequalities. To do anything less is a form of exploitation in and of itself.

It is those working on the frontlines of the drug war, working with the homeless, with people who have been imprisoned, with those who have been murdered by the State or lost loved ones to violence fuelled by the war on drugs, that know deeply that it is structural inequality and structural racism at the heart of these experiences. Poverty is itself a form of trauma, and it is unsurprising that we see some of the worst effects of drug policy in the most deprived parts of the world, whether that be the high rates of drug-related deaths in the poorest parts of the United Kingdom,[73] the similar overdose deaths in the Rust Belt of the United States[74] or Duterte's war being waged in the poorest parts of Manila.[75] The intersectional nature of economic inequalities and the impacts of the drug war are key to understanding what we need to be fighting for as a movement.

A post-prohibition world must seek to untangle the impact of prohibition from the lives of those who have been so egregiously targeted by the carceral/colonial legacies of punitive drug policy: addressing housing rights, immigration rights, education rights, employment rights and all those areas of our lives where drug laws have impeded or limited opportunities. This is why we must learn from our colleagues working in the movement across the world, and learn to recognise when the expertise of those outside the drug policy reform movement is required to create sustainable change. When we are committed to allying ourselves with movements that share our values, understanding deeply the dangers of collaborating with those very same systems that we are trying to eradicate in the pursuit of short-term, short-sighted goals, we will finally be pushing for a transformative drug policy reform beneficial for all.

Notes

1 Carol Black, 'Review of Drugs – Evidence Relating to Drug Use, Supply and Effects, Including Current Trends and Future Risks' (Home Office, UK Government, 2020) 73.
2 Frances Perraudin, 'High Tories: How the Leadership Candidates' Drug Pasts Compare', *The Guardian* (9 June 2019).
3 Michael Shiner, Zoe Carre, Rebekah Delsol and Niamh Eastwood, 'The Colour of Injustice: 'Race', Drugs and Law Enforcement in England and Wales' (Release, 2018) 29.
4 Ibid, 3.
5 Her Majesty's Inspectorate of Constabulary and Fire & Rescue Services, 'PEEL: Police Legitimacy 2017: A National Overview' (2017) 29.
6 Shiner, et al (n 3) 42.
7 Shiner, et al (n 3) 29.
8 Drug Policy Alliance, 'Race and the Drug War' https://drugpolicy.org/issues/race-and-drug-war accessed 17 February 2023.
9 Amnesty International, 'You Killed My Son: Homicides by Military Police in the City of Rio de Janeiro' (Amnesty International, 2015) 7.
10 Kojo Koram, *The War on Drugs and the Global Colour Line* (Pluto Press, 2019).
11 Kenneth B Nunn, 'Race, Crime and the Pool of Surplus Criminality: Or Why the "War on Drugs" Was a "War on Blacks"'(2002) 6 *Journal of Gender, Race & Justice* 381.; Shiner, et al (n 4) 29.
12 Nunn (n 11).
13 Nunn (n 11) 412.
14 Ibid.
15 Nunn (n 11) 415.
16 Harrison Narcotics Tax Act, 1914, ch 1, 38 stat 785.
17 Marihuana Tax Act, 1937, ch 553, 50 stat 551, 2 August 1937.
18 Nunn (n 11) 417.
19 Edward White, 'Unspeakable Affections', *The Paris Review* (5 May 2017).
20 Annie Madden, Pasqual Tanguay and Judy Chang, 'Drug Decriminalisation: Progress or Political Red Herring?' (International Network of People who Use Drugs, 2021) 21.

21 Alex Stevens, Caitlin Hughes, Shann Hulme and Rebecca Cassidy, 'Depenalization, Diversion and Decriminalization: A Realist Review and Programme Theory of Alternatives to Criminalization for Simple Drug Possession' (2022) 19 *European Journal of Criminology* 29, 31.
22 Transform Drug Policy Foundation, 'Drug Diversion in the UK' https://transformdrugs.org/drug-policy/uk-drug-policy/diversion-schemes accessed 1 February 2023.
23 Ibid.
24 Ibid.
25 Katherine Beckett, 'The Uses and Abuses of Police Discretion: Toward Harm Reduction Policing' (2016) 10 *Harvard Law & Policy Review* 77.; Christine Gardiner, '"An Absolute Revolving Door": An Evaluation of Police Perception and Response to Proposition 36' (2012) 23 *Criminal Justice Policy Review* 275.
26 Burcu Borysik, 'Evidence Briefing: Racial Bias Is Pulling Black Young Adults into the Revolving Door' (Revolving Doors Agency, 2022).
27 Judy Hails and Randy Borum, 'Police Training and Specialized Approaches to Respond to People with Mental Illnesses' (2003) 49 *Crime & Delinquency* 52.; Henry J Steadman, Kristin A Stainbrook, Patricia Griffin, Jeffrey Draine, Randy Dupont and Cathy Horey 'A Specialized Crisis Response Site as a Core Element of Police-Based Diversion Programs' (2001) 52 *Psychiatric Services* 219.; Amy C Watson, Patrick W Corrigan and Victor Ottati, 'Police Officers' Attitudes toward and Decisions about Persons with Mental Illness' (2004) 55 *Psychiatric Services* 49.
28 Lauren Gant and Lonnie Schaible, 'The Impact of Policing Styles on Officers' Willingness to Make Referrals into Pre-Arrest Diversion Initiatives' (2022) 23 *Police Practice & Research* 20; Gardiner (n 25); Lonnie Schaible, Lauren Gant and Stephanie Ames, 'The Impact of Police Attitudes towards Offenders on Law-Enforcement Assisted Diversion Decisions' (2020) *Police Quarterly* 24.
29 Gardiner (n 25).; Arthur J Lurigio and Wesley G Skogan, 'Winning the Hearts and Minds of Police Officers: An Assessment of Staff Perceptions of Community Policing in Chicago' (1994) 40 *Crime and Delinquency* 315.
30 Gant and Schaible (n 28).
31 Susan E Collins, Heather S Lonczak and Seema L Clifasefi, 'LEAD Program Evaluation: Recidivism Report' (University of Washington, 2015).; Robert E Worden and Sarah J McLean, 'Discretion and Diversion in Albany's Lead Program' (2018) 29 *Criminal Justice Policy Review* 584.
32 Shiner, et al (n 3).
33 Stanley Cohen, *Visions of Social Control* (Cambridge, 1985).; Stevens, et al (n 21).
34 Robert Ali, Paul Christie, Simon Lenton, David Hawks, Adam Sutton, Wayne Hall and Steve Allsop, 'The Social Impacts of the Cannabis Expiation Notice Scheme in South Australia: Summary Report Presented to the Ministerial Council on Drug Strategy, 4 May 1998' (Department of Health and Aged Care, 1999).
35 Caitlin Hughes and Alison Ritter, *A Summary of Diversion Programs for Drug and Drug-Related Offenders in Australia* (National Drug and Alcohol Research Centre, 2008) 40.
36 Transform Drug Policy Foundation (n 22).
37 Ibid.
38 United Nations Office on Drugs and Crime, *World Drug Report 2016* (United Nations, 2016).
39 Imani Robinson, 'Towards an Abolitionist Drug Policy Reform' in Julia Buxton, Giavana Margo and Lona Burger (eds.), *The Impact of Global Drug Policy on Women: Shifting the Needle* (Emerald Publishing Limited, 2020).

40 Ruth Wilson Gilmore, 'The Problem with Innocence: Human Sacrifice Is the Central Problem That Organizes the Carceral Geographies of the Prison-Industrial Complex' in *Inquest: A Decarceral Brainstorm* (12 May 2022).
41 Stevens, et al (n 21).
42 Ibid.
43 United Nations systems Chief Executives Board for Coordination, 'Summary of Deliberations: Segment 2: Common United Nations System Position on Drug Policy' (18 January 2019) CEB/2018/2.
44 World Health Organization, 'Consolidated Guidelines on HIV Prevention, Diagnosis, Treatment and Care for Key Populations' (World Health Organisation, 2014).
45 Niamh Eastwood, Edward Fox and Ari Rosmarin, 'A Quiet Revolution: Drug Decriminalisation across the Globe' (Release, 2016); TalkingDrugs, 'Drug Decriminalisation across the World: Interactive Map, Portugal' www.talkingdrugs.org/decrim/portugal accessed 2 February 2023.
46 Alex Stevens, 'Is Policy "Liberalization" Associated with Higher Odds of Adolescent Cannabis Use? A Re-analysis of Data from 38 Countries' (2019) 66 *International Journal of Drug Policy* 94.; European Monitoring Centre for Drug and Drug Addiction, 'Cannabis Legislation in Europe: An Overview' (EMCDDA, 2017).; Eastwood, et al (n 45).
47 Eastwood, et al (n 45).
48 Mikhail Golichenko and Sandra Ka Hon Chu, 'Human Rights in Patient Care: Drug Treatment and Punishment in Russia' (2018) 39 *Public Health Review* 12.
49 Eastwood, et al (n 45).
50 TalkingDrugs (n 45).
51 Transform Drug Policy Foundation, '"Diversion", "Decriminalisation", or "Tough Consequences": What's in a Name?' (7 January 2022) https://transformdrugs.org/blog/decriminalisation-drug-offence-diversion-tough-consequences-whats-in-a-name accessed 1 February 2023.
52 Eastwood, et al (n 45).
53 Psychoactive Substances Act, 2016.
54 Misuse of Drugs Act, 1971.
55 In addition to existing quasi-legal models such as the Netherlands and Spain.
56 Transform Drug Policy Foundation, 'Cannabis Legalisation: A Global Change' (11 May 2021) https://transformdrugs.org/blog/cannabis-change-is-happening-across-the-world accessed 3 February 2023.
57 United Nations Office on Drugs and Crime, *World Drug Report: Cannabis and Hallucinogens* (United Nations, 2019).
58 United Nations Office on Drugs and Crime, *World Drug Report 2020: Executive Summary* (United Nations, New York, 2020) 21.
59 Melissa Perlman, 'Reefer Blues: Building Social Equity in the Era of Marijuana Legalization' (2020) 8 *Social Justice and Law Review* 94, 112.
60 City of Sacramento, 'Cannabis Opportunity Reinvestment and Equity (CORE) Program' www.cityofsacramento.org/Finance/Revenue/Sacramento-Marijuana-Information/Core-Program accessed 1 March 2023.
61 Matt Lundy, 'Why B.C. Cannabis Sales Have Struggled to Pick up', *The Globe and Mail* (24 September 2019).
62 Transform Drug Policy Foundation, 'Cannabis Legalisation in Canada – One Year On' (17 October 2019)

https://transformdrugs.org/blog/cannabis-legalisation-in-canada-one-year-on accessed 2 March 2023.

63 DISA Global Solutions, 'Marijuana Legality by State' https://disa.com/map-of-marijuana-legality-by-state accessed 23 February 2023.

64 Perlman (n 59).

65 Jack Reed, 'Marijuana Legalization in Colorado: Early Findings: A Report Pursuant to Senate Bill 13–283' (Colorado Department of Public Safety, 2016).

66 Reed Lindsay, 'Bolivian Coca Growers Fight Eradication', *Washington Times* (25 March 2003).

67 Allie Howell, 'Criminal Conviction Restrictions for Marijuana Licensing' (Reason Foundation, 2018).; Jenni Avins, 'In the Age of Luxury Cannabis, It's Time to Talk about Drug War Reparations', Quartz (25 January 2019) https://qz.com/1482349/weed-and-reparations/ accessed 1 March 2023.

68 Eli McVey, 'Women & Minorities in the Cannabis Industry' (Marijuana Business Daily, 2019).

69 Federal Cannabis Regulations Working Group, 'Legalize It Right: Federal Cannabis Regulation' (Drug Policy Alliance, 2021).; Shaleen Title, 'Fair and Square: How to Effectively Incorporate Social Equity into Cannabis Laws and Regulations' (6 December 2021) Ohio State University Drug Enforcement and Policy Center, 2021.; Health Poverty Action, 'Legal Regulation of Drugs Social Justice Lens' (2021).; International Drug Policy Consortium, 'Principles for the Responsible Legal Regulation of Cannabis' (2022).

70 Laura Garius and Amal Ali, 'Regulating Right, Repairing Wrongs: Exploring Equity and Social Justice Initiatives within UK Cannabis Reform' (Release, 2022).

71 UK Home Office, 'Drugs: International Comparators' (October 2014).

72 Jamie Doward, 'Legalising Cannabis 'Could Earn Treasury £3.5b n', *The Guardian* (2 June 2018).

73 UK Home Office, 'From Harm to Hope: A 10-Year Drugs Plan to Cut Crime and Save Lives' (2021) 18.

74 Adam Dean and Simeon Kimmel, 'Free Trade and Opioid Overdose Death in the United States' (2019) *SSM – Population Health* 8.

75 Amnesty International, 'Philippines: "If you are poor, you are killed": Extrajudicial Killings in the Philippines' "War on Drugs" ' (2017).

2 Drug Policy Reform and Human Rights Post-COVID-19

Kasia Malinowska-Sempruch and Diederik Lohman

Introduction

In his June 2020 Nelson Mandela lecture, UN Secretary General Antonio Guterres likened COVID-19 to an X-ray that has 'reveal[ed] fractures in the fragile skeleton of the societies we have built' and has 'exposed fallacies and falsehoods everywhere'.[1] He described a variety of systemic determinants – inequality, racism, colonial legacies, failures of social protection – that left the world deeply vulnerable to the arrival of the pandemic and all but guaranteed that it would deepen inequalities between haves and have-nots. Yet, Guterres also sounded a positive tone, arguing that by exposing these fallacies and falsehoods, the crisis created a 'generational opportunity to build back a more equal and sustainable world'.[2] To seize this opening, he called for a 'New Social Contract and a New Global Deal that create equal opportunities for all and respect the rights and freedoms of all'.[3]

While Guterres did not mention drugs or drug policy in his speech, COVID-19 did with the drug control system exactly what it did with other flawed systems and institutions: it functioned as an accelerator of its harmful impacts. Most visibly – and grotesquely – millions of people imprisoned for using or selling small amounts of drugs saw their jail time turn into a potential death sentence almost overnight as COVID-19 ripped through prisons.[4] In the United States, for example, the first male and female federal prisoners to die of COVID-19 were a 49-year-old Black man, Patrick Jones, and a pregnant 30-year-old native American woman, Andrea Circle Bear.

Patrick Jones, a 49-year-old Black man from Texas, was arrested in 2007 when police found 40 grams of cocaine at his apartment. He was sentenced to 27 years behind bars, reportedly because he lived in proximity of a college and had previous convictions for burglaries committed as a teenager living on the streets.[5] In October 2019, Jones had sought release under the First Step Act, a 2018 law intended to cut unnecessarily long federal sentences and improve conditions in federal prisons, arguing that his 'conviction and punishment was also a punishment that my child has had to endure'.[6] On 26 February 2020, more than a month after COVID-19 had started spreading in the United States, and one day after the Centers for Disease Control and Prevention warned that COVID-19 was approaching pandemic status,[7] a judge denied his request. Shortly thereafter, he contracted the virus

DOI: 10.4324/9781003169765-4

at the low-security prison in Oakdale Louisiana where he was held and 22 days later he was dead.

Andrea Circle Bear, a 30-year-old native American woman from South Dakota, was arrested for using a residence on the Cheyenne River Indian Reservation to sell drugs in April 2018.[8] During her trial, she admitted that she had sold $850 worth of methamphetamine to a buyer who turned out to be a confidential informant. In January 2020, despite being five months pregnant, she was sentenced to 26 months in prison, followed by 3 years of supervised release. By late March, while at a federal prison in Fort Worth, Texas, Circle Bear developed a fever, dry cough and other symptoms. She was transferred to a hospital and placed on a ventilator. On 1 April, her baby was born by caesarean section. She tested positive for COVID-19 a few days later. On 28 April 2020, Circle Bear passed away without ever seeing or holding her daughter, and leaving behind six children.[9]

These two tragic cases only scratch the surface. The pandemic unleashed a long list of harms. Lockdowns and other restrictions on freedom of movement, combined with enhanced policing powers, made people who use drugs even more vulnerable to arrest. Underfunded health and social services for people who use drugs were disrupted in many countries as lockdowns shuttered or limited their operations and resources were shifted to the COVID-19 response, putting clients at increased risk of HIV, hepatitis C and accidental overdose. Drug markets, destabilised by disruptions in international transportation and commerce, were flooded with more adulterated and unsafe drugs, contributing to a dramatic increase in overdose deaths in the United States.

To seize the generational opportunity, Guterres identified and realise equal opportunities for all, the lessons learned about drug policy before and during the pandemic need to finally be internalised and translated into systemic change. In this chapter, we explore what that change should look like, reviewing the ways in which COVID-19 amplified previously documented harms of drug control policies; how countries and the international community responded to these harms and their root causes; and, finally, describing policy steps that should be taken to reform drug policies post-COVID-19.

COVID-19's Impact on Drugs and Drug Control

The harms of prohibitionist drug control policies are well known. The 2016 Alternative World Drug Report, an NGO alternative to the UN Office on Drugs and Crime's *World Drug Report*, detailed how drug enforcement undermines each of the three pillars – peace and security, development and human rights – that underpin the work of the United Nations, and, causes significant health harms while purporting to protect health.[10] The report argues that drug enforcement has created huge criminal markets that enrich criminal organisations to an extent that, in many regions, their power threatens that of States; that corruption, violence, conflict and instability caused by drug enforcement in producer and transit countries undermine social and economic growth and can 'lock regions into a spiral of underdevelopment'; and that drug enforcement has led to widespread human rights violations through 'the erosion of civil liberties and fair trial standards, the demonization of individuals and groups, and the imposition of abusive and inhuman punishments'.[11] Moreover, it notes that an estimated 246 million people use drugs worldwide despite more than 50 years of prohibitionist drug policies aimed at creating a 'drug-free world'. Similarly, the *Lancet Commission on Public Health and International Drug Policy* concluded that although policies to prohibit drugs are portrayed as necessary to preserve public health and safety, they 'directly and indirectly contribute to lethal violence, disease, discrimination, forced displacement, injustice, and the undermining of people's right to health'[12] and that the harms of 'prohibition far outweigh the benefits'.[13]

The full scope of impacts of the COVID-19 pandemic in the area of drug control policy are not yet understood. Below we describe three broad areas where COVID-19 – and public health measures to respond to it – directly affected people who use drugs: increased risks of harm associated with law enforcement and the criminal justice system; the impact on the safe supply of drugs and the associated increased risk of overdose; and disruptions of health and social services for people who use drugs.

Other harmful effects have also been reported but are not discussed in detail because of a lack of detailed documentation. For example, community organisations in Colombia have pointed out that the pandemic has significantly exacerbated the harmful economic impact of forced eradication campaigns on grower communities, threatening their survival at a time when other economic activity is impossible due to quarantine measures.[14] The International Association for Hospice and Palliative Care has reported stockouts of or limitations on use of morphine, a medicine that is controlled under drug control treaties and laws, in El Salvador, Mexico, Paraguay and Peru because limited supplies of the medicine were redirected to care for COVID-19 patients.[15] In Moldova, closure of international borders led to disruptions of the supply of opioid agonist treatment medications, leaving patients without access to essential treatment.[16] In Lebanon, drug treatment programmes are scrambling to provide buprenorphine to patients after the government stopped subsidising the medicine amidst an economic crisis exacerbated by COVID-19. As buprenorphine is a controlled medicine – and thus subject to myriad regulations – securing a new supply has proven extremely difficult and the Ministry of Health has imposed a dose reduction for all substitution treatment patients, making it hard for them to maintain jobs and other normal life activities.[17]

Many countries have opportunistically used COVID-19 to crack down on civil society organisations, which may harm organisations of people who use drugs or advocate on drug policy issues.[18] The economic devastation COVID-19 has caused around the world could lead to changes in drug markets. The fact that around 100 million people were driven into extreme poverty in 2020[19] is likely to make many people susceptible to involvement in the production or trade of drugs as a survival strategy, putting them at risk of arrest and imprisonment, with all the ripple effects that has for their families. More research is needed to fully understand the diverse direct and indirect impacts of COVID-19.

- **Law Enforcement: Increased Vulnerability to Arrest or Police Harassment**

COVID-19 containment measures, whether complete lockdowns or more localised restrictions on freedom of movement, have a disproportionate effect on people who tend to spend a lot of time on the street, such as people who use drugs – or sell small quantities of them – people experiencing homelessness and sex workers. With streets deserted and police and/or military personnel granted emergency powers to enforce COVID-19-related public health mandates – including stopping people simply for being outside – these people are more visible. This makes people looking to buy or sell illicit drugs an even easier target than they normally are.

While data are limited on how this increased visibility and vulnerability to arrest or harassment played out in practice, the International Network of People who Use Drugs (INPUD) has expressed concern that 'authoritarian power is being left unchecked beyond the limits of containing COVID-19 and deployed against criminalized populations'.[20] Seventy percent of respondents to a web-based survey conducted by INPUD in June 2020 said that policing of drug users for possession and small-scale supply had increased since the pandemic started. Only 16% of respondents said that policing had decreased. Half of survey respondents also believed that emergency powers granted to police were being used to target drug users. Thirty percent said that the same is true for people experiencing homelessness.[21] One respondent to the survey wrote that people who experience homelessness 'have nowhere else to go and are often in parks and other public places' and were therefore 'constantly harassed [or] facing fines that they can't pay'.[22] Another respondent noted that 'people who use drugs are being charged twice if they leave home to buy drugs',[23] once for being outside without a legitimate reason and second for drug possession.

In June 2020, Release, a drug policy reform organisation in the United Kingdom, expressed alarm at data on drug searches carried out by the Metropolitan Police in April 2020, in the middle of a strict lockdown of the city. It noted that police had carried out 30,608 searches, 70% of which were for drugs. This represented a jump of 26% from March 2020 and the 'highest rate of the use of these powers in at least 2 years'. It also noted that Black people were searched four times as frequently as white people, and that the rate of searches of Black people had increased from 7.2 to 9.3 per 1,000 from March to April. It observed that '[d]isturbingly, the highest rate of searches are occurring in boroughs suffering the highest rate of COVID19 deaths'.[24]

- **Fair Trial Concerns for People Facing Drug Charges**

The pandemic threw justice systems worldwide into chaos in 2020 as countries struggled to safely ensure the continued administration of justice. Many countries have imposed restrictions on access to lawyers and moved court proceedings, including criminal trials, into an online regime. These major, unplanned and hastily implemented changes have had significant fair trial implications for parties to any court proceeding but are particularly consequential for people facing (serious) criminal charges.

While the impact of these changes for people facing drug charges generally is not well documented, drug policy advocates and lawyers have raised alarm bells about the consequences for people facing the death penalty on drug charges. Imposition of the death penalty for all but the 'most serious crimes' is a violation of international law, making the erosion of fair trials standards in such cases particularly problematic.[25] In Pakistan, Saudi Arabia and Sri Lanka, for example, lawyers defending clients charged with capital drug offenses have said that access restrictions are so stringent that they have not been able to discuss and develop effective defence strategies with their clients.[26] Lawyers in China have reported needing to comply with onerous COVID-19-related procedures to gain access to clients.[27] In Indonesia, lawyers are barred from in-person visits with clients but have complained that detention facilities in Indonesia often lack the capacity to facilitate video and audio conferences between attorneys and their clients. Such conversations can now often only happen on the cell phones of prison guards, subject to their willingness to agree to this and often in their presence.[28]

Virtual court hearings pose their own sets of challenges. A Harm Reduction International report found that in some countries court hearings were moved into online mode without the consent from defendants, despite a clear stipulation in human rights law that defendants have a right to be 'present at trial'; that virtual court proceedings were not accessible to the public or, conversely, did not provide adequate protection in sensitive cases.[29] Moreover, it noted that virtual hearings rely on the internet connection available in the trial's location and reported 'moments where poor internet connection disrupts the proceedings, raising questions of the ability of courts to examine witnesses and the defendant effectively'.[30]

Despite these fair trial concerns, courts imposed significantly more death sentences on defendants for drug-related offenses in 2020 than in 2019. Harm Reduction International documented 213 cases in ten countries in 2020, a 16.3% increase from 2019. Courts in both Indonesia and Singapore have sentenced people to death on drug trafficking charges in virtual court proceedings. In Indonesia alone, 77 people were sentenced to death for drug trafficking in 2020, an almost 80% increase from 2019.[31]

- **A Drug Possession Charge as a Potential Death Sentence**

Overcrowded jails and prisons were a COVID-19 powder keg. With social distancing impossible, poor hygiene and ventilation, and populations in generally poor health, places of detention presented ideal conditions for explosive outbreaks of the disease, posing serious risks to those deprived of their liberty, prison personnel, as well as surrounding communities.[32] In mid-February, a prisoner in Iran was diagnosed with COVID-19 and within weeks major prison outbreaks were reported in Iran, China and the United States.[33] By December 2021, more than 612,000 cases among prisoners had been reported in 122 countries and more than 4,300 had died in 47 countries.[34]

The criminalisation of drug use and drug possession for personal use has long been a major driver of incarceration. While reliable data on incarceration for drug possession or personal use are lacking, globally, an estimated 21.6% of incarcerated people are deprived of their liberty for drug-related offenses. In some countries, it is as many as 50% or more (Cambodia: 56%, Indonesia: 49%, Nicaragua: 68% and Sri Lanka: 52%).[35] A variety of factors contribute to these extremely high numbers, including legal provisions that criminalise simple possession and use, that deny people arrested on drug offenses access to bail, that impose disproportionately harsh sentences for drug offenses and that ban parole, alternatives to incarceration, amnesty and pardons for drug offenses.[36]

While we were unable to find disaggregated data on COVID-19 cases and deaths in prisons among people deprived of their liberty for drug offenses, unquestionably many of COVID-19's victims in prison will have been people detained on drug charges. As the cases of Patrick Jones and Andrea Circle Bear illustrate, in countries where drug laws are disproportionately enforced against Black and Brown people, this further exacerbated the already disparate impact of COVID-19 on minorities.

- **Safety of Drug Supply**

The pandemic severely disrupted international travel, trade and transportation. This created not just challenges with supply of legal goods, it also upended supply lines for drugs. For example, respondents to INPUD's survey overwhelmingly said that drugs had become harder to get and that their quality had decreased (50–70%)[37], although some other studies stated that drug supply disruptions had been limited.[38] While governments tend to see such volatility as positive – indeed, interrupting supply lines is a central tenet of drug enforcement – unstable drug markets create significant health risks for people who use drugs as it creates incentives for adulteration and changes in drug use patterns, both associated with accidental overdose.

In the United States, drug supply became more unsafe during the pandemic as mixing of fentanyl into the heroin supply – already very common before – increased and reports emerged of fentanyl mixing with cocaine and methamphetamines – a new and deadly phenomenon.[39] As a result of safe supply challenges and changes in drug use behaviour – most importantly an increase in solitary use – overdose deaths in the United States spiked sharply in 2020 and again in 2021 after having shown signs of a gradual decrease in the two previous years preceding the COVID-19 pandemic. In 2020, overdose deaths hit a record high of more than 93,000, a 54% increase from 2019, and 2021 deaths will likely cross 100,000.[40]

- **Disruptions of Health and Social Services for People Who Use Drugs**

Essential health services for people who use drugs – such as needle and syringe programmes, low-threshold community-based drug treatment services, naloxone access and safe injecting sites – are evidence-based services proven to minimise the health harms related to drug use.[41] Yet, these services are grossly underfunded in the best of times in most countries.[42] Moreover, they are often not included in routine packages of health services, in the way that services for smoking or alcohol dependence are.

As countries imposed lockdowns and shut down non-essential services, the ambiguous status of services for people who use drugs led to closures of these services and the diversion of resources to other services that were considered essential. This resulted in reports of at least temporary closures and disruptions of harm reduction and substitution treatment services in every region.[43] Assessments in the United States in early 2020 found that 43% of needle and syringe programmes reported a decrease in availability of services[44] and that more than 50% of such programmes were shut down, at least temporarily, in Ohio.[45] In some cases, personnel and resources were diverted to combat the pandemic. Services for drug users were also sometimes not provided supplies of personal protective equipment (PPE) on the same basis as other essential health services.[46]

The scarcity of services for drug users in combination with restrictions on freedom of movement significantly affected access to services, as people who use drugs who normally travelled to obtain services were no longer able to do so, or were subject to questions by police about the reasons for their travel – obviously problematic in countries where drug use and/or possession are criminalised. This led to disruptions in the use of clean injecting equipment, availability of naloxone and access to antiretroviral treatment for HIV.

While it is not known how much health harm resulted, respondents to the INPUD survey overwhelmingly stated that availability and accessibility of harm reduction services decreased in the early months of the pandemic.[47] Since harm reduction services are often the entry point for people who use drugs to access health services, health education, social protection and other essential life-saving services, the harm is likely to be significant.

Responding to COVID-19's Impact on Drugs and Drug Policy

As COVID-19 exposed the vulnerabilities of societies, global and national leaders spoke about the need to protect those most severely affected in the immediate term, and the need to build back better in the longer term. Many countries took short-term measures to protect frontline workers, to support people who lost their jobs as a result of lockdowns, and to prop up businesses so they could survive the upheaval, while promising more structural reforms to build a more just society on the ruins left by the pandemic.

In the area of drug policy, some steps were taken to address the immediate impacts of the pandemic and containment measures, especially to address the glaring risks faced by people in jails and prisons and, in some countries, to minimise disruptions of health and social services for people who use drugs. The other harms identified earlier went largely or entirely unaddressed. Importantly, there has been a glaring failure in many countries and institutions to look beyond just the symptoms that COVID-19 has highlighted and address the root causes of these harms, which are directly linked to the drug control system.

- **Responding to Immediate Impacts**

Some promising changes have occurred in the area of social and health services for people who use drugs. Traditionally, governments have imposed many restrictive rules and regulations on substitution treatment and harm reduction programmes, including requirements to visit clinics every day to take doses of methadone under supervision, strict limitations on take-home doses, urine testing requirements and limits on distribution of syringes. Ostensibly meant to prevent abuse, drug user advocates have long denounced these regulations as punitive and overly rigid.[48] During the pandemic, these restrictions became unworkable as they required clients to travel regularly during lockdowns and unnecessarily exposed clients and health workers to infection risks. This forced governments to rethink and lift (some of) them. Multiple countries expanded the use of take-home methadone, reduced reliance on urine tests and other control measures and allowed changes to syringe distribution, including secondary distribution through community networks.[49]

These adjustments, however, were not universal and in some countries services for drug users were essentially shuttered, leaving clients at an increased risk of relapse, overdose and contracting HIV and hepatitis C. Moreover, the relaxation of control measures was introduced as an emergency response and it remains a question whether the simplified regulation will continue as the pandemic recedes and pandemic control measures are revoked. In a positive sign, one study in the United States found that take-home doses were not associated with an increase in overdose or failed urine tests in participants while the number of emergency room visits dropped.[50] Significantly, the Global Fund to Fight AIDS, Tuberculosis and Malaria, one of the largest global funders of harm reduction services, explicitly encourages syringe distribution through peer networks.[51] However, national policies and regulations often still impose significant restrictions that impede efficient distribution of clean needles or take-home substitution treatment. It is critical that donors fund civil society organisations to challenge these policies, advocate and build support for greater flexibilities.[52]

Another area where some positive measures have been taken are jails and prisons, although it is unclear how many people facing or convicted of drug charges benefited. As soon as the pandemic started, UN agencies and governments recognised the disastrous potential of exploding COVID-19 cases in prisons and took steps to decongest prisons through release schemes and steps to reduce new entries. A study by DLA Piper found that the 53 jurisdictions globally it studied had released at least 475,000 pretrial and convicted prisoners between March and July 2020, with a focus on people convicted of or charged with minor or non-violent offences.[53] In New Jersey, the governor's office, legislature and human rights advocates joined forces to pass a law that resulted in the release of more than 2,200 people on a single day, including many convicted on drug charges, eventually reducing the state's prison population by 30%.[54] Given that about 21.6% of prisoners worldwide are held on drug charges and that many of them are held on drug possession, use or minor dealing charges, it stands to reason that this included significant numbers of people with drug charges.

However, despite the fact that it is broadly acknowledged that criminalisation of drug use and possession is a driving force behind overcrowding in prisons, few countries specifically sought to release people in prison for non-violent drug use or possession. DLA Piper found that few jurisdictions expressly included people convicted of drug offences as a category of prisoners eligible for release and that at least 15% of jurisdictions, including Cameroon, El Salvador, Ghana and India, took a 'punitive approach to drug users and specifically excluded prisoners who had committed drug-related offences from release'.[55] DLA Piper noted that, in excluding drug offenders, countries often failed to differentiate between drug use and possession for personal use and drug production or trafficking charges, thus treating a drug user the same way as a major drug trafficker. Other countries excluded large swaths of drug offenders from release. For example, Indonesia only allowed the release of people sentenced to 5–10 years for drug use if they had served at least two-thirds of their sentences.[56] Similarly, Harm Reduction International has reported that 28 countries had explicitly excluded people detained for certain drug offenses from decongestion measures.[57] In some countries where drug offenders were not excluded, actual numbers of releases were negligible. For example, in Mexico, only 44 people were amnestied overall, and it remains unclear if any of them were held on drug charges.[58]

While States took some steps that alleviated the impact of the COVID-19 response on access to health and social services for people who use drugs and for those incarcerated, steps to address the other issues described above were limited. Despite unsafe supply contributing to skyrocketing overdose numbers, the US federal government did little to improve the safety of drug supply, although New York became the first state to open a safe injection site in November 2021.[59] To address safe supply challenges, Canada took steps to expand the provision of pharmaceutical-grade opioid and stimulant substances to drug users for whom existing treatments had not succeeded in achieving sustained remission, a solution community advocates had previously proposed, whose implementation became possible or was accelerated as a result of the pandemic.[60]

Building Back Better: Little Appetite for Righting a Historic Wrong

Despite the alarming impacts of COVID-19 on the drug policy arena, there has, with a few important exceptions, been little reflection about the root causes of key vulnerabilities. The approach to drugs at the national and international level has largely remained business-as-usual, firmly based on the prohibitionist model. An April 2021 statement by the United Nations Commission on Narcotic Drugs, the main drug policymaking body within the UN system, is emblematic of this lack of introspection.[61] The statement recognises 'dramatic consequences' of the COVID-19 pandemic on 'all aspects of the world drug problem' but does not mention the links between the prohibitionist approach to drugs and these consequences.[62] It neglects to mention that millions of people remain jailed on minor drug charges because of the criminalisation of drugs, facing the risk of death from COVID-19; that millions of people who use drugs have become more vulnerable to arrest at a time when police powers worldwide are enhanced; or that the pandemic and drug enforcement have combined to make drug supply in some countries dangerously unsafe. The statement also fails to call on Member States to take basic measures to limit the harms associated with the pandemic, such as releasing people imprisoned on non-violent drug charges, recognising health and social services for drug users as essential services, removing onerous regulatory requirements for drug treatment and harm reduction services or improving availability of drug testing and naloxone to reduce the risk of accidental overdoses. Instead, it doubles down on prohibition measures, expressing concern about the development of 'new methods of manufacture, distribution and marketing of, and trafficking in, some types of drugs' and the 'new challenges' this poses for law enforcement authorities.[63]

The Commission statement reflects the reality that at the national level the pandemic does not appear to have prompted much reflection on the root causes of the harms related to drug policy, even where steps were taken to address the harms themselves. For example, in the United States, faced with spiking overdose deaths, government agencies have taken steps to improve access to naloxone and drug treatment services but have done little to effectively address safe supply challenges. In fact, while improving access to services for people who use drugs, the Biden administration is simultaneously proposing to permanently schedule fentanyl-related substances, doubling down on ineffective criminalisation strategies that have fuelled prison overcrowding, especially affecting Black and Brown communities.[64] Various US states are also pursuing 'death by dealer' statutes that allow prosecutors to charge 'drug dealers' with murder – an approach that risks deterring people from calling 911 in case of an overdose and may encourage more solitary drug use.[65]

Given the reluctance of many countries to release minor drug offenders even at the height of a deadly pandemic, it is perhaps unsurprising that discussions about decriminalisation have largely remained static. While UN agencies have recommended that countries decriminalise drug use and possession for personal use,[66] even countries that did release significant numbers of people charged with or convicted of drug offenses have not taken steps to repeal criminalisation provisions in their drug laws.

While the Commission on Narcotic Drugs remains entrenched in the prohibitionist approach to drugs, other parts of the UN system are increasingly questioning it. In a series of reports, the UN's human rights mechanisms have denounced the criminalisation of drugs, the racist application of drug laws, extrajudicial killings in the context of the war on drugs and the use of the death penalty for non-violent drug crimes.[67] A report by the UN Working Group on Arbitrary Detention was particularly forceful in denouncing the harms of a law enforcement-based approach to drugs, raising concerns about abusive drug testing and stop and search, torture, disproportionate sentences, the use of the death penalty, compulsory treatment and discrimination against migrants, indigenous people and other minorities. In 2019, four UN agencies jointly issued the *International Guidelines on Human Rights and Drug Policy*, which, for the first time, provide guidance on the measures 'States should undertake or refrain from undertaking in order to comply with their human rights obligations, while taking into account their concurrent obligations under the international drug control conventions'.[68] While these documents do not yet call for abandoning prohibition altogether, they do make an increasingly forceful case for systemic reform.

Drug Policy and Human Rights Post-COVID-19

By upending normality, the COVID-19 has shone a new light on society, allowing us to see it from a different perspective, evaluate whether policies, systems and institutions do what they should and recreate a better world. The pandemic has led us to question the world and its established practices in many areas of life: the economic order and the burgeoning income inequality it has fuelled; the impact of systemic racism on society; the role of the State in protecting people at a time of emergency and in ensuring access to basic services, including health and education. Most of us have come to the conclusion that the realities that COVID-19 has revealed cannot be accepted and that systemic change is needed to bring society closer to the ideals of equal opportunities and respect for rights and freedoms for all.

These ideals will remain unachievable without a fundamental change in the approach to drugs. We will never live in a drug-free world. But we can live in a world where we reduce the health risks associated with drug use; where people who use drugs are not stigmatised and have access to services that keep them healthy; where jails and prisons are not filled with drug users and people who grow, smuggle or sell drugs as a survival strategy; and where public funds are used for health and social programmes rather than militarised drug enforcement. We did not need COVID-19 to learn these lessons – they have been obvious for years – but the pandemic has created an opportunity to press for and make systemic change and link drug control reform to the broader reform agenda UN Secretary General Antonio Guterres has articulated.[69]

COVID-19 may have changed our lives, but it has not materially changed the core of the drug policy reform agenda. The steps described below are all part of a vision for change that drug policy advocates have long advocated for. The pandemic has just added further urgency to these steps, as the cases of Patrick Jones and Andrea Circle Bear tragically demonstrate.

1 **Do not try to 'build back better'.** While building back better has been the post-COVID mantra, it is not appropriate when applied to drug policy. The drug control system has been fundamentally broken for decades. Rather than trying to build on a flawed system, the new approach to drugs must be built on a new foundation that is anchored in social well-being, health and human rights. Rather than pursuing prohibition and a drug-free world, it should deal with drugs the way we treat other substances that have the potential to cause harm to health, such as alcohol and cigarettes. The role of law enforcement agencies should be drastically reduced in favour of investments in communities and social and health services. The *Lancet Commission on Public Health and International Drug Policy* and the *International Guidelines on Human Rights and Drug Policy* offer detailed roadmaps for drug policies that are anchored in public health and human rights principles.[70]
2 **Decriminalise the use and possession for personal use.** If COVID-19 has taught us one thing, it is that we need to decriminalise drug use so that a drug use charge does not become a death sentence. Various jurisdictions, including

Portugal, Switzerland and Oregon, have decriminalised drug use and possession of some or all drugs, driving down drug arrests, transmission of HIV and hepatitis C and accidental overdoses while drug use has remained stable. As the common UN system position on drug policy recommends, laws that criminalise drug use or possession should be amended to remove criminal sanctions.[71] Moreover, as the UN Working Group on Arbitrary Detention recommends, States should promptly release persons detained only for drug use or possession for personal use and review their convictions with a view to expunging their records.[72]

3 **Decriminalise small-scale production, smuggling and dealing.** As the *Lancet Commission* and the *International Guidelines on Human Rights and Drug Policy* have recommended, petty dealing and production of drugs should be decriminalised.[73] The criminalisation of small-scale, non-violent drug production, smuggling and dealing is a form of criminalising poverty, with multi-generational impacts. Many small players in the drug pipeline get involved in drugs to survive, whether to feed their families or to support their own drug use. Rather than criminalising them, societies should invest in eliminating poverty, supporting communities and ensuring social services are available to help people struggling with poverty, housing, education and employment.

4 **Regulate all drugs.** Decriminalisation is an important first step, but it alone is not sufficient, as it focuses exclusively on the consumer side. It is the criminalisation of drug supplies that lies at the heart of the fiction of a drug-free world, and has led to the militarisation of the response to drugs, the emergence of violent and powerful drug gangs and the destabilisation of entire countries. Drug enforcement, moreover, is a key driver of accidental overdose and other health harms, as it destabilises drug supply and encourages adulteration of drugs. Regulating all drugs is no simple task. While a variety of countries and States have developed models for the regulation of marijuana,[74] experience is thin for regulation of other substances, such as heroin and methamphetamine, that may pose significantly greater public health risks. The Global Commission on Drug Policy has outlined a number of steps for states to follow in regulating drugs.[75] Among others, it recommends an incremental, evidence-based and participatory process that begins with the regulation of lower-potency drugs. It has urged countries to maximise development opportunities offered by regulated drug markets and to ensure that communities most affected by prohibition are beneficiaries of the process.

Prohibition is the cause of one of the metaphorical fractures Antonio Guterres invoked in his Nelson Mandela lecture. For 60 years, prohibitionist policies have done damage to the 'fragile skeletons of the societies we have built'.[76] Like a stress fracture caused by cumulative impact, the damage is not as obvious or immediately debilitating as from an acute break from a single catastrophic event, but no less devastating or extensive, as COVID-19 has highlighted. It is time to put an end to the corrosive effects of prohibition and to allow the fractures it has caused to heal and bone tissue to rebuild and strengthen so that it can withstand the significant challenges that a new approach to drugs will pose. Implementing a drug policy agenda that centres on health, social well-being and human rights will not be easy, but it is essential if we want to seize on Guterres' vision and build back a more equal and sustainable world.

Notes

1 António Guterres, 'Tackling Inequality: A New Social Contract for a New Era' (United Nations, 2020) 3.
2 Ibid, 7.
3 Ibid, 7.
4 Vera, 'If Prison Walls Could Talk: Personal Stories about COVOD-19 and Incarceration' www.vera.org/covid-19-if-prison-walls-could-talk accessed 21 May 2023.
5 Maurice Chammah, 'Coronavirus Ended His Shot at a Second Chance', *The Marshall Project* (3 April 2020).; Rich Schapiro, '1st Prison Inmate to Die of Coronavirus Wrote Heartbreaking Letter to Judge', *NBC News* (5 April 2020).
6 Schapiro (n 5).
7 Eliott McLaughlin, 'CDC Official Warns Americans It's Not a Question of If Coronavirus Will Spread, but When', *CNN* (26 February 2020).
8 Nicholas Bogel-Burroughs and Vanessa Swales, 'Prison with Coronavirus Dies after Giving Birth while on Ventilator', *The New York Times* (29 April 2020).
9 Clara LeBeau, 'The Federal Bureau of Prisons Must Be Held Accountable for the Death of My Granddaughter', *The Washington Post* (22 May 2020).
10 Transform Drug Policy Foundation, 'The Alternative World Drug Report, 2016' (Transform Drug Policy Foundation, 2016).
11 Ibid, 6.
12 Joanne Csete, et al, 'Public Health and International Drug Policy' (2016) 387 *The Lancet* 1427, 1467.
13 Ibid, 1468.
14 Nicholas Sánchez, 'En plena pandemia de COVID-19, el Estado hace erradicación forzada en Catatumbo', *El Espectador* (19 March 2020).; 'Solicitamos al Gobierno suspender los operativos de erradicación forzada durante la contingencia del COVID-19', *Dejusticia* (31 March 2020).; Agencia EFE, 'Erradicación forzada de cultivos de coca, la tensión creciente en medio de la pandemia', *El Heraldo* (14 May 2020).
15 Tania Pastrana, 'Access to Controlled Medicines in Latin America during the Pandemic' Statement of the International Association for Hospice and Palliative Care Delivered at the Commission on Narcotic Drugs (15 April 2021).
16 Harm Reduction International, 'The Global State of Harm Reduction 2020' (Harm Reduction International, 2020).
17 Personal correspondence with Tatyana Sleiman, executive director of Skoun, Lebanese Addictions Center, 21 December 2021.
18 Freedom House, 'Democracy under Lockdown: The Impact of COVID-19 on the Global Struggle for Freedom' (Freedom House, 2020).
19 World Bank, 'COVID-19 to Add as Many as 150 Million Extreme Poor by 2021', 7 October 2020.
20 Judy Chang, Jake Agliata & Mauro Guarinieri, 'COVID-19 – Enacting a "New Normal" for People Who Use Drugs (2020) 83 *International Journal of Drug Policy* 2.

21 International Network of People who Use Drugs, 'INPUD Online Survey on COVID-19 & People who Use Drugs (PWUD) Data Report 2' (International Network of People who Use Drugs, 2020).
22 Ibid, 24.
23 Ibid, 21.
24 Jesse Bernard and Imani Robinson, 'UK Policing during the COVID-19 Pandemic', *TalkingDrugs* (2 June 2020) www.talkingdrugs.org/uk-policing-during-the-covid-19-pandemic accessed 1 March 2023.
25 Patrick Gallahue, 'Drugs and the Death Penalty' (Open Society Foundations, 2015).; Rick Lines, 'A "Most Serious Crime?" – The Death Penalty for Drug Offences and International Human Rights Law' (2010) 21 *Amicus Law Journal* 21.
26 Ajeng Larasati and Giada Girelli, 'The Death Penalty for Drug Offences: Global Overview 2020' (Harm Reduction International, 2021).
27 Ibid.
28 Ibid.
29 Ibid, 23.
30 Ibid, 29.
31 Larasati and Girelli (n 26).
32 United Nations Office on Drugs and Crime, World Health Organization, UNAIDS and the Office of the United Nations High Commissioner for Human Rights, 'UNODC, WHO, UNAIDS and OHCHR Joint Statement on COVID-19 in Prisons and Other Closed Settings' (13 May 2020).
33 DLA Piper, 'A Global Analysis of Prisoner Releases in Response to COVID-19' (DLA Piper, 2020).
34 Justice Project Pakistan, 'COVID-19 and Prisoners' https://jpp.org.pk/covid19-prisoners/ accessed 1 March 2023.
35 UN Working Group on Arbitrary Detention, 'Arbitrary Detention Related to Drug Policies' (18 May 2021) A/HRC/47/40.
36 Ibid.
37 International Network of People who Use Drugs (n 21).
38 Judith Aldridge, et al, 'Drugs in the Time of COVID: The UK Drug Market Response to Lockdown Restrictions' (Release, 2021).
39 Caroline Lewis, 'Overdoses Involving Cocaine and Fentanyl Are on the Rise', *National Public Radio* (7 July 2021).
40 Centers for Disease Control and Prevention, Press Statement: 'Drug Overdose Deaths in the U.S. Top 100,000 Annually' (17 November 2021).; Mike Stobbe, 'US Overdose Deaths Hit Record 93,000 in Pandemic Last Year' *Associated Press* (14 July 2021).
41 World Health Organization, United Nations Office on Drugs and Crime and UNAIDS, 'WHO, UNODC, UNAIDS Technical Guide for Countries to Set Targets for Universal Access to HIV Prevention, Treatment and Care for Injecting Drug Users – 2012 Revision' (United Nations, 2012).
42 Harm Reduction International (n 16).
43 International Network of People who Use Drugs (n 21).; Lincoln Choudhury, 'The Impact of COVID-19 on Harm Reduction in Seven Asian Countries' (Harm Reduction International, 2020).; Adrian Dunlop, Buddhima Lokuge, Debbie Masters, et al, 'Challenges in Maintaining Treatment Services for People Who Use Drugs during the COVID-19 Pandemic' (2020) 17 *Harm Reduction Journal* 26.; L Nedda Dastmalchi, 'HIV in the Era of COVID-19: Why Experts Are Concerned about an Increase in Cases', *ABC News* (29 April 2020).; Peter Sarosi, 'Harm Reduction Responses to COVID-19 in

Europe', *Drogreporter* (16 March 2020) https://drogriporter.hu/en/how-harm-reducers-cope-with-the-corona-pandemic-in-europe/ accessed 1 March 2023.

44 Sara N Glick, et al, 'The Impact of COVID-19 on Syringe Services Programs in the United States' (2020) 24 *AIDS and Behavior* 2466.

45 Harm Reduction Ohio, 'HEALTH ALERT: Canton Latest to Close Its Syringe Program (Updated)' (29 March 2000) www.harmreductionohio.org/covid-19-updates-syringe-programs-ongoing/ accessed 1 March 2023.

46 Harm Reduction International (n 16).

47 International Network of People who Use Drugs (n 21).

48 Chang, et al. (n 20).

49 Harm Reduction International (n 16).; Choudry (n 43).; Eurasian Harm Reduction Association, 'Harm Reduction Service Delivery to People Who Use Drugs during a Public Health Emergency: Examples from the COVID-19 Pandemic in Selected Countries' (Eurasian Harm Reduction Association, 2020).

50 Ofer Amram, Solmaz Amiri, Victoria Panwala, et al, 'The Impact of Relaxation of Methadone Take-Home Protocols on Treatment Outcomes in the COVID-19 Era' (2021) 47 *American Journal of Drug and Alcohol Abuse* 722.

51 Global Fund to Fight AIDS, Tuberculosis and Malaria, 'Harm Reduction for People Who Use Drugs: Priorities for Investment and Increased Impact in HIV Programming' (The Global Fund, 2022).

52 Shona Schonning, 'The Impact of a Multi-Country Harm Reduction Advocacy Grant in South-East Asia: Changing Hearts and Minds, Policies and Practices' (Harm Reduction International, 2020).

53 DLA Piper (n 33).

54 Tracey Tully, '2,258 N.J. Prisoners Will Be Released in a Single Day', *The New York Times* (4 November 2020).

55 DLA Piper (n 33) 23.

56 Ibid.

57 Giada Girelli, 'COVID-19, Prisons and Drug Policy: Global Scan March-June 2020' (Harm Reduction International, 2020).

58 Pedro Villa y Cana, 'Bajo la Ley de Amnistía 44 personas fueron liberadas: Encinas', *El Universal* (23 December 2021).

59 Jeffery C Mays and Andy Newman, 'Nation's First Supervised Drug-Injection Sites Open in New York', *The New York Times* (30 November 2021).

60 Paxton Bach, et al, 'Innovative Strategies to Support Physical Distancing among Individuals with Active Addiction' (2020) 7/9 *The Lancet Psychiatry* 731.

61 UN Commission on Narcotic Drugs, 'Statement of the Commission on Narcotic Drugs on the Impact of the Coronavirus Disease (COVID-19) Pandemic on the Implementation of the Joint Commitments of Member States to Address and Counter All Aspects of the World Drug Problem' (31 March 2021) E/CN.7/2021/L.2.

62 Ibid, 2.

63 Ibid, 3.

64 Drug Policy Alliance, 'Press Release: Nearly 100 Civil Rights, Policy Organizations Urge Congress to Reject Biden's Harmful Sentencing Proposal' (21 October 2021).

65 Sarah Maslin Nir, 'The Cocaine Was Laced with Fentanyl. Now Six Are Dead from Overdoses', *The New York Times* (31 August 2021).

66 United Nations systems Chief Executives Board for Coordination, 'Summary of Deliberations: Segment 2: Common United Nations System Position on Drug Policy' (18 January 2019) CEB/2018/2.

67 UN High Commissioner on Human Rights, 'Promotion and Protection of the Human Rights and Fundamental Freedoms of Africans and of People of African Descent against Excessive Use of Force and Other Human Rights Violations by Law Enforcement Officers' (1 June 2021) A/HRC/47/53.; UN High Commissioner on Human Rights, 'Conference Paper: Promotion and Protection of the Human Rights and Fundamental Freedoms of Africans and of People of African Descent against Excessive Use of Force and Other Human Rights Violations by Law Enforcement Officers' (28 June 2021) A/HRC/47/CRP.1.; United Nations Working Group on Discrimination against Women and Girls, 'Women's and Girls' Sexual and Reproductive Health Rights in Crisis' (28 April 2021) A/HRC/47/38.; UN Special Rapporteur on extrajudicial, summary or arbitrary executions, 'Extrajudicial, Summary or Arbitrary Executions' (7 June 2021) A/HRC/47/33.

68 UN Development Program, World Health Organization, UNAIDS, Office of the High Commissioner on Human Rights & International Centre on Human Rights and Drug Policy, *International Guidelines on Human Rights and Drug Policy* (2019) 4.

69 Guterres (n 1).

70 *The Lancet* (n 13).; UN Development Program, et al (n 68).

71 Chief Executives Board (n 66).

72 UN Working Group on Arbitrary Detention (n 35).

73 *The Lancet* (n 13).; UN Development Program, et al (n 68).

74 See Chapters 1 and 4 of this book.

75 Global Commission on Drug Policy, 'Regulation: The Responsible Control of Drugs' (Global Commission on Drug Policy, 2018).

76 Guterres (n 1) 3.

3 Debunking the Three Myths about Reforming Asian Drug Policies

Michelle Miao and Gloria Lai*

Introduction

While global drug policies and practices have started to make tectonic shifts in the past decades,[1] Asia remains home to countries and territories which adopt the most punitive approaches to drug use and supply. Paradoxically, Asia's lag in the global process of drug liberalisation is also why it can significantly shape the future of international drug policy. This is because an approach to gauge the likely course of global drug policy is to analyse trends and obstacles to reform in jurisdictions that are the most resistant to policy change and attitudinal shifts. To predict the dynamic patterns of future change thus requires close attention to nations in Asia, where about 60% of the world's population resides. In terms of drug use and supply around the world, it is estimated that this region accounts for 58% of people who use opioids, over one-third of people who use amphetamines, 35% of the people who inject drugs living with hepatitis C and 38% of the quantities of synthetic new psychoactive substances seized.[2]

Besides its practical influence in the global landscape of drug use and supply due to its sheer size, Asia may also play a prominent role in shaping drug policy debates and legal changes because it is home to hard-line political and legal regimes which are the most resistant to harm reduction and human rights approaches.[3] Many Asian countries, especially those governed by authoritarian political regimes, embrace zero-tolerance approaches of criminalisation and punishment that have reformed only slightly over the years. The legal changes adopted in Thailand in 2021 and 2022 towards the legal regulation of the use (and other activities such as commercial sale, household cultivation, import and export) of cannabis, hemp and kratom plants represent significant change in the region, and these may well trigger support for similar reforms in neighbouring countries.[4] During the same period, Thailand also adopted legal reforms aimed at reducing the numbers of people imprisoned for low-level drug offences.[5] However, it fell short of removing criminal and other punishment for drug use and possession. Given that most people in prison for drugs in Thailand are held for methamphetamine-related offences, and methamphetamine

* One of the authors (Michelle Miao) is grateful for the support of a Direct Grant for Research (Project Code 4059034) at the Faculty of Law, Chinese University of Hong Kong.

DOI: 10.4324/9781003169765-5

is far from becoming legalised, it remains to be seen whether the changed laws will achieve its aim of reducing levels of imprisonment in the long term.[6] In Malaysia, where most of the over 1,000 people on death row are convicted of drug offences, the government abolished mandatory use of the death penalty. However, the death penalty remains a sentence that may be given.[7] Notably, despite the international trend towards abolition around the turn of the century, 'the number of countries expanding the application of the death penalty to include drug offences' increased in the first decade of the 21st century, especially in Asia.[8] Overall, the gap between entrenched punitive drug policies in many parts of Asia and drug liberalisation reforms in other areas of the globe has widened recently.[9] This growing divide has been marked by ongoing extrajudicial killings by law enforcement in wars on drugs in the Philippines, Bangladesh and Indonesia, over-incarceration for low-level drug offences in countries such as Myanmar and Cambodia, ongoing use of compulsory drug rehabilitation programmes and unwavering use of the death penalty in countries such as China, Singapore and Viet Nam.[10] In many of these countries, punitive drug policies are not only a symbol of hard-line politics but a significant part of the nation's operative criminal justice regime.[11]

These harsh realities invite enquiries about the potential of current reform initiatives to inspire changes away from exceptionally punitive policies in Asia. Indeed, it would be helpful to debunk three myths common to current drug policies and discourses in Asia. Here, we do not intend to claim that these Asian countries, with considerable variations in their political, social, economic and legal contexts, can be classified as an identical or unified 'Asian approach' concerning drug prohibition. There are, however, shared characteristics in their reliance on State-centred ideological preferences and political interests for tailoring drug policies. These salient characteristics shape the *status quo* of drug policies in this region and set out conditions for future reforms.

This chapter seeks to challenge the following three myths associated with Asian drug law, policies and practices. First, we claim that Asian countries' historical paths do not causally determine their current and future reliance on prohibition, and criminalisation in particular, as the primary approach to solve drug-related social and public health problems. Second, we refute the assumption that a criminal justice approach and harm reduction are mutually exclusive and disconnected regulatory strategies of drug control. From a practical perspective, a genuine and meaningful transition from prohibition to harm reduction remains a significant challenge for many drug reformers in Asia. Third, we disagree that human rights approaches have limited normative and practical significance in shaping future Asian drug policy reform.

Are Asia's Drug Policies Determinately Shaped by History?

The contemporary prohibitionist policies in many Asian countries are believed to be inextricably tied to their colonial legacy in the early 20th century.[12] In the late-Qing period in China, military defeat in the 1839–1842 Opium War with Britain and the subsequent forced acceptance of British opium imports into China marked the start of what has been labelled a 'Century of Humiliation'.[13] Despite the varying interpretations of the ethics of the opium trade and the associated military conflicts,[14] the Opium War is widely believed to be a pivotal part of the Chinese collective memory of drugs.[15] The unsaid statement about the political salience of this historical chapter, however, is that a nationalist interpretation of the Opium War is fundamental to cementing the legitimacy of the contemporary Chinese political regime.[16] As the failure of the late-Qing government to stop domestic opium use and ban opium importation is perceived to have significantly weakened the power of the imperial throne,[17] the harsh stance of the Chinese government today against drug production, importation and distribution similarly bolster its political legitimacy.

The rationale behind the punitive approach to illicit drugs in China today is multidimensional. Besides claimed benefits – such as safety, health, moral purity, and order – to the Chinese society and individuals, the prohibitionist approach is also a political statement, a rejection of a nation's historical failure and the proud success of a new approach of social control,[18] which is believed to be effective, powerful and independent of Western influences.[19] It is in this sense that contemporary drug policies in China are not solely determined by historical experiences but rather contingent on a politicised, reconstructed narrative of history. Furthermore, in framing drug-related activities as morally corruptive and life-threatening and claiming success through its implementation of prohibition-based strategies, the Chinese State has been able to extend its political control to other spheres of social life through the imposition of administrative sanctions[20] and criminal punishment.[21]

Indeed, a brief survey of China's modern history reveals that drug prohibition is far from being a dominant trend. After the Opium War, the Chinese government ended its ban on opium and levied taxes on the trade to raise revenue, opening the way for domestic cultivators to enter the market and increasing the overall availability of opium in the country.[22] After the demise of the imperial regime, opium consumption and trade in the post-Qing era remained widespread through to the establishment of the People's Republic of China (PRC). Drug policies and practices during this period of modern China could hardly be characterised as punitive. The brutally punitive prohibitionist campaign after the founding of the PRC in 1949, which combined forced detoxification programmes, incarceration and summary executions, was so effective that China proclaimed it rehabilitated 10–20 million 'drug addicts' and became a 'drug-free nation' within three years.[23] The country's new image served as a powerful symbol of national pride and a rejection of old China's 'century of humiliation' plagued by what was portrayed as 'foreign-induced drug addiction'.[24]

With China opening its national borders to facilitate economic marketisation and globalisation in the late 1970s, illicit drugs were increasingly smuggled into China, starting in Yunnan Province bordering the infamous Golden Triangle region where the borders of China, Thailand, Laos and Myanmar meet. Interestingly at that time, despite adopting a prohibitionist approach, lawmakers were relatively lenient towards drug supply activities. The first criminal statute in the history of the PRC, which was enacted in 1979, prescribed a maximum five-year fixed term of imprisonment or penal servitude for producing, selling and trafficking illicit drugs without aggravating circumstances.[25] Drug possession was not a criminal offense. This is to be compared with the 1997 Criminal Law, which prescribes capital punishment for smuggling, manufacturing, selling and transporting illicit drugs[26] and life imprisonment for drug possession.[27] It was also not until the 1980s that China created its first specialist drug enforcement police force in southern Yunnan province along the drug trafficking routes from the Golden Triangle.[28] In other words, the highly punitive approach to drug control in China today is hardly a product of a consistent historical track record. The current extensive use of China's criminal justice system to control illicit drugs, from imposing the death penalty for drug trafficking to the forced rehabilitation of people dependent on drugs, is only about two-decades-old. Throughout the region, prohibitionist drug policies are a recent phenomenon, compared with century-old practices of drug cultivation and consumption.[29]

Drug policies in other Asian jurisdictions have been shaped by their respective colonial experiences to varying degrees and in different ways.[30] However, the politicised use of moralised rhetoric and criminal punishment against illicit drugs as a means of political and social control follows a similar political logic to China.[31] Compared with the long history of drug use and cultivation in Asia, often by indigenous peoples and ethnic minorities,[32] criminalisation has been a new addition to the domestic government's arsenal to control and regulate drug-related activities.[33] Moreover, the policy shift and attitudinal hardening towards prohibition in Asia during the last two decades of the 20th century was at least partially a product of changing international politics, illustrated by a prohibitionist international legal environment and the United States' leadership in waging a global 'war on drugs'.[34]

This suggests that transforming the way in which the issue of drug use and supply is politically framed in public and policy discourses may induce paradigm shifts in attitudes and policies. It has been argued that reclaiming one's own traditional practice of drug consumption (e.g. opium, cannabis, and kratom) is also a nationalist project.[35] Arguably, establishing legally regulated markets for currently prohibited drugs would actually afford governments greater control over drug use and supply. To some extent, such arguments partially underpin reform measures in Thailand, where legally regulated markets for the use and supply of cannabis (limited to research and medical purposes), hemp and kratom have been established, driven by political interests and economic motivations, but also with the support of civil society advocacy.[36] However, the shrinking spaces for civil society and NGOs to engage in drug policymaking processes throughout the region in recent years[37] bode ill for prospects for further reform.

In sum, a review of drug-related practices and policy development in this region does not provide convincing evidence that the punitive orientations of contemporary drug policies and practices are decisively shaped by historical experiences or traditional approaches. Instead, they seem to be products of domestic and international political dynamics and social conditions, which are promising yet challenging battlegrounds for reform-minded legal scholars, policymakers and civil society advocates striving to chart a different future.

From Criminalisation to Harm Reduction: Old Wine in New Bottles?

In the last two decades of the 20th century, the HIV epidemic spreading throughout Asia helped drive drug policy reforms away from a criminal justice-centred approach towards harm reduction.[38] Region-wide restrictions and criminalisation of opium use and supply led to the increasing popularity of heroin in Hong Kong, Thailand and Laos.[39] A major negative health consequence associated with the growing injection of heroin was surging HIV transmission through the sharing of used syringes. For example, in Yangon, Myanmar, there was an 80% HIV prevalence among people who injected drugs, and HIV prevalence among people who injected drugs in Thailand rose from 2% to 43% in 1988.[40]

As a direct response to the increasing rate of HIV transmission in the region, HIV prevention measures were introduced for people who inject drugs,[41] some of which became a constituting part of what has been widely referred to as a 'harm reduction' approach.[42] Harm reduction seeks to provide novel remedies that the existing criminalisation approach did not offer. Recent regional changes in drug policies and practices generally reflect this paradigm shift, including the introduction of harm reduction measures such as opioid substitution therapy and needle/syringe programmes in countries that impose the harshest penalties against drug-related activities (e.g. China, Vietnam and Malaysia). For example, in Vietnam, the political leadership 'emerged as strong proponents of including harm reduction in the new HIV law' and became forces pushing for policy and legal changes for HIV prevention.[43] Subsequently, the National Assembly in 2008 amended its Drug Law to introduce a generic reference to harm reduction.[44]

Drug rehabilitation programmes were introduced in China, Vietnam, Laos, Cambodia, Nepal, Myanmar, Thailand, Indonesia and Malaysia,[45] alongside reduction in the use of the death penalty for drug offences in Thailand, Vietnam, Singapore and Malaysia, and the permitted use of cannabis for medical purposes in Thailand and South Korea (with a proposal being considered in the Philippines).[46] In China, people who use or are dependent on drugs are increasingly seen as requiring medical treatment. They are perceived as 'sick' and 'victims of their dependency', rather than being evil or dangerous.[47] In Vietnam, for instance, 'it has become a commonly held belief among many Vietnamese leaders that drug dependence is a chronic relapsing medical condition, not a crime'.[48] This criminal-to-patient attitudinal shift led to a legislative amendment that removed the previously required criminal arrests and incarceration of people who use drugs.[49]

Harm reduction and criminalisation are distinct approaches that represent different paradigms of drug policies. These two approaches agree on the *need* to minimise harm, but they disagree on *how* to define and control those harms. The latter approach uses criminal sanctions, including deprivation of life, liberty and property, to condemn offenders. This is justified as a way to deter or eliminate the perceived harms to others of drug use and dependence, such as the misguided assumption that people who use drugs will inevitably steal, rape and kill. The former approach directs resources and strategies to minimise the adverse health, social and legal impacts of drug use and punitive drug policies.[50] Under the harm reduction approach, harm is also understood to include the negative consequences of drug prohibition,[51] but without any perceived 'moral corruption' about drug use itself.[52]

While several governments in the region claim to take a drug policy approach whereby people who use drugs are 'patients' instead of criminals, in practice, however, harm reduction and criminalisation approaches coexist in many Asian countries.[53] The drug rehabilitation programmes implemented by governments in the region are overwhelmingly coercive and punitive and have become sites of widespread human rights violations.[54] These circumstances indicate the lack of progress towards genuinely health-based responses to drug use and dependence. The approach of harm reduction in these countries often inherits coercive and stigmatising genes from its criminal justice predecessor. Under Vietnam's Ordinance on Administrative Violations, for instance, illicit drug use is still considered an administrative violation and subject to two-year compulsory treatment with longer terms of detention and forced labour. In response to the changes, some people who use drugs purposefully commit petty crimes to be arrested and sentenced to shorter prison terms.[55] In some rehabilitation centres in South Vietnam, an economic incentive in building and running treatment centres constitutes a self-reinforcing system that disregarded the well-being of people who use drugs.[56] Governments in such countries use a diluted concept of decriminalisation to justify their losing sight of (or willingly disregarding) the fundamental values and principles behind the health-led approach of harm reduction.

The blurry boundary between these two approaches is an inherent danger in juxtaposing a supposedly humane, health-centred approach and a highly punitive method of drug control. Indeed, sometimes programmes are clothed in 'harm reduction' while in reality are initiatives resembling the characteristics of a criminal justice approach to drug control. Given the fragile rule-of-law conditions and weak rights-awareness in many Asian countries, attention to the intertwinement and conflation of these two approaches is urgently needed. In this way, Asian drug policy reformers can promote a genuine transition from an oppressive ideology of drug control to a dignity-protecting, humane approach to drug policy.[57]

In many Asian countries, it is within immense political and institutional constraints that drug policy reform and advocacy will take shape in the short term. A fundamental rejection of criminal justice responses – which is often central to power control and authoritarian legitimacy – is conditioned on successful broader reforms and restructuring the existing power dynamics among government and civil society. This will demand considerable resources and time. Eliminating State control from the formulation and implementation of drug policies at the moment is virtually impossible. Therefore, it is likely that harm reduction-oriented reforms, which circumvent State dominance, will compete alongside State institutions for opportunities to regulate drug-related activities for a considerable time.[58]

Despite the limited space for critical civil society engagement on drug policy in many Asian countries,[59] enhanced participation by NGOs that meet the diverse needs and concerns of the population is critically important to remedy State dominance in this field. For example, civil society's active participation in drug dependence treatment and harm reduction programmes help safeguard the interests of individuals involved, in particular those from socially marginalised and economically disadvantaged groups.[60] This is because NGOs have the advantage of reaching out to people who use drugs, including those in more vulnerable situations due to gender, race, ethnicity, sexual orientation and socio-economic status, without necessarily provoking fears of arrest or stigmatisation.[61]

Policy transformation requires the reallocation of resources and transfer of power between criminal justice and administrative agencies. A criminal justice approach demands funding for police, courts and prisons, while a harm reduction approach requires health and social services, personnel support and facilities such as drug consumption rooms, needle and syringe programmes, non-abstinence-based housing and employment initiatives, drug checking, overdose prevention and reversal, psychosocial support and the provision of information on safer drug use.[62] Both regimes require resources, and these resources may be derived from funding, capacity building, personnel training and institutional support emanating from the same State agencies.[63]

Therefore, a paradigm shift from criminalisation to harm reduction may not always exclude criminal sanctions, but instead merely redistribute criminal justice resources so that they are directed 'not at nonviolent drug users and sellers but at violent and other predatory criminals'.[64] In many Asian countries, police oversee both harm reduction and drug prohibition approaches, and there is, therefore, a similarity in how the police perceive and implement health versus punishment.[65] But this intertwinement of harm reduction and criminal justice may not be desirable as it opens the gate for rights-abusive practices. This might explain the failures to tame the harms associated with drug use throughout the region, in both government-run and private drug treatment and rehabilitation centres. Abuses have been documented in these places, from torture resulting in death to extortion and kidnappings to extract money from family members of 'patients' in Nepal, Bangladesh and Thailand. In China and Southeast Asia, economic incentives are vital for the proliferation and continued operation of many compulsory centres.[66]

These unintended consequences of drug policy reforms suggest that drug law reform should not focus on promoting a shift away from police and prisons alone. Instead, reform towards a harm reduction approach needs to engage on a much broader footing with a reorientation and reshaping of the totality of multiple stakeholders, including, but not restricted to, State agencies and grassroots civil society organisations alike to effectively prevent harms associated with drug use, including the provision of voluntary, evidence-based treatment services. The real consequences of a reallocation of power and resources among and between different State organs and social institutions warrant scrutiny by civil society and public oversight bodies in countries where changes are underway. In comparison, debates are urgently needed where an emerging global commitment to 'harm reduction' still meets strong resistance from local governments.[67]

Are Human Rights Incompatible with the Asian Approach to Drugs?

Distinct political, social and cultural conditions in Asia may appear to render limited possibilities for progress towards human rights approaches, and even more so when it comes to the topic of punitive drug policies.[68] The above section demonstrated the challenges posed to transforming the issue of drug use and dependence from an issue of criminal justice into a matter of health and harm reduction. Redefining drug use and dependence as a human rights issue faces still more scepticism in Asia, partly due to issues of political palatability[69] and cultural acceptance[70] of international human rights language. These controversies are explicable by the central concern of human rights (in particular civil and political rights): the relationship between individual rights and State power. Many authoritarian governments in the region are deeply allergic to limits on State power and find the rhetoric of human rights unappealing. Hence the past years saw the increased normative salience of human rights yet with limited implementation in the region.

As in other policy areas,[71] human rights are a hard sell in debates about drug policy in general and Asia in particular.[72] Many Asian politicians and policymakers believe a human rights approach would bring few benefits or improve the efficacy of drug control in the region.[73] Nonetheless, human rights have transformative potential. They are indispensable in achieving the deeper goals of drug policy reform, which technical solutions cannot sufficiently provide.[74] Vietnam is a case in point. Despite being the first country in Southeast Asia to decriminalise drug use in 2009, the implementation of the reform measures was undermined by the cultural inertia of Vietnam's police.[75] The reforms made positive steps towards a health-led and harm reduction-oriented approach, but these technical shifts failed to shed the punitive nature of police-led implementation. It seems that, compared with changes in technicalities and strategies, transformation of underlying values generates more enduring impact. There are at least three reasons why a human rights-based approach will be a critical tool to shatter the once-unshakable regional reliance on the 'courts-and-cops' approach and achieve fundamental attitudinal shifts in the area of drug policy.

First, in addition to a cultural relativist assertion of 'Asian values',[76] one of the central claims used by various Asian governments to contest the legitimacy and universality of human rights-based approaches has, for a long time, been that the priority of developing countries should be to protect economic, social and cultural rights, rather than civil and political rights.[77] The catalogue of human rights relevant to drug law, policies and practices, however, includes a wide range of economic, social and cultural rights, to which these human rights-sceptics, for decades, claimed to have a firm commitment.[78] International and regional agencies and institutions, therefore, should meet less ideological resistance when they monitor whether respective countries fulfil their obligations under binding legal instruments to enforce and protect economic, social and cultural rights, such as the right to the highest attainable standard of health, right to an adequate standard of living and the right to social security.[79] In addition, some other rights – such as the right to life[80] and the right to privacy[81] – are commonly classified as civil and political rights but nonetheless are pregnant with social and cultural connotations in the context of drug policy.

In sum, the possibility of reframing drug policies as a human rights issue in Asia is promising. At least theoretically, such a transformation will encounter fewer thorny ideological, cultural and political challenges in the jurisdiction of many self-proclaimed guardians of economic, social and cultural rights. The alleged primacy of economic, social and cultural rights over civil and political rights, a major ideological obstacle to human rights protections in many Asian countries, can no longer be used to shield these governments from obligations and accountabilities from practices such as compulsory or coerced treatment.[82] Moreover, in the case of human rights violations, due to the relatively non-sensitive nature and justiciability of these rights, individual victims and affected groups have a greater chance of securing judicial remedies in domestic courts in addition to administrative, financial, educational and social measures.[83]

Second, there are considerable variations in Asian countries' attitudes towards human rights due to varying perceptions of its nature, scope and suitable enforcement mechanisms. Yet, despite these disagreements, most governments would concede at least some minimal role of human rights in regulating domestic drug policies.[84] Cross-border transfusion of human rights norms is feasible given both the regional integration of the drug trade market and the cross-country social impact of drug abuse and prohibition.[85] Due to the trans-local connections and influences of drug supply and demand in this region, countries will inevitably monitor, learn and imitate each other's behaviours and policies. This opens the possibility of acculturation as a powerful mechanism to reshape regional practices with the aid of human rights frameworks.[86] In terms of compliance, it seems that most Asian governments are susceptible to not only material inducements and consequences but also what has been called the 'logic of appropriateness' of their activities.[87] Traditional arguments of 'non-interference in the internal affairs of sovereign States' lose their appeals as the drug policy issue is no longer the isolated concern of any individual State or government.

The third benefit of reframing drug policy using human rights-based language is its potential to fundamentally shift attitudes and practices away from stigmatisation, coercion and discrimination. Alongside punitive approaches, compulsory drug rehabilitation programmes in the region pose the most formidable challenges to reformers seeking to establish genuine paradigms of harm reduction and voluntary treatment. During the first decade of the 21st century, compulsory drug treatment became a regional fad. Most Asian countries introduced some form of compulsory treatment or rehabilitation programmes in response to the rise in drug use and new types of drugs such as methamphetamine.[88]

Despite their seemingly humane, health-centred approach, abusive practices in both government and private drug rehabilitation centres have been documented, from denial of medical care to torture resulting in death.[89] These practices and the lack of public outrage over their extensive abuses raise serious concerns about the efficacy of prior reforms. Drugs are still seen as a social evil, and people who use drugs are viewed as moral culprits and public enemies.[90] The need to ground drug control and regulatory practices upon principles of individual autonomy, privacy, dignity, safety and welfare is precisely the reason why a human rights-based approach is urgently needed. With its penetrating force and clarity, such a promising approach may dismantle the outdated mindset and stigmatising practices, fundamentally changing the way illicit drugs are perceived, regulated and controlled in the region. Without such a thorough revamp, even if drugs are regulated by legalised markets in the future, it will be bureaucrats and politicians that benefit the most. Stigma and coercion will be an enduring part of the practice.

Conclusion

What is known about the contemporary drug policies and practices in Asian hardline regimes? In this chapter, we challenge the three myths surrounding Asian drug policy discourses, debates and mindset from historical, strategic and human rights angles. We claim that the current punitive orientation of Asian drug policies, rather than being historically determined, is shaped by contemporary domestic, regional and international political dynamics and interests. We also believe that the alleged policy and practice shift from a heavy reliance on criminalisation and punishment to an ostensibly humane, treatment-centred approach of harm reduction in many Asian countries recently warrants close scrutiny due to institutional inertia and inadequate legal safeguards surrounding the control, management and treatment of people who use drugs. Last but not least, a human rights approach, despite being subject to intense scepticism in this region, is promising and pivotal to cultivating a human dignity-based right awareness and remould the mindset of various stakeholders involved in drug-related policy formulation, enforcement and implementation.

These clarifications are made keeping in mind the perennial epistemic obstacles, policy dilemmas and practical constraints facing drug policy reformers in the region. In this sense, it is the hope that this chapter could provide useful insights and framework of analysis for Asian advocates and reformers to form and implement their strategies and initiatives, free from some of the common misconceptions and controversies. The arguments highlighted in this chapter are framed and posited to echo a broader paradigm shift to harm reduction and human rights-based approaches in the governance of drug-related issues across the globe, which has already inspired multifaceted institutional, discursive and policy transformations from discipline and punishment to human dignity, health and welfare.

Notes

1 Since mid-2010s, a chorus of international and regional agencies has called for a human rights-based approach to drug policy worldwide. See, e.g. United Nations Development Program, World Health Organization, UNAIDS, International Centre on Human Rights and Drug Policy, *International Guidelines on Human Rights and Drug Policy* (2019).; Office of the United Nations High Commissioner for Human Rights, 'Implementation of the Joint Commitment to Effectively Addressing and Countering the World Drug

Problem with Regard to Human Rights – Report of the Office of the United Nations High Commissioner for Human Rights' (September 2018) A/HRC/39/39.; 'A Public Letter to UN Secretary General Ban Ki-moon' (14 April 2016) www.drugpolicy.org/ungass2016 accessed 2 February 2023. In addition, harm reduction has been at the heart of debates against a criminal justice approach to drug use and possession for the past two decades. See generally, David R Bewley-Taylor, *International Drug Control: Consensus Fractured* (CUP 2012).

2 United Nations Office on Drugs and Crime, *World Drug Report 2021* (United Nations, 2021).

3 Gideon Lasco, 'Drugs and Drug Wars as Populist Tropes in Asia: Illustrative Examples and Implications for Drug Policy' (2020) 77 *International Journal of Drug Policy* 1.

4 'One-Stop Cannabis Knowledge Shop Opens', *Bangkok Post* (17 June 2022); 'Anutin: Cannabis Decriminalisation a Success', *Bangkok Post* (14 June 2022).

5 'Drug Bill Changes to Lighten Sentences', *Bangkok Post* (16 October 2021).

6 Gloria Lai and Unchisa Eaimtong, 'Thailand Reforms Drug Laws to Reduce Impacts of Criminal Justice System', *IDPC Blog* (23 December 2021).

7 Amnesty International, 'Current Status of the Death Penalty in Malaysia' (Amnesty International, 2023).

8 Rick Lines, 'The Death Penalty for Drug Offences: A Violation of International Human Rights Law' (Harm Reduction International, 2007) 6.

9 Banyan, 'Asia Is Still Saying No to Drugs', *The Economist* (14 January 2017).

10 Amnesty International, '2021 World Day against the Death Penalty: The Additional Burden of the Death Penalty on Women' (Amnesty International, 2021).; Amnesty International, 'Death Sentences and Executions 2019' (Amnesty International, 2020).; Amnesty International, 'Substance Abuses: The Human Cost of Cambodia's Anti-drug Campaign' (Amnesty International, 2020).; Gloria Lai and Claudia Stoicescu, 'Drug Policy in Asia: The Origins and Extremities of Prohibition' in David R Bewley-Taylor and Khalid Tinasti (eds.), *Research Handbook on International Drug Policy* (Edward Elgar, 2020).

11 See, for instance, David T Johnson and Franklin E Zimring, *The Next Frontier: National Development, Political Change, and the Death Penalty in Asia* (Oxford University Press, 2009) 308–309.

12 See, for instance, William O Walker, *Opium and Foreign Policy: The Anglo-American Search for Order in Asia, 1912–1954* (UNC Press, 1991) (arguing that it is impossible to fully understand foreign and security policy in Asia without understanding the fight against opium in the region).;"中国的禁毒" ['Anti-drug in China'] (2000) 27.; 中华人民共和国国务院公报 [Gazette of the State Council of the People's Republic of China] 29 (stating that waging wars on drugs was the 'historical responsibility' of the Chinese government).; James Windle, 'A Slow March from Social Evil to Harm Reduction: Drugs and Drug Policy in Vietnam' (Brookings, 2016) 2 (in Vietnam, the punitive approach started in early 1990s).

13 William B McAllister, 'Foundations of the International Drug Control Regime: Nineteenth Century to the Second World War' in David R Bewley-Taylor and Khalid Tinasti (eds.), *Research Handbook on International Drug Policy* (Edward Elgar, 2020) 3–4.; Julia Lovell, *The Opium War: Drugs, Dreams and the Making of China* (Picador, 2012) 32–33.

14 Harry G Gelber, 'China as "Victim"? The Opium War That Wasn't' (2006) Center for European Studies Working Paper Series 136 (the Opium War was to maintain the principle of free trade and defend British civilians).; Jasper Ridley, *Lord Palmerston* (Constable, 1970) 254–256.; Arthur Waley, *The Opium War through Chinese Eyes* (Allen

and Unwin, 1958) (Britain imposed its superior military power to guarantee the profitable trade and disregard the horrible moral evils of opium).

15 Sheldon X Zhang and Ko-lin Chin, 'A People's War: China's Struggle to Contain Its Illicit Drug Problem' (Brookings, 2016) 9.

16 Yongming Zhou, 'Anti-drug Campaigns and State Building: China's Experiences in the 1950s' (2001) 32 *CEMOTI, Cahiers d'Études sur la Méditerranée Orientale et le monde Turco-Iranien* 233.

17 William O Walker, 'Drug Trafficking in Asia' (1992) 34 *Journal of Interamerican Studies and World Affairs* 201, 204.

18 Michelle Miao, 'The Penal Construction of Drug-Related Offenses in the Context of "Asian Values": The Rise of Punitive Anti-Drug Campaigns in Asia' (2017) 1 *International Comparative, Policy & Ethics Law Review* 47, 76; Patrick Tibke, 'Drug Dependence Treatment in China: A Policy Analysis' (*International Drug Policy Consortium*, February 2017).; McAllister (n 13) 3.

19 See Walker (n 12).

20 中华人民共和国治安管理处罚法 [Public Security Administration Punishments Law of the People's Republic of China], amended in 2012, arts 71–74.

21 中华人民共和国刑法 [Criminal Law of the People's Republic of China] (1997刑法 [1997 Criminal Law]), most recently amended in 2020, pt II, ch VI, s 7.

22 McAllister (n 13) 3.

23 Chongde Zhang and Yuan Chen, *China's Battle against Narcotics* (New Star Publishers, 1998).

24 Alison Adcock Kaufman, 'The "Century of Humiliation," Then and Now: Chinese Perceptions of the International Order' (2010) 25 *Pacific Focus* 1.

25 中华人民共和国刑法 [Criminal Law of the People's Republic of China], amended in 1979, art 171.

26 1997刑法 [1997 Criminal Law], art 347.

27 Ibid, 348.

28 张齐云 [Zhang Qiyun], '云南西双版纳禁毒34年战果累累' [Xishuangbanna City of Yunnan Province Has Achieved Fruitful Results in Drug Control for 34 Years] (Central Political and Legal Affairs Commission of the Communist Party of China, 28 June 2016). www.chinapeace.gov.cn/chinapeace/c53628/2016-06/28/content_12152065.shtml accessed 18 March 2022.

29 John Collins, 'Imperial Drug Economies, Development, and the Search for Alternatives in Asia, from Colonialism to Decolonisation' in Julia Buxton, Mary Chinery-Hesse & Khalid Tinasti (eds.), *Drug Policies and Development: Conflict and Coexistence* (Brill and Nijhof, 2020).

30 Ander Permanyer-Ugartemendia, 'Opium after the Manila Galleon: The Spanish Involvement in the Opium Economy in East Asia (1815–1830)' (2014) 10 *Investigaciones de Historia Económica-Economic History Research* 155.; Anne L Foster, 'Models for Governing: Opium and Colonial Policies in Southeast Asia, 1898–1910' in Anne L Foster (ed.), *The American Colonial State in the Philippines* (Duke University Press, 2003).; Gary Reid and Nick Crofts, 'Historical Perspectives of Drug Use in Southeast Asia' in Fifa Rahman and Nick Crofts (eds.), *Drug Law Reform in East and Southeast Asia* (Wiley-Blackwell, 2013).; Tripti Tandon, 'Drug Policy in India' (*International Drug Policy Consortium*, February 2015) 7.

31 Lasco (n 3).; Kieu Truong and Pip Nicholson, 'Drugs Prosecutions in Vietnam: the Modern Propaganda Trial' (2008) 34 *Monash University Law Review* 430.; Tim Lindsey

and Pip Nicholson, *Drugs Law and Legal Practice in Southeast Asia: Indonesia, Singapore and Vietnam* (Bloomsbury, 2016).

32 Nguyễn Thị Phương Hoa, 'Drug-Related Crimes under Vietnamese Criminal Law: Sentencing and Clemency in Law and Practice' (*Asian Law Center Briefing Paper Series*, 2014) 7.; Martin Booth, *Opium: A History* (Simon and Schuster, 1996).; Peter Lee, *Opium Culture: The Art and Ritual of the Chinese Tradition* (Inner Traditions/Bear & Co, 2006).

33 Daniel JP Wertz, 'Idealism, Imperialism, and Internationalism: Opium Politics in the Colonial Philippines, 1898–1925' (2013) 47 *Modern Asian Studies* 467.; Bobby Anderson, 'People, Land and Poppy: The Political Ecology of Opium and the Historical Impact of Alternative Development in Northwest Thailand' (2017) 1 *Forest and Society* 48.; Lindsey and Nicholson (n 31) 213.

34 Former US President Richard Nixon was the one who coined the phrase, 'war on drugs'. See Emily Dufton, 'The War on Drugs: How President Nixon Tied Addiction to Crime', *The Atlantic* (26 March 2012).; Ann Fordham, 'How the United States Fueled a Global Drug War, and Why It Must End' (Open Society Foundations, 2021).; Istvan Bayer and Hamid Ghodse, 'Evolution of International Drug Control, 1945–1995' (1999) 51 *Bulletin on Narcotics* 1 (mentioning the different approach adopted by the United States and other countries in defining illicit drugs since early 20th century).

35 Ann Fordham, 'The Meaningful Participation of 'Stakeholders' in Global Drug Policy Debates – A Policy Comment' in Julia Buxton, Mary Chinery-Hesse & Khalid Tinasti (eds.), *Drug Policies and Development: Conflict and Coexistence* (Brill and Nijhof, 2020).; Minxin Pei, 'Drugs, Gunboats and China's Score to Settle' (*Project Syndicate*, 24 August 2018).

36 Virginia Macdonald and Supatra Nacapew, 'Drug Control and Harm Reduction in Thailand' (*International Drug Policy Consortium*, 2013).; Chokwan Kitty Chopaka, 'Medical Cannabis Moving ahead in Thailand, but Who Stands to Benefit?' (*IDPC Blog*, 14 May 2019) https://idpc.net/blog/2019/05/medical-cannabis-moving-ahead-in-thailand-but-who-stands-to-benefit accessed 17 November 2021.; Pascal Tanguay, 'Can Medical Cannabis in Thailand Balance Profits and Patients?' (*East Asia Forum*, 13 May 2021) www.eastasiaforum.org/2021/05/13/can-medical-cannabis-in-thailand-balance-profits-and-patients/ accessed 17 November 2021.; Jake Pesaruk, '"An Unprecedented Achievement Anywhere" – Thailand's Decriminalization of Kratom', *Filter* (21 July 2021).

37 'Shrinking Civic Space in ASEAN: Indonesia and Thailand' (*Lokataru Foundation*, 15 March 2021) https://lokataru.id/shrinking-civic-space-in-asean-indonesia-and-thailand/ accessed 17 November 2021.; James Gomez and Robin Ramcharan, 'COVID-19 Shrinks Civic Space in Southeast Asia', *The Jakarta Post* (25 April 2020).; 'A Matter of Regional Concern: Shrinking Civil Society Space in Central Asia' (OSCE Human Dimension Implementation Meeting, Warsaw, 23 September 2015).; Edward Wong, 'Clampdown in China Restricts 7,000 Foreign Organizations', *The New York Times* (28 April 2016).

38 Thu Vuong, et al, 'Drug Policy in Vietnam: A Decade of Change?' (2012) 23 *International Journal of Drug Policy* 319, 319–320.

39 Reid and Crofts (n 30) 5.

40 Ibid, 6.

41 'Rampant HIV Spread in Developing Countries' (1991) 38 *International Nursing Review* 167.

42 UNAIDS, 'Health, Rights and Drugs: Harm Reduction, Decriminalization and Zero Discrimination for People Who Use Drugs' (UNAIDS, 2019).
43 Vuong, et al, (n 38) 322.; Theodore M Hammett, ' "Social Evils" and Harm Reduction: The Evolving Policy Environment for Human Immunodeficiency Virus Prevention among Injection Drug Users in China and Vietnam' (2008) *Addiction* 137–145.
44 Vuong, et al, (n 38) 323.
45 Adeeba Kamarulzaman and John L McBrayer, 'Compulsory Drug Detention Centers in East and Southeast Asia' (2015) 26 *International Journal of Drug Policy* Suppl 1:S33.; Lee Edson P Yarcia, 'It's Time to Decriminalize: Drug Policy Reform under a Public Health Framework' in Gideon Lasco (ed.), *Drugs and Philippine Society* (Bughaw 2021) 310–311.; Rick Lines, Julie Hannah & Giada Girelli, ' "Treatment in Liberty": Human Rights and Compulsory Detention for Drug Use' (2021) 22 *Human Rights Law Review* 1, 5.
46 Claudia Stoicescu and Gideon Lasco, '10 Years of Drug Policy in Asia: How Far Have We Come? A Civil Society Shadow Report' (*International Drug Policy Consortium*, 19 February 2019).
47 Tibke (n 18).; Simon Baldwin, 'Drug Policy Advocacy in Asia: Challenges, Opportunities and Prospects' (*International Drug Policy Consortium*, 2013) 19.
48 Law No. 16/2008/QH12 on Amending and Supplementing a Number of Articles of the Law on Drug Prevention and Control (National Assembly of Vietnam, 12 June 2008).
49 Law No. 13/2009/L-CTN on Amending and Supplementing a Number of Articles of the Penal Code (National Assembly of Vietnam, 29 June 2009).
50 Ethan Nadelmann, 'Learning to Live with Drugs', *The Washington Post* (Washington, 2 November 1999).
51 An alternative view is that the harm reduction approach includes harm of drug use but not harm of prohibition. See Jarrett Blaustein, Miki McLay & Jude McCulloch, 'Secondary Harm Mitigation: A More Humanitarian Framework for International Drug Law Enforcement' (2017) 46 *International Journal of Drug Policy* 66, 67.
52 Nadelmann (n 50).; Bernard E Harcourt, 'The Collapse of the Harm Principle' (1999) *Journal of Criminal Law and Criminology* 109.
53 Stoicescu and Lasco (n 46).
54 Vuong, et al, (n 38) 321.; Human Rights Watch, 'The Rehab Archipelago: Forced Labor and Other Abuses in Drug Detention Centers in Southern Vietnam' (Human Rights Watch, 2011).
55 Vuong, et al, (n 38) 323.
56 Human Rights Watch (n 54).
57 Toby Seddon, 'Markets, Regulation and Drug Law Reform: Towards a Constitutive Approach' (2020) 29 *Social and Legal Studies* 313, 321.
58 Clifford Shearing, 'A Constitutive Conception of Regulation' in Peter Grabosky and John Braithwaite (eds.), *Business Regulation and Australia's Future* (Australian Institute of Criminology, 1993).
59 Gloria Lai, 'Asia: Advocating for Humane and Effective Drug Policies' (2015) 21 *Sur: International Journal on Human Rights* 1.; Lai and Stoicescu (n 10).
60 Pham Nguyen Ha, et al, 'The Evolution of HIV Policy in Vietnam: From Punitive Control Measures to a More Rights-based Approach' (2010) 3 *Global Health Action* 1.
61 Han-Zhu Qian, et al, 'Injection Drug Use and HIV/AIDS in China: Review of Current Situation, Prevention and Policy Implications' (2006) 3 *Harm Reduction Journal* 1.; Vuong, et al, (n 38).

62 Harm Reduction International, 'What Is Harm Reduction?' www.hri.global/what-is-harm-reduction accessed 17 November 2021.
63 This is not to deny that funding for HIV prevention, treatment and care, e.g. from the Global Fund to fight AIDS, Tuberculosis and Malaria, has contributed significantly to the introduction and scale-up of harm reduction measures in countries that retain punitive drug policies.
64 Nadelmann (n 50).
65 Kamarulzaman and McBrayer (n 45).; Vuong, et al, (n 38).
66 Vuong, et al, (n 38) 321.; Human Rights Watch (n 54).
67 Ricky Gunawan and Gloria Lai, 'Consensus and Contradictions in ASEAN: An Analysis of Southeast Asia at and after UNGASS 2016' in Axel Klein and Blaine Stothard (eds.), *Collapse of the Global Order on Drugs: From UNGASS 2016 to Review 2019* (Emerald, 2018) 155.; Jennifer Hasselgard-Rowe, Naomi Burke-Shyne & Ann Fordham, 'Public Health and International Drug Control' in David R Bewley-Taylor and Khalid Tinasti (eds.), *Research Handbook on International Drug Policy* (Edward Elgar, 2020) 257.
68 Miao (n 18).
69 Bilahari Kausikan, 'Asia's Different Standard' (1993) 92 *Foreign Policy* 24, 26.
70 Yash Ghai, 'Human Rights and Governance: The Asia Debate' (1994) 15 *Australian Year Book* of *International Law* 1, 4.; Amartya Sen, *Human Rights and Asian Values* (Carnegie Council on Ethics and International Affairs, 1997).
71 Diane K Mauzy, 'The Human Rights and "Asian Values" Debate in Southeast Asia: Trying to Clarify the Key Issues' (1997) 10 *The Pacific Review* 210; Kausikan (n 69).; Ghai (n 70).
72 Miao (n 18).
73 See, e.g. Rodrigo Duterte, '"I Don't Care about Human Rights": Philippines' Duterte Acknowledges Abuses in Drug War but Refuses to Back Down', *South China Morning Post* (6 August 2016).; 'China Will Never Allow Drug Traffickers from Any Country to Kill and Poison Its People: Chinese Embassy in Canada', *Global Times* (11 August 2021).; Tee Zhuo, 'Singapore Has Sovereign Right to Use Death Penalty against Drug Offenders: Ministries Respond to Malaysian Minister', *The Strait Times* (22 November 2019).
74 Damon Barrett, Julie Hannah & Rick Lines, 'What Does It Mean to Adopt a Human Rights-based Approach to Drug Policy?' (2020) 22 *Health and Human Rights Journal* 355 (stating that 'Some of the biggest debates needed in drug policy are not about evidence, as such, but underlying principles or ideals.').
75 Vuong, et al, (n 38).
76 Miao (n 18).
77 Ghai (n 69) 27.; John D Ciorciari, 'Institutionalizing Human Rights in Southeast Asia' (2012) 34 *Human Rights Quarterly* 695, 702.
78 Prime Minister's Office, *White Paper on Shared Values* (Cmd 1, 1991).; 'Human Rights in China' (Information Office of the State Council of the People's Republic of China, November 1991).; 'White Paper on Human Rights Progress in China', *China Daily* (23 September 2019).
79 See *International Guidelines on Human Rights and Drug Policy* (n 1).
80 *International Covenant on Civil and Political Rights* (adopted 16 December 1966, entered into force 23 March 1976) 999 UNTS 171, art 6(1).
81 Ibid, art 17.; *Universal Declaration of Human Rights* (10 December 1948) A/RES/217 A (III), art 12.

82 Simon Flacks, 'Drug Control, Human Rights, and the Right to the Highest Attainable Standard of Health: A Reply to Saul Takahashi' (2011) 33 *Human Rights Quarterly* 856, 863.

83 Scott Leckie and Anne Gallagher, *Economic, Social, and Cultural Rights: A Legal Resource Guide* (Penn Press, 2011) xvi–xvii.

84 Many countries, despite their varying degrees and patterns of reservation, enshrined human rights in their Constitutions. See, e.g. 中华人民共和国宪法 [Constitution of the People's Republic of China], most recently amended in 2018, art 33.; Hiến pháp nước Cộng hòa xã hội chủ nghĩa Việt Nam [Constitution of the Socialist Republic of Vietnam], most recently amended in 2013, art 3.; Ang Konstitusyon ng Republika ng Pilipinas [Constitution of the Republic of the Philippines] 1987, art II, s 11.; Konstitusi Republik Indonesia [Constitution of the Republic of Indonesia] 1945, ch XA.

85 Cláudia Costa Storti and Paul De Grauwe, 'Globalization and the Price Decline of Illicit Drugs' (2009) 20 *International Journal of Drug Policy* 48.; Ben Bowling, 'Transnational Criminology and the Globalization of Harm Production' in Mary Bosworth and Carolyn Hoyle (eds.), *What Is Criminology* (Oxford University Press, 2011).

86 Ryan Goodman and Derek Jinks, 'How to Influence States: Socialization and International Human Rights Law' (2004) 54 *Duke Law Journal* 621.

87 Sangmin Bae, *When the State No Longer Kills: International Human Rights Norms and Abolition of Capital Punishment* (SUNY Press, 2007) 126.

88 Kamarulzaman and McBrayer (n 45).; Stoicescu and Lasco (n 46) 31.; Lee Edson P Yarcia and Jan Michael Alexandre C Bernadas, 'Articulating Key Obligations of States to Persons Deprived of Liberty under A Right to Health Framework: the Philippine Case Study' (2021) 14 *International Journal of Human Rights in Healthcare* 310; Lines, Hannah & Girelli (n 45).

89 See, e.g. Human Rights Watch, 'Torture in the Name of Treatment: Human Rights Abuses in Vietnam, China, Cambodia, and Lao PDR' (24 July 2012).; Zhang and Chin (n 15).; George Havenhand, 'Reorienting Drug Policy in Indonesia: Pathways to the Sustainable Development Goals' (*LBH Masyarakat and Reprieve*, March 2020) 12.; 'Coalition of NGOs on Human Rights and Drug Policies for UPR – Nepal' (*Universal Periodic Review*, July 2020) http://fileserver.idpc.net/library/UPR-Submission-People-Who-Use-Drugs-in-Nepal(1).pdf accessed 17 November 2021.; Alia Shoaib, 'Photos Show Homeless Heroin Addicts in Afghanistan Rounded up and Forced into Grim Rehab by the Taliban', *Business Insider* (11 October 2021).; Ambika Satkunanathan, 'A Broken System: Drug Control, Detention and Treatment of People Who Use Drugs in Sri Lanka' (Harm Reduction International, 2021) 16–18; Lines, Hannah & Girelli (n 45).

90 Miao (n 18) 66–67.

Part II

Tracking Progress

4 Lessons Learned from Legal Regulation of Cannabis

Zara Snapp, Jorge Herrera Valderrábano and Luis Daniel Santiago Vidargas

Introduction

The drug policy reform movement has advanced its agenda substantially in recent years, spurring harm reduction strategies, strategic litigation and, perhaps most successfully, legally regulating cannabis in numerous jurisdictions for both medicinal and recreational adult use. However, the looming question remains whether regulation can promote social justice, development, equity and human rights or whether capitalism and economic interests will overwhelm these possibilities as an industry emerges.

At the time of writing in 2022, only two national governments have fully regulated cannabis markets for adult use, Uruguay (2013) and Canada (2018), along with 21 states in the United States, while Malta[1] and Luxembourg have approved home-grow and cannabis associations, without designing a commercial adult use market. Many more countries have moved forward with medicinal cannabis, including Argentina, Colombia, Germany, Greece, Israel, Jamaica, Portugal, Switzerland, and numerous others, as well as 36 states in the United States.[2] Thanks to strategic litigation, Mexico has legalised home-grow, without yet approving a more comprehensive bill that would allow for a commercial market.[3] The green wave of regulation has been steady but not as swift as some forecast when Uruguay became the first country to regulate under the leadership of President José 'Pepe' Mújica.

Most of the states that have regulated cannabis for personal use in the United States have subsequently passed reforms including social equity programmes to promote minority cannabis business ownership, equitable license distribution and record expungement to combine criminal justice and economic opportunity elements into a comprehensive social justice effort.[4] In other contexts, such as Mexico, the conversation has centred on how to include cultivating communities in policy discussions and the transition to a legal market considering that the country is one of the top illegal cannabis producers in the world.[5] Canada is slowly integrating social justice components into its already implemented regulatory framework, with few successful applicants in its expungement programme due to high barriers to

DOI: 10.4324/9781003169765-7

access.[6] As of August 2020, only 467 applications had been received by the Parole Board of Canada (PBC), and 265 record suspensions had been ordered.[7] Automatic expungement is a key part of promoting social justice through reducing obstacles.

Based on the authors' organising and academic work, four principles of social justice have emerged in the context of cannabis law reform, although many more could be included within the cannabis regulation sphere. For our purposes, we will focus on how legal regulation has confronted the dynamics of privilege and oppression, recognised the communities that have been historically vulnerable or vulnerated, implemented affirmative action to level the balance of justice and power and repaired the harms of prohibition.[8] In Latin America, the transitional justice pillars – including truth, justice, reparations and guarantees of no-repetition –must be transversal and integrated within drug policy reform. While jurisdictions have identified diverse objectives for legally regulating cannabis, our analysis as public policy practitioners centres on the institutional and societal capacity during implementation to meet these four principles and hopes to serve as a guide for future policymaking.

Health, Equity and Justice in Cannabis Regulation

Cannabis reform campaigns have primarily centred around two general arguments. The first is that the plant should be regulated rather than criminalised because it is safer for consumers than legal substances such as alcohol and tobacco. The other is that legal regulation is the best policy to achieve wider public goals, such as reducing underage consumption, shrinking the criminal market and promoting human rights, whether through reducing rights violations from drug law enforcement or the capacity of criminal justice reforms to advance social equity.

For those of us within the reform movement who seek to strictly regulate all psychoactive substances, the second argument holds greater weight because it provides a blueprint, a way to consider the risks and benefits of all substances without stigmatising the use of others. If we believe that all substances should be regulated, we must also recognise there will be substances that are not necessarily 'safer' than alcohol and tobacco that still require differentiated legal regulation, rather than blanket criminalisation.[9] It is this understanding that will allow us to have a more extensive and profound conversation about how lessons learned from cannabis reforms can be used to inform our work in regulating other substances such as cocaine and heroin. Regulating substances beyond cannabis may have a much more powerful social impact in countries such as Mexico and Colombia that have borne the burden of punitive, prohibitionist policies over the past 100 years. The United States and Canada should also consider the safe supply of substances as a public health response to the overdose crisis, while seeking criminal justice mechanisms to expunge records, release people from prison and eliminate the criminalisation of people who use any type of drug.[10]

Reviewing the cannabis reforms implemented over the past ten years, primarily related to recreational adult use, four main lessons can be extrapolated:

1 A public health approach is a first step that should be taken but is not sufficiently comprehensive in contexts that have experienced the devastating judicial, economic, social and cultural impacts of prohibition. This is particularly true in countries where the cultivation and production of psychoactive plants is a development issue related to poverty and inequality.
2 Integrating social equity or social justice mechanisms in the newly legal market is key. However, access to capital, licenses or institutional support is required to reduce barriers to entry.
3 Cannabis reform should, but does not always, include judicial reforms. Expungement of cannabis-related criminal convictions, prisoner releases for those incarcerated on cannabis charges, early release and effective decriminalisation of possession for personal use must be explicitly integrated to any regulatory policy.
4 The greatest risk in cannabis regulation is that corporate capture of the market allows it to become an industry with economic practices that do more harm than good in communities.

As we glean lessons from the various regulatory models being implemented, future-focused thinking, research and practice require us to forecast diverse outcomes that put equity-based objectives at the centre to inform prospective initiatives, particularly at an international level.

A Public Health Approach: Balancing Risks and Outcomes

The world has witnessed the growing contradictions between the international drug control system and the objective of protecting public health. Despite the more than 60 years of an international regime based on prohibition, drug production and use remains stable on a global level. Production can be reduced in one area, only to increase in a neighbouring zone or country, known commonly as the balloon effect.[11] While individual statistics vary, the aggregate whole remains largely stable. The same is true for prevalence of drug use which increases due to population growth but maintains relatively stable with greater increases in developing countries.[12] The revenues of illegal markets have increased, particularly during the COVID-19 pandemic, due to disruptions in trafficking routes,[13] empowering criminal organisations who seek to maximise revenues and territorial control, while weakening institutional capacity.[14] This has delivered several 'unintended consequences', as outlined by the United Nations in 2008.[15] But most importantly, it has posed risks for communities and individuals.

Prohibitionist policies have disproportionately affected people who use drugs. Not only do they face security threats because of their interactions with illegal markets, as well as risks related to exposure in public spaces where corruption and violence are constant, they also face increased risk of health harms. Many incentives exist for illegal groups that produce drugs clandestinely to distribute products that are lower in quality and higher in revenue. The lack of legal mechanisms for government supervision on the production chain of drugs poses high risks to people using drugs, who are uncertain about the substance's origin, its composition, the materials used for its production and the process for its transformation into a final product.[16] Evidence suggests that these are factors that contribute to serious mental health issues, substance use disorder or fatal overdoses.[17]

Illegality is the foundation of this situation. Legal regulation attempts to open a safer supply chain, reducing the harms of prohibition, which could lead to better outcomes in health, personal security or access to human rights and basic services.[18] Several models already exist that balance risk within the context of a legally regulated market in psychoactive substances, the most common being alcohol and tobacco.

The history of alcohol in the United States offers one of the few examples of transition from illegal markets to legal markets. Following the Volstead Act, alcohol was banned in the United States beginning in 1920. Alcohol prohibition lasted for more than a decade, and as law enforcement increased, it created incentives for illicit producers to increase their return on investment from alcohol production. Following the 'iron law' of prohibition,[19] liquor production focused on more potent products, able trafficked in smaller, more compact quantities to reduce risk of detection while maximising profits. Information on production standards, quality and possible risks was not available to consumers, much like illegal drug markets today. The Temperance Movement produced propaganda regarding alcohol use focused on fear.[20]

However, it eventually became clear that the problems created by prohibition surpassed the risks of legal alcohol access. The failure to decrease alcohol use over the long term,[21] combined with a surge in crime related to alcohol and the increased power of organised criminal groups,[22] pressure from industry as well as general societal concerns[23] led to the decision of Congress with the support of President Franklin D. Roosevelt to end alcohol prohibition in 1933.[24] Today we can see a similar coalescence of concerns and interests fuelling the movement to legally regulate drugs such as cannabis, as well as psychedelics and stimulants such as psilocybin and MDMA, which are currently being explored through a therapeutic framework.[25]

Public Health in Uruguay

In the case of cannabis, protecting public health has been at the centre of transitioning from an illegal market to a legal one. Following an increase in the perception of insecurity related to the illegal drug market in 2013, Uruguay moved forward with regulating cannabis. The government, which promoted the legislative bill, framed its arguments around separating markets to ensure that people who use cannabis would not be offered other, often riskier substances, to reduce the power of organised criminal groups and to improve the quality of the cannabis which was being consumed in the country.[26]

José 'Pepe' Mújica, President of Uruguay at the time, sought to address security issues related to the illegal market, which was supplied principally by organised criminal groups, and to increase the quality of products consumed to protect the health of Uruguayan citizens. Cannabis regulation was presented as a valuable mechanism to confront both issues, while maintaining a consistent discourse regarding the protection of human rights of people who use cannabis within both national and international fora. The government of Uruguay grounded its defence of legal regulation at the United Nations as a means of prioritising their human rights obligations above drug control requirements.[27]

Uruguayan authorities considered that legal regulation was a safer route when balancing the risks of prohibition versus the risks of consuming. A type of Paraguayan cannabis, known as *prensado paraguayo* for its pressed form, was abundant in the Uruguayan market. This product posed health risks because it often contained mould and because production standards were low since it had to be trafficked clandestinely to its destination.[28] *Prensado* smells acidic because of the fermentation and decomposition due to a lack of care during production. Paraguayan growers could increase the quality but the illegal market forced them to go to great lengths to mask the product they were transiting. By pressing the plant, producers could traffic larger quantities and the plastic wrapping process reduced its distinctive odour. Based on these health risks, the government determined that providing legal access was a means to respect the health of people who use cannabis in Uruguay.

Uruguayan residents who use cannabis have three methods of legal access: they may cultivate up to six plants in their home for personal use, following a governmental registration process; they may join a cannabis social club, which can have between 15 and 45 members and up to 99 plants (proportional to the number of members); or they can purchase cannabis in pharmacies.[29] Cannabis in the regulated market is grown by the private sector, the government buys it and then distributes it to pharmacies around the country. Residents registered to access cannabis can exclusively utilise one of these three ways and are allowed to have up to 40 grams per month.[30]

Cultivation for personal use is the second most utilised mode of access, with 12,902 people participating. There are 213 cannabis social clubs which supply 6,452 people, and 46,375 people who purchase their cannabis from 23 pharmacies.[31] Cannabis clubs can use any seeds they choose, motivating greater genetic diversity, while the regulated market is restricted to five varieties, two indica dominant, two sativa dominant and one high in CBD. This strict government regulation ensures that only residents over 18-years old have legal access to the plant. In order to ease the concerns of its neighbouring countries, Uruguay only allows people who reside in the country or are citizens to have access, although this policy is currently being reviewed in order to reduce diversion of legal cannabis to the illegal market.

Uruguay chose to regulate based on priorities of protecting health and human rights. Recognising that the previous, illegal supply of cannabis was causing harm in their country, both due to the social and economic externalities of the illegal market as well as the low-quality of cannabis, they designed a policy based on separating markets and providing legal access to all adult residents. This has not translated into greater health harms but rather a greater understanding regarding both the possible risks and the benefits of legal cannabis. The policy change has also been shown to have an impact on the judicial system, with fewer arrests and incarceration of people for cannabis-related offenses.[32]

Social Equity and Industry: A Delicate Balance

Social equity programmes aim to provide resources proportional to the needs of each individual, often as a means of increasing their opportunities in a given situation.[33] A drug arrest and conviction in the United States and other parts of the world can lead to a loss of rights and social services, including government services, the right to vote, access to public housing or deportation in the case of being undocumented.

Black, Indigenous and people of colour have been disproportionately affected by punitive, prohibitionist policies.[34] The impacts of drug convictions have created intergenerational cycles of poverty and reduced opportunities as people, primarily men, are taken from their communities and incarcerated for low-level drug offences. Numerous studies, along with seminal works such as *The New Jim Crow*,[35] demonstrate that the criminalisation of drug offenses have been disproportionately leveraged against people of colour, even though white people consume illegal substances at the same rate.[36] Integrating social equity, including access to capital as a means of increasing the participation of communities negatively impacted by prohibition, in the emerging cannabis industry has become both a lesson learned and a path which must still be followed. Although progress has been slow, there are clear examples that demonstrate this is possible if jurisdictions are flexible and committed to incorporating social equity in their policy design.[37]

In the United States, when states such as Colorado and Washington regulated cannabis for adult use in 2012, issues of industry social equity were not on the table. Colorado explicitly prohibited people who had been criminalised from participating in the market, something which has since been rectified. There was discussion around how to ensure that people would no longer be criminalised for an activity that was now legal, and reducing arrests generally for cannabis.[38] However, it was unclear how to incorporate social justice principles. Additionally, the main concern on the part of state governments was how the federal government would react to legal regulation for adult use, given that cannabis remains prohibited under federal drug laws.

As time has passed, and more states have regulated, social equity has become the most important issue during campaigns, regardless of whether reforms are proposed at the legislative level or through citizen referendums.[39] It is no longer sufficient to regulate; there must be a social justice purpose behind the regulatory framework.

Numerous US states have passed innovative laws with social equity provisions. At the same time, companies have brought cases against state governments for implementing these affirmative action approaches.[40] The push and pull between rights and reparations has been at centre stage regarding legal regulation. Since the use and possession of cannabis is illegal under federal law and states set their own policies regarding the medical and recreational commercialisation and use of cannabis, the guidelines for the issuance of licenses to participate in the cannabis industry chain as a producer, manufacturer or seller vary widely. With 21 states currently regulating the adult use of cannabis, each one is an experiment, both in the regulatory framework and in the social justice purpose proposed in the law.[41] Although most states that initially regulated allocated tax revenue to finance public health and educations services such as prevention and treatment,[42] only one state, Massachusetts,[43] had a commissioner specifically focused on social equity during the implementation of cannabis regulation. There has been a greater interest in this as more states regulate.

Unfortunately, a prevailing trend among the legal cannabis industry across the United States is the perpetuation of structural inequity based on class and race, including a lack of access to capital, property, technical assistance and connections.[44] A disproportionate market share of the legal industry is held by upper-middle class white people, when compared to Black, Latino/Hispanic, Asian or other minorities' shares, even as minorities are criminalised at a much higher rate for drug-related offenses[45]. According to a *Marijuana Business Daily* survey, 81% of cannabis business owners are white, while 6% are Latino/Hispanic, 4% are Black and 2% are Asian.[46] Now that the medical use of cannabis is legal in 36 US states, and adult use of cannabis is legal in 21, bias exists regarding who gets to participate in the legal cannabis industry. Access to capital, previous engagement in the medical market and inequity in licensing guidelines have shown to benefit big businesses and disregard small, minority-led initiatives.[47] Social equity programmes, with varying levels of success, seek to shift the balance of economic power, by increasing opportunities through affirmative actions to repair the harms previously waged by cannabis prohibition.

There have been positive and negative developments. In Florida, for businesses to qualify for a medical license, they must have vertical integration, which means they control the entire production chain for the products they sell, including cultivation, extraction, manufacturing, retail and laboratory testing.[48] Such rules limit access to the legal medical market, since it closes the door to small or medium entrepreneurs who cannot afford a complex production chain, leaving it to a small group of big cannabis or pharmaceutical companies that can develop these operations. As of 2020, according to the Office of Medical Marijuana Use, five companies control 65% of the medical cannabis market in Florida, which is one of 11 states that require vertical integration for a cannabis license.[49] Regulatory agencies should be aware of the intent behind the model in order to achieve stated objectives of avoiding corporate capture or spurring social equity.

On the positive side, Massachusetts has an innovative social equity programme. As part of the policy design prior to implementation, one of the five Commissioners of the Cannabis Control Commission was appointed to specifically focus on the issue of equity. This means that there was always a voice at the table integrating and motivating a discussion around social equity, but more importantly, pushing for affirmative actions to achieve stated objectives. The Social Equity programme provides technical assistance and training and expedited license application review, as well as reduced licensing fees. Beneficiaries of the programme have to demonstrate eligibility through the following means: living in designated areas, income and residency requirements, having a previous drug-related criminal record or a parent or spouse who had been criminalised for drug offences or demonstrating an articulable experience that would be relevant.[50] Social consumption and delivery-only licenses are exclusively for social equity participants during a minimum of three years.[51] These types of licenses have fewer barriers to entry since there is low investment required and can provide economic opportunities for communities that have been disproportionately affected by previous prohibitionist policies.

In September 2021, New York regulated adult cannabis use following years of debate, with a clear social equity framework. Priority has been given to social equity licensing, with the stated goal of 50% of cannabis business licenses for social equity participants in the state and a funded incubator programme is expected to provide grants, access to capital and technical assistance for disproportionately impacted communities and small-scale farmers.[52] Housing Works became the first operator of a dispensary in New York City bringing in over $12 million dollars in the first six months. This money goes directly to fulfilling their mission of providing healthcare, housing, sexual health and harm reduction services, advocacy for health equity and social justice initiatives, LGBTQ+ youth programs and job training to New Yorkers.[53] In order to motivate additional interventions, the bill also created categories of license for cooperatives, social consumption spaces, delivery and small businesses to target people who do not have access to large investments.

Countries around the world are exploring ways to integrate social justice mechanisms into cannabis regulation. In Mexico, following the Supreme Court declaration of unconstitutionality regarding the absolute prohibition of cannabis, the Senate and Congress have advanced the discussion on cannabis reform with a social justice framework. The proposed law from the Senate includes creating a quota system where, for the first five-years of implementation, at least 40% of cultivation licenses would be exclusively granted to the social sector such as *ejidos* (agricultural land farmed communally under a system supported by the state), cooperatives and communal property or communities that had been affected by prohibition through crop eradication.[54] According to the proposal, which has not been approved, after the first five-years, a minimum of 20% of cultivation licenses must be granted to communities. As a cannabis-producing country, the goal with this mechanism is to transition people and communities from the illegal to the legal market by reducing barriers to entry and creating affirmative actions. Additional restrictions exist on the number of points of sale allowed per company to reduce the possibility of corporate capture.[55]

Inclusive approaches such as those in Massachusetts and New York can boost equity in the cannabis industry, while the measures being proposed in Mexico demonstrate a willingness to acknowledge and transition the illegal market to a formal space. However, experience has shown that inclusion in the design and flexibility in implementation, as well as a strong regulatory agency, are key to ensure that good intentions become effective policies.

Finally, it is worth noting the barriers that national and international mechanisms pose to prevent money laundering and to address corruption, which has resulted in significant challenges for small cannabis businesses to access banking services. This situation has obliged companies to operate in cash only, increasing security risks and operating costs, in addition to promoting informality. Uruguay experienced this with the implementation cannabis regulation when licensed pharmacies participating in the industry were not able to charge cannabis operations because they have a multinational bank (namely, HSBC or Bank of America).[56] US federal law does not permit people with 'drug trafficking activities' to have bank accounts, even if companies operate within a legal scheme.[57] A regulatory model to counter the current global challenges in the cannabis industry would need to provide banking guidelines and consider negotiations with public and private actors, to allow for the creation of bank accounts within the cannabis industry.

Cannabis Regulation: Judicial Reform as a Means of Reparations

Mass criminalisation and prohibition of cannabis have resulted in millions of people being incarcerated around the world for low-level crimes such as possession or sale.[58] Noted academics have demonstrated that punitive drug policies were used to justify social control, oppression and criminalisation.[59] While the United States has some of the gravest examples of mass incarceration and overcriminalisation, in other countries certain populations have also been disproportionately affected through punitive policies related to both supply and demand.

As states in the United States move towards the legal regulation of cannabis, there has been a parallel movement to excarcerate, expunge criminal records and decriminalise activities that were previously illegal. Involvement in the justice system, for any length of time, is strongly linked to reduced life opportunities,[60] including employment, education or in gaining social capital. It has been widely documented that criminalisation of the use of cannabis has disproportionately affected Black, Indigenous and people of colour, although rates of use are relatively similar across racial lines.[61] Data show that drug enforcement in the United States has carried a racial and ethnic bias that affected primarily Black and Latino communities. According to the Drug Policy Alliance, as of 2018 nearly 80% of people in federal prison and almost 60% of people in state prison for drug offenses are Black or Latino/Hispanic.[62] If social justice is a goal of regulating cannabis, then judicial reform is a key component of repairing the harms as jurisdictions move towards legally regulating cannabis or any psychoactive substance.

Sealing or expunging criminal records related to cannabis could impact the largest number of people compared with the economic development and social equity opportunities explored previously. Expungements also have a broader effect if done automatically, without requiring the criminalised person to submit paperwork or 'opt in'.[63] The best case scenario is to integrate both social equity programmes and judicial reform into the policy design and subsequent implementation concurrently. One of the most recent and most far-reaching judicial reforms is in New York, which automatically expunges records and contemplates releasing people who are incarcerated for crimes which would now be legal or decriminalised. The Office of Court Administration will have up to two years to carry out the process, and making it automatic, eliminates barriers witnessed in other states.[64]

There are also policy options that reduce contact with law enforcement and the opportunity to be criminalised, such as addressing consumption in public spaces or while driving a vehicle. The New York regulation model addresses these by allowing for consumption of cannabis in any space in which tobacco consumption is permitted. Legislators also approved criteria that establish sanctions for driving under the influence of cannabis, but clearly identified that the smell of cannabis would not be considered as a cause to stop or detain a vehicle. The regulatory framework implements a decriminalisation process for minors, imposing a fine of no more than $50 and explicitly stating that there can be no other consequences or revocation of privileges or rights. Law enforcement has no mechanism for acting against people under 21 for possessing up to three ounces since it is a civil matter and possession cannot be cause for stop, search or arrest.[65]

Caution: Possible Corporate Capture Ahead

As jurisdictions move towards regulation, the hunger for market domination runs parallel with companies exploring options for expansion. Several jurisdictions with cannabis regulation for adult use began with a medical cannabis model whose companies were the first to receive licenses for the 'recreational' market, as in the case of Colorado and Washington State.[66]

Canadian companies, many of which have histories of cut-throat practices, as in the case of Canadian companies mining in countries such as Mexico,[67] have a first-mover advantage and have invested capital in other countries with cannabis regulations. In 2018, Aurora Cannabis acquired the first Mexican company to obtain a medical cannabis distribution license,[68] following medical cannabis reforms. In June 2019, Canopy announced a $3.4 billion deal to purchase US-based cannabis company Acreage,[69] with a specific requirement being that the United States legalises non-medical cannabis at the federal level within the next 7.5 years. Canopy reportedly has at least two other similar deals with US companies.[70] This is the fear of corporate capture and the risk of commercialising cannabis (and other substances) without incorporating social equity mechanisms into the initial policy design and implementation.

While these acquisitions are primarily undertaken by the largest companies, domestically in Canada, there has also been a trend of losing stock value following a merger of this type, with some smaller companies gaining market share as consumer demands shift. Companies such as Tilray and Aurora have seen their market share decrease in 2021,[71] while other companies are gaining strength. It is unclear over the long term how this will play out, however, the involvement of US and Canadian companies in jurisdictions such as Uruguay and Colombia have been broadly documented.[72]

There is also a focus on exporting cannabis-derived products from Latin America to other countries with medical cannabis regulations, including the European

Union, Australia and Brazil. This has created an emphasis on export, often at the expense of domestic markets. In the case of Colombia, 93% of the licenses granted by the Ministry of Health have been for export.[73]

Future regulation needs to create a better balance between lifting the restrictions of prohibition and ensuring the new markets promote social well-being. Governments must innovate in the issuance and implementation of a regulatory model, to prevent corporate capture, avoid monopolisation and actively promote market access to communities which have been historically marginalised. Some policy levers include the use of social equity programmes and licenses, ensuring minimum standards of transparency and accountability, establishing limits to the participation of foreign investment in domestic markets and supporting domestic production and consumption. This is crucial to motivate a diverse, horizontal market that allows for many actors to participate and distribute resources more equitably along the value chain. It is desirable that governments set restrictions on corporate political funding and lobbying, to assure that these issues can be discussed during the policy design process.

Conclusion

Lessons from cannabis regulation are evolving with each new legal framework. Jurisdictions are recognising the need to implement judicial reforms, including expungements, pardons and sealing of records as a means of repairing the harms of prohibition. These mechanisms will also prove to be crucial when considering regulation in places where organised crime has played a large role, and where non-state actors are willing to transition to a legal market in exchange for pardons or amnesty.

Less than a decade has passed since the first adult use regulation models were implemented, and while several key lessons can be captured from these first jurisdictions, there is still much to be learned in the practice of legal regulation. As governments and societies seek to place social equity at the centre of cannabis regulation, it will be necessary to use policy levers that have the desired impact.

As explored in this chapter, placing the health and human rights of the population at the centre of policies begins with ensuring access to quality products and implementing effective decriminalisation models. Social equity mechanisms are key to facilitating the participation of people who have been criminalised or been negatively affected by prohibition to engage in the legal market. Avoiding corporate capture can be a policy objective as a means of reparations to ensure a horizontal, diverse and more just legal cannabis market. Finally, judicial reforms are urgently required and should be implemented concurrently with any regulatory scheme in order to reverse some of the existing harms of prohibition.

Regulation may not only be used to provide safer channels for drug use to reduce the risks and harms of prohibition. When implemented from a social justice approach, it can also be used for addressing the negative outcomes of repressive drug policies that have threatened social development in many countries. As more jurisdictions explore legal regulation of cannabis and other psychoactive plants or substances, it is both wise and necessary to undertake a clear contextual diagnosis with clearly defined policy objectives. Rather than importing models from others, governments should be flexible in meeting the needs of its population, with human rights, health and social justice as cross-cutting goals.

Notes

1 Daniel Boffey, 'Malta to Legalise Cannabis for Personal Use in European First', *The Guardian* (13 December 2021).
2 Terry Hacienda, 'The 2021 Guide to Cannabis Laws around the World', *Chicago Tribune* (15 July 2021).
3 David Agren, 'Mexico Supreme Court Strikes down Laws That Ban Use of Recreational Marijuana', *The Guardian* (28 June 2021).
4 Drug Policy Alliance, 'From Prohibition to Progress: A Status Report on Marijuana Legalization' https://drugpolicy.org/legalization-status-report accessed 20 February 2023.
5 Oscar Lopez, 'Mexico Set to Legalize Marijuana, Becoming World's Largest Market', *The New York Times* (19 March 2021).
6 Tyler Choi, 'Canada Passes Law to Speed Pardons for Pot Possession', *Reuters* (20 June 2019).
7 Public Safety Canada, 'Cannabis Pardons' www.publicsafety.gc.ca/cnt/trnsprnc/brfng-mtrls/prlmntry-bndrs/20201201/001/index-en.aspx accessed 12 February 2023.
8 Ozlem Sensoy and Robin Diangelo, 'Developing Social Justice Literacy: An Open Letter to Our Faculty Colleagues' (January 2009) 90 *Phi Delta Kappan* 345.
9 David J Nutt, Leslie A King & Lawrence D Phillips, 'Drug Harms in the UK: A Multicriteria Decision Analysis' (1 November 2010) 376 *The Lancet* 1558.
10 Zara Snapp and Jorge Herrera Valderrábano, 'Tracing a Path for Opium Gum from Mexico as a Safe Supply Harm Reduction Measure for Canada' (May 2021) 91 *International Journal of Drug Policy* 103066.
11 Pat Paterson and Katy Robinson, *Measuring Success in the War on Drugs* (Perry Center Occasional Paper, 2014).
12 United Nations Office on Drugs and Crime, '2020 World Drug Report: Impact of COVID-19, Policy Implications' (June 2020).
13 United Nations, 'Covid-19 Causes Some Illegal Drug Prices to Surge, as Supplies Are Disrupted Worldwide', *UN News* (7 May 2020).
14 Zara Snapp, Khalid Tinasti & Jorge Herrera Valderrábano, 'Regulation of Illegal Drugs: State Control and Fragile Institutional Capacity' (2019) 1(3) *Journal of Illicit Economies and Development* 255.
15 United Nations Office on Drugs and Crime, *2008 World Drug Report* (United Nations, 2008), 21.
16 Neil Hunt, 'A Review of the Evidence-Base for Harm Reduction Approaches to Drug Use' (2003) *Forward Thinking on Drugs*.
17 Global Commission on Drug Policy, 'War On Drugs: Report of the Global Commission on Drug Policy' (2011).
18 Global Commission on Drug Policy, 'Regulation: The Responsible Control of Drugs' (2018).
19 Harry Levine and Craig Reinarman, 'From Prohibition to Regulation: Lessons from Alcohol Policy for Drug Policy' (1991) 69/3 *The Milbank Quarterly* 461, 466.

20 Leah Rae Berk, 'Temperance and Prohibition Era Propaganda: A Study in Rhetoric' (February 2005) Alcohol, Temperance & Prohibition: Brown University Library Center for Digital Scholarship https://library.brown.edu/cds/temperance/essay.html accessed 12 February 2023.

21 Alcohol consumption fell at the beginning of Prohibition to approximately 30% of its pre-Prohibition level. During the next several years, however, alcohol consumption increased sharply, to about 60–70% of pre-Prohibition levels. Jeffrey Miron and Jeffrey Zwiebel, 'Alcohol Consumption during Prohibition' (April 1991) National Bureau of Economic Research, Working Paper No. 3675.

22 Mark Thornton, 'Alcohol Prohibition Was a Failure' (17 July 1991) CATO Institute, Policy Analysis No. 157 www.cato.org/policy-analysis/alcohol-prohibition-was-failure accessed 12 February 2023.

23 Levine and Reinarman (n 19).

24 Mark Thornton, 'The Real Reason for FDR's Popularity' (20 October 2010) Mises Institute https://mises.org/library/real-reason-fdrs-popularity accessed 12 February 2023.

25 Transform Drug Policy Foundation, 'How to Regulate Stimulants: A Practical Guide' (Transform Drug Policy Foundation, 2020).

26 Guillermo Garat, 'El Camino: cómo se reguló el cannabis según sus actores políticos' (2014) Junta Nacional de Drogas Presidencia de la República de Uruguay.

27 Milton Romani Gerner, 'Uruguay's Advances in Drug Policy'(August 2015) 12 *Sur: International Journal on Human Rights* 1.

28 Matias Maxx, 'Cómo nace el prensado paraguayo', *El Surti* (11 November 2017).

29 República Oriental del Uruguay Poder Legislativo, *Ley N 19172, Marihuana y sus Derivados: Control y regulación del Estado de la Importación, Producción, Adquisición y Almacenamiento, Comercialización y Distribución* (7 January 2014).

30 Geoff Ramsey, 'Entendiendo la regulación: un análisis de la ley histórica sobre cannabis en Uruguay' (November 2016) Washington Office on Latin America.

31 Instituto de Regulación y Control de Cannabis, Uruguay www.ircca.gub.uy accessed 21 February 2023.

32 Cecilia González, 'Marihuana legal en Uruguay: más de 50,000 usuarios inscritos, menos tráfico y descenso de detenciones', *Actualidad RT* (28 August 2020).

33 Massachusetts Cannabis Control Commission, 'Equity Programs' https://masscannabis control.com/equity-programs/ accessed 13 February 2023.

34 Drug Policy Alliance, 'The Drug War, Mass Incarceration and Race' (25 January 2018) https://drugpolicy.org/resource/drug-war-mass-incarceration-and-race-english spanish accessed 20 February 2023.

35 Michelle Alexander, *The New Jim Crow: Mass Incarceration in the Age of Colorblindness* (New Press, 2010).

36 Drug Policy Alliance (n 4).

37 Shaleen Title, 'Fair and Square: How to Effectively Incorporate Social Equity into Cannabis Laws and Regulations' (6 December 2021) Ohio State University Drug Enforcement and Policy Center.

38 Beau Kilmer, et al, 'Cannabis Legalization and Social Equity: Some Opportunities, Puzzles and Trade-offs' (2021) 101 *Boston University Law Review* 1003.

39 Beau Kilmer and Erin Kilmer Neel, 'Being Thoughtful about Cannabis Legalization and Social Equity' (2020) 19 *World Psychiatry* 194.

40 John Schroyer, 'More California Marijuana Companies Sue State over Revoked Licenses', *Marijuana Business Daily* (17 September 2021).

41 Zara Snapp and Jorge Herrera Valderrábano, 'United States Drug Policy: Flexible Prohibition and Regulation' in Axel Klein and Blaine Stothard (eds.), *Collapse of the Global Order on Drugs: From UNGASS 2016 to Review* 2019 (Emerald, 2018).
42 Drug Policy Alliance (n 4).
43 Massachusetts Cannabis Control Commission (n 33).; Title (n 37).
44 Megan U Boyanton, 'Entrepreneurs of Color Fight for Fair Share of Legal Weed Wealth', *Bloomberg Law* (30 November 2021).
45 Marisa Omori, '"Nickel and dimed" for Drug Crime: Unpacking the Process of Cumulative Racial Inequality' (2019) 60 *The Sociological Quarterly* 287.
46 Eli McVey, 'Percentage of Cannabis Business Owners and Founders by Race', *Marijuana Business Daily* (11 September 2017).
47 Title (n 37).
48 *Public Health: General Provisions – Medical Use of Marijuana*, Florida Statute 381.986 (2022).
49 Jeff Smith, 'Florida's High Court Upholds Medical Marijuana Vertical Licensing and Caps', *Marijuana Business Daily* (27 May 2021).
50 Massachusetts Cannabis Control Commission (n 33).
51 Ibid.
52 New York State Office of Cannabis Management and Social Equity, 'Adult-Use Cannabis for New Yorkers Ages 21 and over' https://cannabis.ny.gov/adult-use accessed 22 February 2023.
53 Cision PR Newswire, Nonprofit Housing Works Cannabis Co Garners $12 Million in Sales During First Six Months of Operation in New York (Housing Works Cannabis Co) www.prnewswire.com/news-releases/nonprofit-housing-works-cannabis-co-garners-12-million-in-sales-during-first-six-months-of-operation-in-new-york-301888677.html
54 Senado de la República,

> Dictamen de las comisiones unidas de justicia, de salud, y de estudios legislativos segunda, con opinión de la comisión de seguridad pública por el que se expide la ley federal para la regulación del cannabis y se reforman y adicionan diversas disposiciones de la ley general de salud y del código penal federal.
>
> (2020)

55 Adrián Jiménez, et al, 'Hacia una Regulación Por La Paz' (Friedrich-Ebert-Stiftung, 2022).
56 Ernesto Londoño, 'Pot Was Flying off the Shelves in Uruguay. Then U.S. Banks Weighed in', *New York Times* (25 August 2017).
57 Pablo Gracia García, 'Marihuana Legal: aprendiendo del modelo uruguayo', *El Sol de México* (7 July 2019).
58 Drug Policy Alliance (n 34).
59 Louise Arbour, et al, 'Are We Addicted to Prison?', *The Daily Star* (26 September 2020).
60 Akiva Liberman and Jocelyn Fontaine, 'Reducing Harms to Boys and Young Men of Color from Criminal Justice System Involvement' (Urban Institute, February 2015).
61 American Civil Liberties Union, 'A Tale of Two Countries: Racially Targeted Arrests in the Era Marijuana Reform' (American Civil Liberties Union, 2020).
62 Drug Policy Alliance (n 34).
63 Kilmer, et al (n 38).
64 New York State Unified Court System, 'Cannabis (Marihuana) and Expungement under New York State Law' (June 2021) www.nycourts.gov/courthelp/Criminal/marihuanaExpunge.shtml accessed 20 February 2023.

65 Start Smart New York, 'New York Marijuana Legalization Explainer' http://smart-ny.com/mrta-explainer/ accessed 20 February 2023.
66 John Ingold, 'Colorado Issues First Licenses for Recreational Marijuana Businesses', *The Denver Post* (23 December 2013).
67 'Canadian Miners Do in Mexico What They Aren't Allowed at Home', *TeleSur* (15 May 2018).
68 'Aurora Cannabis Acquires Mexico's Farmacias Magistrales after Signing Partnership', *The Globe and Mail* (10 December 2018).
69 Canopy Growth, 'Canopy Growth Announces Plan to Acquire Leading US Multi-state Cannabis Operator, Acreage Holdings' (18 April 2019) www.canopygrowth.com/investors/news-releases/canopy-growth-announces-plan-to-acquire-acreage-holdings/ accessed 20 February 2023.
70 Transform Drug Policy Foundation, 'How to Regulate Cannabis: A Practical Guide', 3rd ed (Transform Drug Policy Foundation, 2022) 301.
71 'Organigram Doubled Canadian Cannabis Market Share since January', *Marijuana Business Daily* (7 January 2022).
72 Juan Mauricio Ramírez, 'La industria del cannabis medicinal en Colombia, December 2019', Fedesarrollo: Centro de Investigación Económica y Social.; Carlos Alberto Valdivieso-Valdivieso, 'El contexto económico-productivo y político social de la industria del cannabis en Colombia' (Universidad Católica de Colombia, 2021).
73 Mayra Iglesias, Aníbal Nicolás Saldías & Gregory Ross, 'Marijuana: Made in Uruguay'(19 February 2021) Woodrow Wilson Center Blog www.wilsoncenter.org/blog-post/marijuana-made-uruguay accessed 23 February 2023.

5 The Regulation of Legal Drug Markets

Key Lessons from Alcohol Control Policy in Africa

Ediomo-Ubong E. Nelson and Isidore S. Obot

Introduction

Global drug prohibition, framed by the three UN drug conventions, has failed to eliminate the production, trafficking and non-medical use of drugs. The failure has undermined the capacity of the regime to maintain the loyalty of signatory States to its normative principle.[1] Consequently, there have been defections from legal prohibition towards various forms of government control of drugs,[2] and the legal regulation of drugs is gaining traction in drug policy discussions. Regulation is a responsible approach to managing the risks associated with all aspects of the drug market by moving control of drugs from criminal markets onto the government. In this sense, drug regulation is rooted in a long history of government regulation of other risky products such as tobacco and alcohol.[3] Lessons could, therefore, be drawn from these other commodities to inform the regulation of currently illegal drugs.

In this chapter, we consider lessons from alcohol control for drug regulation, highlighting the tension between profit and public health. In terms of our position on drug policy, we are of the view that legal regulation is an imperfect, but realistic, approach to the control of psychoactive drugs, which offers greater prospect for the reduction of harms than does legal prohibition. It is, therefore, a preferable policy option. We also recognise that realisation of the public health goals of regulation depends on the design of the regulatory system, that is, whether it is driven by public health goals and incorporates measures that are known to be effective in achieving these ends.

Global Drug Prohibition

The global drug prohibition regime is built on the three UN drug conventions (1961, 1971 and 1988). The 1961 Single Convention on Narcotic Drugs,[4] which harmonised previous international agreements, created a stricter and more prohibitive drug control system. It imposed strict controls on plant-based drugs (e.g. opium poppy, coca and cannabis). The 1971 Convention on Psychotropic Substances established controls on synthetic substances such as amphetamines, barbiturates,

DOI: 10.4324/9781003169765-8

benzodiazepines and psychedelics.[5] But compared to the control of plant-based drugs in the 1961 treaty, the control of so-called psychotropic drugs in the 1971 treaty were weaker due to lobbying by western-based pharmaceutical industry.[6] The 1961 and 1971 Conventions outlawed traditional uses of plant-based drugs, limited their cultivation to medical and scientific uses and curbed diversion of psychoactive pharmaceutical drugs for non-medical or illicit purposes.[7]

The 1961 and 1971 Conventions did not prohibit consumption but placed drug production and trade under control in order to limit their use to medical and scientific purposes.[8] The International Narcotics Control Board (INCB) was established to provide the technical expertise needed to implement the drug control system and guarantee supply of narcotic and psychotropic substances for their licit uses. But as Bewley-Taylor, Blickman and Jelsma have argued,[9] the INCB has morphed into an inflexible defender of the policy status quo, increasingly taking a proscriptive, rather than an adjudicatory, stance towards reformist approaches that build on the inbuilt flexibility of the Conventions, particularly in relation to cannabis markets. Stricter measures, adopted in response to the rapid expansion of drug supply from producer countries to markets in North America and Europe, led inevitably to the criminalisation of users through the prohibition of possession.

During the 1970s and 1980s, there was an explosion in demand for non-medical use of cannabis, cocaine and heroin in the western world, which led to large-scale production in the traditional producing countries to supply the expanding western markets.[10] International trafficking in illicit drugs by organised criminal groups also expanded significantly. These developments prompted the negotiation of what became the 1988 Convention against Illicit Traffic in Narcotic Drugs and Psychotropic Substances.[11] The new treaty contained provisions to curb illicit cultivation, production and trafficking of drugs and diversion of chemical precursors. It also placed increased obligations on States parties to apply criminal sanctions to eliminate all aspects of illicit production, possession and trafficking of narcotic drugs.

The treaties support enforcement-based responses to the rapidly expanding global trade in illicit drugs. In the United States, for example, this provided support for counternarcotic operations targeting producing countries, especially those in South America. As the US-led counternarcotic operations squeezed supply chains from South Asian and Latin American sources to North American and European markets, new trafficking routes (and consumer markets) emerged in West Africa.[12] On the other hand, Latin America became increasingly sceptical of the US-styled war on drugs. These developments have led to a shift in the focus of the prohibition regime from Latin America to West Africa,[13] a development that is bolstered by the region's dependence on foreign aid and susceptibility to diplomatic pressures.[14]

The Failure of Prohibition and Defections

The global drug prohibition regime has not succeeded in eliminating international drug production and trafficking, although it has occasionally been able to interrupt or displace illicit drug flows.[15] Its implementation over the past 100 years has been associated with significant negative consequences. These include an increase of the global prison population, human rights violations, restricted access to essential medicines (e.g. pain medications) and criminalisation of drug use, which creates barriers to health services for people who use drugs, including HIV prevention.[16] With treaty reform unlikely, the system has witnessed increased 'defections' from the prohibition model towards decriminalisation and harm reduction. Some countries have gone as far as legalising substances that they once legally prohibited. Recent developments, including new flexibilities highlighted by the 2016 United Nations General Assembly Special Session (UNGASS) on drugs[17] and the rescheduling of cannabis by the Commission on Narcotic Drugs (CND) in 2020,[18] have fuelled the crisis in what is known as the 'Vienna consensus' on drugs.

The political consensus on prohibition is breaking down.[19] An increasing number of States have questioned the effectiveness of zero-tolerance measures to reduce the scale of illicit drug markets. This scepticism has persisted despite the INCB's insistence that the solution lies in greater implementation of the measures contained in the existing strategy, and not in new approaches.[20] Beginning from the 1990s, some European countries such as Portugal and the Netherlands implemented measures based on public health and harm reduction. Latin American and Caribbean countries (e.g. Uruguay, Jamaica and Costa Rica) have also adopted alternatives to the prohibition model, even calling for treaty reforms at the 2016 UNGASS. Even in the United States, the bastion of prohibition, a growing list of states have decriminalised or legalised scheduled drugs at state levels, most notably cannabis.

In Africa, there have also been defections from what has been regarded as a traditional continental consensus on prohibition to positions that are aligned with the global drug policy reform movement.[21] Some countries on the continent have begun to explore alternatives to prohibition through adoption of policy reform measures. In countries such as Lesotho, Zimbabwe, South Africa and Zambia, we have witnessed the legislation of cannabis cultivation for medicinal purposes. Other countries, for example Ghana and Morocco, are in the process of decriminalising cannabis cultivation and/or personal use. Still others have adopted an even more lenient position, treating cannabis as *de facto* legal through their lax-enforcement or non-enforcement of laws.[22]

The end point of global drug policy reforms, including decriminalisation of possession for personal use, is to regulate currently illegal drugs the same way alcohol and tobacco are regulated in most countries. Experience with alcohol and tobacco regulation offers lessons for the regulation of currently illegal drugs. Before turning to consider these lessons, we will look at how alcohol production and marketing are currently regulated, and the challenges involved.

The Regulation of Alcohol

Alcohol was the first psychoactive substance to be placed under some form of international control.[23] European colonial powers agreed a treaty which prohibited or banned the availability of alcohol (e.g. distilled spirits) in many parts of Africa.[24] By the 1940s, however, these treaty provisions had fallen out of use.[25] Temperance movements had become prominent in many English-speaking and Scandinavian countries during the 19th and early 20th century, resulting in prohibition of alcohol in some States or sub-national jurisdictions.[26] In the United States, a law prohibiting the production, importation, transportation and sale of alcoholic beverages was enacted in 1920. Prohibition, however, proved ineffective in reducing alcohol consumption and related health and social harms. By 1933, prohibition in the United States was repealed and was replaced by a regulatory framework that allowed government intervention in every aspect of the alcohol market.[27]

Although alcohol policy often operates at the national and sub-national levels, the World Health Organization (WHO) has promoted a coordinated global strategy on alcohol control based on a public health perspective.[28] For example, the WHO Global Strategy to Reduce the Harmful Use of Alcohol,[29] endorsed by the 63rd World Health Assembly in 2010, calls for greater international cooperation based on the view that national and local action can yield better results if supported by regional and global action based on agreed policy frameworks. Regional strategies or action plans have been adopted by the WHO Regional Office for Europe, Western Pacific Region, the Regional Committee for Africa and the Pan American Health Organization.[30]

Alcohol policy encompasses a broad range of interventions, including rules and regulations that aim to reduce the availability and consumption of alcoholic beverages. Rooted in the public health perspective of the WHO, these measures target the wider environment, only indirectly affecting individual behaviours (e.g. increase in price due to taxation can affect an individual's ability to purchase alcohol). Apart from the individual, alcohol policy also impacts the economy since alcohol production creates employment and revenue through excise tax. Policymaking involves balancing these considerations. As Nicholls explained, the aim of policy on alcohol is to reduce harms, but also to support industry, employment and the rights of individuals to consume alcohol in ways that do not harm others.[31] He further noted that alcohol policy development involves trade-offs between the reduction of health and social harms, consideration of economic impacts and the protection of personal freedom.

The alcohol market is regulated through a number of policy measures, recently developed by the WHO into a package of proven interventions to reduce alcohol-related harms known by the acronym SAFER. The package is designed to guide governments on five high-impact strategic actions prioritised for implementation to reduce alcohol harms and to promote health and development. This includes **strengthening** restrictions on alcohol availability; **advancing** and enforcing drink-driving countermeasures; **facilitating** access to screening, brief interventions and treatment; **enforcing** complete restrictions or bans on alcohol advertising, sponsorship and promotion, and **raising** prices on alcohol through excise taxes and pricing policies. We elaborate briefly on controls on availability, restrictions on advertising and marketing, and taxation and pricing policies, which together compose the 'three best buys' of alcohol regulation.[32]

Availability controls, as measures for regulating the alcohol market, are based on findings from international studies which show that increased availability of alcohol is associated with increased consumption.[33] There is also evidence that restrictions on availability are linked to decreasing consumption of alcohol.[34] Availability and retail accessibility of alcohol can be regulated through licensing, state monopolies and prohibition laws.[35] Studies have shown that, on balance, licensing systems are associated with higher consumption.[36]

The cost of alcohol to consumers is generally known to have a significant influence on consumption. Existing evidence shows that consumers are responsive to price, although this may apply differently to different products and different sets of consumers.[37] Taxation of alcohol products at different levels from production to consumption leads to increase in the price of retail alcohol, which in turn influences per capita consumption. It also enables governments to control the scale of the alcohol market.[38] The use of taxation as a means of revenue generation for the State, instead of using it to reduce consumption, often results in lower taxation to reduce the risk of illicit production and cross-border importation known to be associated with higher taxation.[39] Further, policies that establish minimum unit prices for retail alcohol have been shown to reduce consumption among some subgroups, including hazardous and low-income drinkers.[40]

Marketing restrictions are important in reducing overall alcohol consumption.[41] This has inspired calls for greater controls on alcohol marketing, including increased demand for a legal framework for the control of alcohol similar to the Framework Convention on Tobacco Control (FCTC).[42] Contrary to industry claims that marketing only changes brand allegiance, alcohol marketing strategies are often aimed at expanding the market, and studies have shown an association between exposure to alcohol marketing and consumption.[43]

In developing countries (especially in Africa), alcohol producers use voluntary self-regulation codes of marketing developed by industry bodies to avoid formal regulations that may curtail key marketing practices such as associating alcohol with music, sports and other aspects of popular culture. Affluent countries in the West may be able to impose restrictions on alcohol marketing despite industry resistance. But, as the 2014 World Cup tournament in Brazil revealed, global alcohol producers can easily override national legislations in developing countries.[44] It can, therefore, be expected that similar patterns of North-South inequality may unfold in the regulation of currently illegal drugs.

The Challenges of Alcohol Regulation – Focus on Africa

In this section, we briefly discuss the challenge of industry influence on alcohol regulation, focusing on sub-Saharan Africa where the majority of countries do not have a written alcohol policy and action plan. A major goal of global alcohol producers is to increase sales of their products by promoting European styles of drinking in developing markets, particularly Africa.[45] Africa is a key area for alcohol market growth,[46] with large populations of non-drinkers including women and young people. Global alcohol producers have sought to capture new markets in the continent using diverse strategies that pose significant challenges for regulation.

Part of the strategy used by alcohol producers has been to limit statutory regulation of alcohol marketing and to direct government policy into protecting their own interests.[47] There have been cases of industry involvement in writing national policy drafts that privilege business interests. For example, Bakke and Endal have shown how the alcohol producer SABMiller and the industry-funded organisation, International Centre for Alcohol Policies (ICAP), were involved in preparing draft alcohol policies for four African countries: Lesotho, Malawi, Uganda and Botswana.[48] These policies underplayed evidence-based public health approaches to addressing alcohol harms, focusing instead on individually focussed interventions that usually have a more limited effect.[49] Such policy focus is based on the representation of the problem as one of individual choice,[50] and this undermines the population-based measures suggested by the WHO strategy.

In other countries, alcohol producers have opposed or delayed policies that may pose a threat to their interests. In Botswana, alcohol producers opposed a bill that proposed a tax levy on locally produced liquor, leading to a significant reduction in the levy as of 2018.[51] In South Africa, alcohol producers have fought and stalled a proposal for a marketing ban and a Liquor Amendment Bill (2016) that aims, among other things, to raise the drinking age from 18 to 21.[52] Few African countries have binding regulations on alcohol advertising, and in the absence of such regulations, industry groups use self-regulation codes that specify the type of content and market segment the industry will voluntarily exclude. This allows alcohol producers to use sophisticated marketing techniques to promote drinking among new segments of the population in African countries.[53] Similar strategies may be adopted, indeed are already being used, by corporations in the legal drug market. In the next section, we argue that industry influence in the regulatory process is potentially the most significant challenge to regulating legal drug markets. We also argue that State monopolies offer better scope for regulating drugs than licensing systems.

Regulating Drugs – Lessons from Alcohol Control

Legal regulation of drugs involves moving previously illicit drugs from the control of criminal markets to the control of the government. Drug regulation aims to promote public health goals through government control of the various aspects of the market. Under a licensing system, this includes licensing of producers and vendors and regulating the price, potency, packaging and preparation of products. It also applies to sales, including location, design, opening hours as well as marketing, advertising, branding and promotion.[54] It also involves controlling availability and access through age limits, medical prescription systems and licensing of buyers or club membership schemes.[55] Under a monopoly system, the government serves as the economic actor controlling the different levels of the market (i.e. wholesale, retail).

Experience with alcohol regulation offers some lessons for the regulation of legal drug markets. First, the regulation of alcohol shows that it is possible to regulate currently illegal drugs, however imperfectly. Alcohol regulation is generally considered to be more effective in protecting public health than alcohol prohibition.[56] As earlier noted, there are proven measures for reducing per capita alcohol consumption and associated harms. Stockwell and colleagues have shown that similar measures could also be used to regulate currently illegal drugs.[57] They described the technicalities of applying policies on pricing and physical availability of alcohol to regulation of legal cannabis markets, including finding a balanced pricing system that could prevent the undercutting of prices by a parallel illegal market.

A key lesson from alcohol regulation is that the major challenge with regulating legal markets has to do with how to protect the regulatory system from industry influence.[58] Alcohol producers attempt to oppose regulatory controls (including taxation, minimum pricing, outlet density, opening hours and marketing) by promoting ineffective approaches such as industry self-regulation, public education campaigns and individual responsibility.[59] They utilise what has been described as the 'three chains of influence' to circumvent regulation.[60] The 'public good chain' uses corporate social responsibility programmes on high anxiety public issues (e.g. COVID-19 pandemic) to bolster industry legitimacy and divert attention from questionable marketing practices. The 'knowledge chain' involves influencing knowledge production by defining research priorities, providing biased funding and review processes and hiding industry links by transferring funds through intermediaries. The 'political chain' involves lobbying or directly influencing policymakers.

These strategies, some of which have been perfected over many years, are transferrable across industry contexts (e.g. from tobacco to alcohol industry), and there is evidence that some of these strategies have been adopted by cannabis corporations in some developed countries.[61] Increased investment in medicinal cannabis by alcohol and tobacco producers portend greater corporate influence on the regulation of legal cannabis markets,[62] including deployment of the strategies used to circumvent government regulation. Regulation should, therefore, aim to promote public health and welfare and restrict over-commercialisation. Protecting legal drug markets from corporate capture also requires regulation of foreign investments as well as support for small-scale farmers (e.g. local cannabis and coca farmers in Africa and South America, respectively) to secure a place in the legal market. Without such protections, local farmers could revert to the illegal market, which could potentially undermine the legal market in a regulated system.

Alcohol regulation also teaches that State monopolies, for example the Finnish alcohol monopolies, may be better suited for achieving public health goals such as reducing consumption and harms.[63] Licensing or privatised systems, as practised in some US states, could create an industry that is capable of opposing the public health goals of regulation.[64] State monopolies have direct controls over the policies that have the most impact on consumption and related harms, such as pricing, availability, advertising and marketing.[65] The existence of commercial actors with resources and incentives to lobby governments to relax control measures makes licensing systems less congenial to public health and safety.[66] On the other hand, monopoly systems that are motivated by government's interest in revenue generation may be at cross-purposes with public health concerns about reducing harms by limiting consumption.[67] What is needed are assertive systems whose mission is to reduce health harms, and not those that merely insist that the rules be followed.[68]

The Framework Convention on Tobacco Control, designed to reduce the health costs associated with long-term use of smoked tobacco, provides a model for the regulation of legal drug markets. There is currently no such framework for alcohol, partly due to industry interference, and this has constrained progress in the reduction of alcohol consumption and harms. In addition to taxation and pricing policies, the FCTC includes restrictions on advertising, marketing and sponsorship, and controls on the physical availability of tobacco products.[69] These measures, implemented along with public health education, have contributed to the reduction of tobacco consumption and harms in many countries within a legal market that allows for production and trade in tobacco products.[70] Such a framework could be used to control marketing by the legal drug industry and to promote public health goals, assuming it is possible to negotiate it.[71]

The regulation of alcohol (and to some extent, tobacco) products also highlights the importance of political commitment at all levels (international, regional and national). At the international level, the development of a framework for the regulation of currently illegal drugs similar to the Framework Convention on Tobacco Control would require funding and capacity building for civil society organisations.[72] The domestication and implementation of such a framework at regional and national levels also require commitment to prioritise public health over profits. Experience with alcohol regulation allows little optimism regarding the feasibility of such commitment, most notably in Africa.

Even potential fiscal benefits from excise tax may not be a sufficient incentive. As Levine and Reinarman observed three decades ago in America,[73] and experience with alcohol taxation in Africa bears out, there is little reason to believe that excise tax on legal drugs will provide a fiscal boom for States. A shift to legal regulation could even mean loss of foreign aid, since a significant proportion of funding for law enforcement in Africa comes from international partners (e.g. the United States). On the other hand, revenue generation through taxation could trump public health and welfare goals, which may be better protected by State monopolies that report to health ministries.

Experience with alcohol regulation in Africa, amply illustrated by the liquor levy controversy in Botswana,[74] is instructive of the importance of involving relevant stakeholders (e.g. the public health community) for ensuring success in alcohol policy development and implementation. The Botswana experience also highlights the need for reliable data on alcohol consumption and problems to inform policy-making. Governments need to support large-scale, nation-wide surveys to generate relevant data. At the international level, there is a need to strengthen international cooperation in research, including providing technical support to developing countries. Research should be protected from industry influence through disclosure of conflict of interest. Non-industry funding for research is also important in restricting industry influence on evidence production.

Conclusion

In this chapter, we have considered some of the lessons that may be drawn from alcohol for the regulation of currently illegal drugs. We have shown that a major challenge is how to manage the tension between profits and public health. Experience with alcohol (and to some extent, tobacco) regulation instructs that, contrary to celebratory opinions, regulation of drug markets will not automatically ensure the reduction of drug use and health-related harms. While it will bring drugs under the remit of State control, consumption and related health and social problems could still increase unless the right set of policy measures are adopted. The realisation of the public health goals of drug regulation will depend on the capacity and willingness of governments at the global, regional and national levels to develop, implement, monitor and update evidence-based policy measures to check the production and marketing of drugs.

Notes

1 David Bewley-Taylor, *International Drug Control: Consensus Fractured* (Cambridge University Press, 2012).
2 Ibid.
3 Global Commission on Drug Policy, *Regulation – The Responsible Control of Drugs* (Global Commission on Drug Policy, 2018).
4 *Single Convention on Narcotic Drugs 1961* (as amended by the 1972 Protocol) (30 March 1961) 520 UNTS 7515.
5 *Convention on Psychotropic Substances 1971* (21 February 1971) 1019 UNTS 14956.
6 William McAllister, 'The Global Political Economy of Scheduling: The International-Historical Context of the Controlled Substances Act' (2004) 76 *Drug and Alcohol Dependence* 3–8.
7 Martin Jelsma, 'The Development of International Drug Control: Lessons Learned and Strategic Challenges of the Future' (2010) Transnational Institute Series on Legislative Reform of Drug Policies Nr 10, 2.
8 David Bewley-Taylor, Tom Blickman & Martin Jelsma, 'The Rise and Decline of Cannabis Prohibition: The History of Cannabis in the UN Drug Control System and Options for Reform' (2014) Global Drug Policy Observatory.
9 Ibid.
10 Jelsma (n 7).
11 *UN Convention against the Illicit Traffic in Narcotic Drugs and Psychotropic Substances* (20 December 1988) 1582 UNTS 27627.
12 Jason Eligh, 'The Evolution of Illicit Drug Markets and Drug Policy in Africa' (2019) ENACT Report, Global Initiative against Transnational Organised Crime Continental Report 03.
13 Joanne Csete and Constanza Sánchez, 'Telling the Story of Drugs in West Africa: The Newest Front in a Losing War?' (2013) Global Drug Policy Observatory.
14 Axel Klein, 'Nigeria & the Drugs War' (1999) 26 *Review of African Political Economy* 51.

15 Eligh (n 12).
16 Jelsma (n 7).; Isidore Obot, 'Assessing Nigeria's Drug Control Policy, 1994–2000' (2004) 15 *International Journal of Drug Policy* 17.
17 Mike Trace, 'After UNGASS – Where Do Governments Go from Here?' (2017) 17 *Drug and Alcohol Today* 81.
18 Commission on Narcotic Drugs, 'Consideration of the Notification from the World Health Organization Concerning Scheduling under the Single Convention on Narcotic Drugs of 1961 as Amended by the 1972 Protocol, and the Convention on Psychotropic Substances of 1971' (23 November 2020) E/CN.7/2020/CRP.19.
19 Bewley-Taylor (n 1).
20 Eligh (n 12).
21 Ibid.
22 Ibid.
23 Robin Room, 'International Control of Alcohol: Alternative Paths Forward' (2006) 25 *Drug and Alcohol Review* 581.
24 Lynn Pan, *Alcohol in Colonial Africa* (FFAS, 1975).
25 Room (n 23).
26 Jack Blocker, *American Temperance Movements: Cycles of Reform* (Twayne, 1989).
27 Harry Levine and Craig Reinarman, 'From Prohibition to Regulation: Lessons from Alcohol Policy for Drug Policy' (1991) 69/3 *The Milbank Quarterly* 461.
28 James Nicholls, 'Alcohol Policy in Global Context' in Torsten Kolind, Betsy Thom & Geoffrey Hunt (eds.), *The Sage Handbook of Drug and Alcohol Studies: Social Science Approaches* (Sage, 2016).
29 World Health Organization, *Global Strategy to Reduce the Harmful Use of Alcohol* (World Health Organization, 2010).
30 Nicholls (n 28).
31 Ibid.
32 World Health Organization, *Tackling NCDs Best Buys* (World Health Organization, 2017).
33 Thomas Babor, et al, *Alcohol: No Ordinary Commodity: Research and Public Policy* (Oxford University Press, 2003).
34 Michela Baccini and Giulia Carreras, 'Analyzing and Comparing the Association between Control Policy Measures and Alcohol Consumption in Europe' (2014) *SUM* 1684.
35 Nicholls (n 28).
36 Thor Norström, et al, 'Potential Consequences of Replacing a Retail Alcohol Monopoly with a Private Licence System: Results from Sweden' (2010) *Addiction* 2113.; Tim Stockwell, et al, 'Estimating the Public Health Impact of Disbanding a Government Alcohol Monopoly: Application of New Methods to the Case of Sweden' (2018) *BMC Public Health* 1–16.
37 Nicholls (n 28).
38 Ibid.
39 Ibid.
40 Heng Jiang, et al, 'Modelling the Effects of Alcohol Pricing Policies on Alcohol Consumption in Subpopulations in Australia' (2020) *Addiction* 1038.; Anurag Sharma, Kompal Sinha & Brian Vandenberg, 'Pricing as a Means of Controlling Alcohol Consumption' (2017) *British Medical Bulletin* 1–10.
41 Babor, et al (n 33).
42 Room (n 23).
43 Peter Anderson, et al, 'Impact of Alcohol Advertising and Media Exposure on Adolescent Alcohol Use: A Systematic Review of Longitudinal Studies' (2009) *Alcohol*

and Alcoholism 229.; David Jernigan, et al, 'Alcohol Marketing and Youth Alcohol Consumption: A Systematic Review of Longitudinal Studies Published Since 2008' (2016) 112 *Addiction* 7.

44 Jonathan Gornall, 'World Cup 2014: Festival of Football or Alcohol?' (2014) 348 *British Medical Journal* 1–4.

45 Nicholls (n 28).

46 David Jernigan and Thomas Babor, 'The Concentration of the Global Alcohol Industry and Its Penetration in the African Region' (2015) 110 *Addiction* 551.

47 Carina Ferreira-Borges, Charles Parry & Thomas Babor, 'Harmful Use of Alcohol: A Shadow over Sub-Saharan Africa in Need of Workable Solutions' (2017) 14 *International Journal of Environmental Research and Public Health* 4.

48 Oysten Bakke and Dag Endal, 'Alcohol Policies out of Context: Drinks Industry Supplanting Government Role in Alcohol Policies in Sub-Saharan Africa' (2010) 105 *Addiction* 22.

49 Charles Parry, 'African Experience Supports View That the Global Alcohol Industry Should Have No Role in the Formulation of Public Health Policies' (2014) 109 *Addiction* 1211.

50 Carol Bacchi, 'Problematizations in Alcohol Policy: WHO's "Alcohol Problems"' 42 *Contemporary Drug Problem* 120.

51 Mbogeni Mguni, 'Alcohol Levy Cut by 20%' *MmegiOnline* (3 October 2018) www.mmegi.bw/business/alcohol-levy-cut-by-20/news accessed 1 February 2023.; Refilwe Sinkamba, 'Alcohol Abuse and Interventions Strategies in Botswana and China: A Preliminary Study' (2015) 29 *PULA: Botswana Journal of African Studies* 1.

52 Carina Ferreira-Borges, et al (n 47).

53 Bakke and Endal (n 48).

54 Global Commission on Drug Policy (n 3).

55 Ibid.

56 Ibid.

57 Tim Stockwell, et al, 'Lessons Learned from the Alcohol Regulation Perspective' in Tom Decorte, Simon Lenton & Chris Wilkins (eds.), *Legalizing Cannabis* (Routledge, 2020).

58 Chelsea Shover and Keith Humphreys, 'Six Policy Lessons Relevant to Cannabis Legalization' (2019) 45 *American Journal of Drug and Alcohol Abuse* 698.

59 Peter Adams, Marta Rychert & Chris Wilkins, 'Policy Influence and the Legalized Cannabis Industry: Learnings from Other Addictive Consumption Industries' (2021) *Addiction* 1–15.

60 Ibid.

61 Ibid.

62 Ibid.

63 Stockwell, et al (n 57).

64 Ibid.

65 Levine and Reinarman (n 27).

66 Norman Giesbrecht, et al, *Strategies to Reduce Alcohol-related Harms and Costs in Canada: A Comparison of Provincial Policies* (Centre for Addictions & Mental Health, 2013).

67 Stockwell (n 57).

68 Robin Room and Jenny Cisneros Ornberg, 'Government Monopoly as an Instrument for Public Health and Welfare: Lessons for Cannabis from Experience with Alcohol Monopolies' (2019) 74 *International Journal of Drug Policy* 223.

69 Jonathan P Caulkins and Beau Kilmer, 'The US as an Example of How Not to Legalize Marijuana' (2016) 111 *Addiction* 2090.
70 Jane Landon, et al, 'International Codes and Agreements to Restrict the Promotion of Harmful Products Can Hold Lessons for the Control of Alcohol Marketing' (2016) 112 *Addiction* 102.
71 Allyn L Taylor and Ibadat S Dhillon, 'An International Legal Strategy for Alcohol Control: Not a Framework Convention – at Least Not Yet' (2012) 108 *Addiction* 450–455.
72 Landon, et al (n 70).
73 Levine and Reinarman (n 27).
74 Joseph MN Pitso and Isidore S Obot, 'Botswana Alcohol Policy and the Presidential Levy Controversy' (2011) 106 *Addiction* 898.

6 Legal Epidemiology in Post-Prohibition Scenarios

Scott Burris, Corey S. Davis and Elizabeth Platt[*]

Introduction

The dominant paradigm of international drug policy for the past century has been a prohibition on the manufacture, distribution, possession and use of controlled drugs for non-medical or scientific uses.[1] Primary reliance on criminal law has been a constant in drug control in countries throughout the world, even as the drugs of concern and the social factors driving drug use have changed.[2] The other notable constant in this history has been a high level of iatrogenic harm to individuals and societies created by criminalisation and the tendency of criminalisation to interfere with effective measures of misuse prevention, harm reduction and substance use disorder treatment. When it comes to reducing the harms of drugs, the 'cure' of prohibition has consistently proven worse than the disease.[3]

Recognition of the net harms visited upon individuals throughout the world by prohibition has helped create both political will and space for reforms, marginal and radical.[4] The willingness to experiment with alternative approaches, however, does not on its own produce healthier policies. Drug use, substance use disorders and drug markets are all complex phenomena. While we have some well-studied models for regulated drug markets, none of them promise easy solutions to the problems we face today.[5] Virtually all drugs, however regulated, can cause harm to at least some users. Virtually all laws, no matter how framed, can operate in ways that are inequitable, unjust or that cause harm to health. Conscious policy experimentation, in which new approaches are tested and evaluated in a timely manner, is crucial to developing and maintaining regulatory approaches that improve on the status quo. As better regulatory models are validated, the speed at which they are adopted across jurisdictions – the degree to which communities gain access to these better drug policy 'treatments' – is of the highest importance to health and health equity.

Legal epidemiology is the scientific study of the health effects of laws and legal practices.[6] Policy surveillance, the systematic scientific tracking of laws of public health importance, is a legal epidemiology tool for measuring law for evaluation research and supporting the diffusion of legal innovation. Both are key to a global effort to identify and spread healthy drug policies.[7] Empirical evaluation of drug policies is already conducted at a high level of sophistication, and it is no criticism of the people doing this work to suggest we need more and even better

DOI: 10.4324/9781003169765-9

such research. The contributions of a legal epidemiology approach include a more precise and granular measurement of law in evaluation research, a theory-driven attention to the mechanisms of legal effect in theorising research and drawing causal inferences, and a more explicit concern with using this research to support the diffusion of healthier drug policies as well as accountability for the failure to adopt them.

Introducing Legal Epidemiology and Policy Surveillance

Legal epidemiology as a field emerged from efforts in the United States to improve the quality and increase the quantity of empirical studies illuminating law's health effects and side effects.[8] It rests on the fact that law is a ubiquitous feature of social organisation and a powerful influence on norms and behaviours in most societies. While it does not fundamentally depart from the broad field of policy evaluation research, legal epidemiology pursues more seriously and with greater specificity the ways that law can exert this influence.

Laws may be used explicitly as an intervention to change behaviours and environments. For example, laws criminalising drug possession may be intended to reduce individual consumption and break down drug markets or to reduce drug-related harm, and can be evaluated in relation to those goals. Law also works by creating the legal-institutional infrastructure of regulation. Law, to carry on the drugs example, defines what agencies have authority to regulate drug-related matters, and these agencies' jurisdiction and powers. It is this infrastructural law that has installed police and criminal justice agencies as the primary actors in matters of drug control in many places, giving them huge discretion in the crafting of 'law on the streets'. These interventional and infrastructural laws are plain to see in relation to a particular topic such as drugs.

Less obvious perhaps, but often more important to health, are the 'incidental' health effects of laws that do not purport to be, or are only loosely related to, a particular health issue. These laws influence or mediate the 'social determinants of health' – access to resources of money, social status and environmental amenities that substantially determine both individual lifespans and the level and distribution of health in a community.[9] As policymakers become more aware of and accepting of the proposition that the prevalence of unhealthy drug use is influenced by structural factors such as educational and economic opportunity, 'drug policy' may come to embrace tax, labour and social welfare legislation. In all these modes – interventional, infrastructural and incidental – law is properly understood as a mass 'treatment' to which its subjects are routinely exposed and, like all treatments, should be studied for its effects and outcomes. Systematic evaluation of law allows us to understand not only the general impact of a law but also the impact of specific features of the law and their impact on specific populations.[10]

Legal epidemiology differs from traditional policy research in its treatment of the independent variable. What the policy research field calls 'policy' is usually a combination of several distinct elements: the observable form of the rule (the 'law on the books'), the activity or standard the rule stipulates (variously measured in implementation practices, outputs and outcomes) and, in some studies, the social constructions of the 'policy'.[11] Common definitions of policy also often include settled practices of organisations. Legal epidemiology insists that 'policy' not be understood as the standard of behaviour or intervention itself (though that is fine in colloquial expression) but as *the social means through which a practice, standard or other form of intervention is deliberately put into wide use through laws or law-like rules*. A desirable standard is put into the form of a policy so that it will, in the future, take place more widely, more thoroughly, more consistently and (hopefully) more effectively. The *diffusion* of some desirable thing through a policy is complementary but distinct from the instrumental efficacy of that thing.

For example, research that shows that the practice of providing individuals with naloxone can reduce overdose mortality does not answer the question of whether liberalising law regulating naloxone access will result in wider adoption of that practice or fewer opioid overdose deaths.[12] Because the fundamental purpose of policy is the diffusion of healthy behaviours and conditions, the crucial work of policy research is to find out whether the policy is resulting in the diffusion of the desired conditions/behaviours and whether the policy has effects at scale that are consistent with its effects observed 'in the lab' and in intervention trials.

Legal epidemiology thus starts with attention not to 'policy' in some general sense but to what one might call 'formal policy' – a statute, regulation, order, ordinance, guideline, standard operating procedure, contractual clause or other formalising text purporting to define a required course or standard of action within a jurisdiction or organisation. Starting with 'laws on the books' – the observable text defining the policy – allows us to more readily distinguish policymaking, implementation and impact from each other as research questions and from the policy itself. The 'law on the books' is the formally adopted, written expression of the thing to be done and primary instrument of its scale-up. Law on the books can be measured and mapped across space and time. It is the independent variable in an evaluation study, or at least the thing that defines what actions are to be implemented. The overall policy process works through changes in behaviours and environments to produce (or not) the desired policy outcomes.

Around the world and within individual countries, laws and other formal policy texts on the same subject go into effect with different requirements in different places at different times.[13] Studying this variation over time allows us to evaluate real-world legal interventions with a level of scientific accuracy, validity and strength of causal inference functionally equivalent to randomised trials.[14] A good example of this was road safety in the United States, where policy was developed, implemented, evaluated and revised over many years in a systematic manner.[15] Identifying the consequences, both good and bad, of specific laws provides an evidence base for the adoption of more healthy public policies.[16] On an international level, policy surveillance methods can produce studies using cross-national policy surveillance data to understand the factors and ideas that might influence a government to adopt a specific type of drug policy.[17] Legal epidemiology research using these legal data can evaluate which policies are associated with healthy outcomes, while controlling for a variety of national characteristics that could drive differences in those outcomes.[18]

The remainder of this chapter suggests three ways legal epidemiology as an approach to drug policy research can contribute to better research and legal practice. It also discusses some of the methodological and cultural challenges in furthering the adoption of this method for evaluating and improving policy.

Three Contributions of Legal Epidemiology to Future Drug Policy Research and Implementation

- **Better Measurement of Law for Evaluation**

If researchers and policymakers want to understand the impact of law and law-like rules of all kinds, they first need to understand what the law requires and where and to whom it applies. Taking the written form of the policy seriously starts with observing the differences between formal policies in detail, as well as key features like effective dates that, along with theory, help define the time points and resolution for observing potential effects.[19] Policy surveillance fills that need as a process of transforming the words of law into numeric data through rigorous, transparent and reproducible scientific methods.[20] The term 'surveillance' comes from public health, where it refers to the ongoing tracking of diseases and other events of public health significance.[21] Policy surveillance is the logical extension of that practice to the law, as the law is a phenomenon subject to change, differing across space, and of enduring importance to public health.[22]

Policy surveillance had its start in drug policy research, though not by that name. The first comprehensive resource tracking the characteristics of law across jurisdictions to support evaluation research was the US Alcohol Policy Information System (APIS), launched in 2003 and funded by the National Institutes of Health as a project of the National Institute on Alcohol Abuse and Alcoholism as part of a systematic effort to gauge the effectiveness of a wide range of legal interventions directed at alcohol-related harm.[23] The Center for Public Health Law Research at the Temple University Beasley School of Law drew on the APIS model to produce two resources for systematically capturing and presenting laws: LawAtlas and the Prescription Drug Abuse Policy System (PDAPS).[24] All of these sites provide no-cost access to data produced through rigorous and transparent methods of observation—data that have been used in hundreds of scientific papers. Although there are challenges (to which we will return), these methods are also being applied internationally.[25]

Policy surveillance as a scientific method is a multi-step process of measurement that includes the development of a conceptual model and legal framework, a process of iterative coding and rigorous quality control.[26] The process supports quantitative evaluation, implementation research, case studies and qualitative research. By documenting the specifics of the law, it captures valuable information at the outset to define the implementation inputs and outputs that should be observed in further research to address implementation problems and amend the law as needed.[27]

As a process of measurement, scientific legal mapping aims to accurately observe the apparent features of a legal text, and in so doing to minimise interpretation as to what the law 'means'.[28] For example, a researcher conducting policy surveillance would document that a law on its face authorises the establishment of a syringe service programme. That researcher will not aim, at least as an initial matter, to determine whether such a law could be interpreted to allow a syringe service programme to provide supervised injection services or make qualitative assessments as to the 'breadth' or 'narrowness' of the law. Rather, the researcher should aim to objectively observe the apparent features of the legal text, such as the specific services explicitly required to be provided, or a stated requirement of local government approval prior to operation.

It follows that scientific legal mapping should ordinarily begin with measurement and avoid any sort of qualitative coding or categorisation. If the research aims ultimately to categorise syringe service laws as 'narrow' and 'broad', the researchers should first measure the apparent features of a legal text on which such a categorisation would be based, and then, in a second operation, sort laws based on the measured features. This approach not only has the advantage of transparency but can be embodied in code that can automatically classify (and update classifications) across a large dataset. It should also be observed that a system of measurement based initially on what the law says, rather than what it means, is more suited for the adoption of machine-assisted coding approaches as machine learning is integrated into standard research processes over the next decade.

Crucial to the process is quality control, and measures are taken throughout to ensure the reliability of data.[29] Although the specifics vary, this is primarily accomplished through the redundant implementation of each step in the process, with research and coding completed independently by two separate researchers at varying rates of redundancy. The results are then compared, divergences are identified and rates of divergence are calculated. All divergences are discussed and causes identified; these learnings are then integrated into the research protocol going forward. Although this sort of inter-rater comparison is used during the work to identify problems with research and coding protocols, an interrater-reliability statistic is not used as the final measure of the accuracy of the dataset. Since the premise of policy surveillance is that the apparent features of a text can be objectively and consistently measured, the final quality assessment of a dataset is a measurement of the rate of error. When all the data have been created, it undergoes post-production statistical quality control, which provides an estimate for the overall error rate of the dataset. As in other similar processes of mass production, the degree of error to be considered acceptable is a function of resources. In our work, we typically aim to guarantee with 95 percent confidence that the overall dataset error rate is below five percent.

A final but important step is publication of the data, codebooks and protocol for use without cost by researchers and the public. A simple Creative Commons license provides guidelines for non-commercial use. One of the advantages of scientific legal mapping methods is that they produce basic legal data that can be reused, expanded forward or back in time or revised by other researchers. The cost and difficulty of obtaining and coding laws, particularly in settings where law is not universally or freely available, does not need to be expended by every researcher interested in evaluating a particular kind of law. In this, policy surveillance represents an application of open science principles.

- **Theory for Better Design and Causal Inference**

Methodological work in legal epidemiology has pointed to the importance of theory in constructing studies and assessing inferences of causality. Law is capable of being usefully theorised from many disciplinary points of view, including criminology, economics, epidemiology, sociology and social psychology. To facilitate the application of diverse theories in legal epidemiology research, the field deploys the concept of 'mechanisms of legal effect'. These are the theory-based and empirically observable phenomena like deterrence, procedural justice or expected utility that support testable hypotheses not just to whether but through what observable processes a law may have an effect.[30]

There are manifold risks of bias and error even in sophisticated causal inference studies. Drawing causal connections between laws and outcomes in the world is challenging, for many reasons. No law operates by itself: in any given setting, many laws may affect the same behaviour simultaneously, and within and across jurisdictions there may be complex variations in enforcement or the characteristics of the regulated parties. A scientific approach to understanding *how* law influences health is crucial to assessing *whether it* does so. Theories of how law influences structures, behaviours and environments – theories of the mechanism of legal effect – can be used to define the phenomena to be observed in an evaluation or implementation study. This enables researchers to determine where to look, at what point in time one might expect to see effects, how effects might evolve over time and what sort of intended and unintended effects might arise.

To take an example from drug policy research, a study aiming to assess the effects of naloxone access laws on overdose mortality is logically making observations along a causal chain the links of which include enactment of the law and access to the drug by people in the target population. The effect of the law on access is obviously a highly important question of implementation and a sine qua non of effectiveness. Even if the law is associated with reduced (or increased) overdose mortality, if there is no measurable impact of the law on access to the drug, law is unlikely to be a major cause. As this shows, it is a mistake to use enactment or existence of naloxone law as a measure of naloxone access;[31] indeed, it begs the question of the research.

As this example also suggests, a clear and explicit hypothesis of the mechanism of effect supports causal inference by postulating plausible mechanisms to explain an observed association. If a study shows a strong and significant association between enactment of a naloxone access law and reduced drug overdose, but other evidence shows that naloxone was largely unavailable to the drug using population during the period of the study, one must assume that the correlation between the law and the reduction of naloxone is spurious or has come about by another mechanism. It is unlikely but not logically impossible, for example, that the enactment of the law so powerfully communicated the risks of overdose that a large number of users sought treatment, resulting in a decline in overdoses and deaths even in the absence of a direct effect on supply.

Finally, mechanism evidence is useful to guide reform and implementation. Understanding how law works can also guide legislators and regulators in crafting innovative interventions aimed at newly recognised problems.[32] In the naloxone example, if research shows that distribution systems are not able to actually deliver naloxone to the people who need it, policymakers can take further action, such as appropriating funds to pay for the product and expanding the range of individuals and organisation authorised to distribute it.

Researchers can draw on a rich and diverse literature to understand mechanisms of law. There is no single correct theory, and therefore no need to make an exclusive choice. Rather, the choice of what theory or theories to draw upon is a practical one based on research questions and designs, types of law or regulatory approach under study and state of current knowledge about the matter being investigated. The message of legal epidemiology is the importance of having one.

- **Policy Surveillance to Promote Diffusion of Healthier Policies and Accountability for Unhealthy Ones**

A future of drug policy experimentation, change and meaningful diversity is possible. This creates an opportunity for research to influence the shape of future policy decisions with evidence about implementation and effects of these diverse policy choices. The influence of evidence on policy is not automatic. Enacting policies is a social-informational and political process: actors need to know that the policy alternatives exist, and have the motivation and resources to change existing law to more closely resemble that which has shown to be effective in other jurisdictions. Knowledge, capacity and motivation to improve the law can be influenced by informational campaigns that capture the current state of the law in a way that supports comparisons to distinguish places that have enacted healthy policies and those that retain unhealthy ones. Policy surveillance is a foundation of efforts to target, carry out and assess the success of advocacy efforts.

HIV policy provides an apt example. For nearly four decades after the epidemic began, it was recognised that law was an important mediator in causing, preventing and treating HIV. Confidentiality and voluntariness of testing, protection against discrimination, criminalisation of HIV-related behaviour, access to care and even the cost of medicines were all matters in which the law was both significantly different across jurisdictions and an important factor in shaping the HIV-related risk environment. The notions that the overall social environment should be 'enabling' of HIV prevention and care and that respect for human rights was integral to an effective control programme were cornerstones of global policy guidance and national prevention plans. Yet at the global, national and local level, there was no real-time (or even annual) tracking of the actual state of the law, and therefore no basis for making countries accountable for their policies or focusing advocacy efforts—let alone data for quantitative research.[33] Only with the launch of the HIV Policy Lab project by Georgetown University in 2020 did the world finally have a comprehensive policy surveillance resource and a real opportunity to assess and promote compliance with WHO guidance and best practice.[34]

A similar US example is CityHealth.org ('CityHealth'), an initiative designed to push the 75 largest cities in the United States to adopt 12 selected health policies. It includes a public, web-based performance ranking system[35] as well as an active government relations element that works with interested stakeholders in the cities to leverage the rankings and supporting information to change city policy. Supported by a foundation and a major health system, the website uses an Olympic-style medal system (from no medal to gold) to rank each policy based on its internal characteristics and awards each city an overall medal computed from its individual policy scores.

CityHealth utilises policy surveillance[36] to capture individual features of the nine policies that make them stronger or weaker, and thus serve as the criteria for ranking.[37] For example, earned sick leave policies are ranked based on the following: (1) whether the city has an earned sick leave law, (2) whether an employee can use earned sick leave to care for family members (including spouses, children, parents, grandparents, grandchildren, siblings and domestic partners), (3) whether an employee can use earned sick leave for domestic violence recovery, (4) the minimum amount of earned sick leave time an employee can earn and (5) the smallest business size covered under the earned sick leave law. Cities earn a bronze medal in the earned sick leave category if the city's policy allows leave to care for family members and to deal with certain issues related to domestic violence. If the city's policy provides at least 40 hours of earned sick leave, it gets silver, while if it provides at least 48 hours and covers all sizes of employers, it earns a gold medal. The same criteria, based on observable features of the policy, are measured for every city being evaluated, leading to a both qualitative and quantitative assessment of earned sick leave policies that can be directly and consistently compared across cities.[38] Over five years, the proportion of cities earning an overall medal nearly doubled (from 19 to 37), the number of individual policy gold medals earned went from 84 to 142, and one policy was retired because 40 of 40 cities adopted it.

By creating accessible legal data that present patterns and variation in the law, policy surveillance facilitates the spread of innovative policies and a greater understanding of their important attributes.[39] Policy surveillance can also enable advocacy for policy reforms, and accountability of those reforms, by informing diffusion strategies and policy decisions while making those decisions transparent for the public.[40]

Challenges of Drug Policy Research in a Post-Prohibition World

Both policy surveillance and evaluation have a foothold in the realm of drug policy. The US National Institutes of Health (NIH) has supported at least two policy surveillance programmes (PDAPS and APIS), and the data they generate have been used in numerous evaluations – though not nearly as many as needed. NIDA and other NIH agencies still have a long way to go to adequately fund studies – and research careers – in drug policy and legal epidemiology more generally.[41] Europe has also seen efforts to track policy changes in cannabis and other drugs,[42] and some important policy evaluation work has been carried out.[43]

Drug policy evaluation research, limited though it sometimes is, has been instrumental to policy change in several countries. In one notable shift, following studies into feasibility, safety and cost-effectiveness, Switzerland legalised the medical prescription of heroin.[44] In Australia, following a report to Parliament on the establishment of safe injection sites that reviewed existing laws in Europe and policy implications, legislation was passed to operate a site in Sydney.[45] Portugal famously decriminalised possession for personal use of all drugs based on the opinion of a multidisciplinary committee of experts brought together by the government.[46]

Despite advances in legal information and research methods, there are challenges to collecting and accurately coding the features of law at the global level. Access to legal information is an ongoing problem for analysts around the world.[47] International efforts to share legal information, like the WHO's *International Digest of Health Legislation*, have largely failed, and new initiatives are only slowly appearing.[48] In recent years, the United Nations Office on Drugs and Crime has developed an online legal library of legislation from around the world, including 866 pieces of legislation involving drug offenses.[49] The European Monitoring Centre for Drugs and Drug Addiction has also carried out efforts to document national policy in Europe. While these efforts are a good start, they must be expanded and enhanced to facilitate international policy surveillance, evaluation and, hopefully, adoption of more health-oriented policy.

Obtaining the relevant legal text is only the first problem. While national policy surveillance can rely on a mostly shared language and legal tradition, international policy surveillance is hampered by variation across countries on measures such as the structure and operation of legal systems, language and translation issues, inaccessibility and differing legal cultures.[50] Legal systems can vary greatly as to the division of authority, so comparing national laws may not capture the full legal reality on the ground within a country.[51] Even within States, policy surveillance raises many issues related to the collection of local laws, including conflicts in standardisation and access.[52] Legal data are a starting point for evaluation, but data capturing health and other outcomes – not to mention information about implementation – are also essential. Challenges in acquiring these data are significant, though beyond the scope of this article to address.

Even where legal, implementation and outcome measures are all available, larger challenges of politics and culture remain. As Kaplan writes:

> The entire enterprise [of policy surveillance and evaluation] … requires a truly transdisciplinary effort in evaluating global health information and its effect. This ecosystem at the nexus of law, policy, and health is complex, and, in my view, such monitoring and evaluation … similarly requires the coalescence of disciplines that normally may not interact. Moreover, all the policy surveillance and legal epidemiology in the world will not matter if the disparities in social determinants of health remain as they are. The field requires concerted political action.[53]

The evaluation of the health effects of law is inherently a transdisciplinary enterprise, requiring the expertise of a range of scientific disciplines as well as a diversity of forms of expertise. In framing and conducting drug policy research, the expertise of drug users, of regulators and of people living in communities affected by drug- (or drug-enforcement) related problems all can contribute to properly designing studies, selecting measures and interpreting results. Building this sort of collaborative research culture is no easy task, as Kaplan observes.

And then come culture and politics. Not everyone who conducts or funds drug policy research is free of stigmatised beliefs about drug use and drug users, or willing to consider the failure of prohibition. There can be pressure on researchers to conform to existing prejudices in the selection, design and reporting of their research. Researchers who hew to the science still face the challenge of translating their findings to policymakers who by conviction or political convenience remain addicted to punishment as the treatment of choice for drug problems. Even researchers who successfully navigate those waters must be prepared for the fact that policymakers may decline, for a variety of reasons, to implement what the data suggest are best practices for improving the health of people who use drugs.

Conclusion

The world is currently at a drug policy crossroads. It is clear that the era of prohibition has not met any of the markers its supporters claimed and has caused enormous harm. Effective, public health focused and equity-driven drug regulation is needed. Legal epidemiology can help accomplish this by supplying objective legal data and rigorous policy evaluation as an evidence base for comprehensive, equity-focused and health-oriented drug policy.

Notes

* The authors thank Joshua Waimberg, J.D., M.B.A., for his contributions to the original draft of this chapter.

1 Joanne Csete, et al, 'Public Health and International Drug Policy' (2016) 387 *The Lancet* 1427.; Dan Werb, 'Post-war Prevention: Emerging Frameworks to Prevent Drug Use after the War on Drugs' (2018) 51 *International Journal of Drug Policy* 160.

2 Peter Reuter, 'Why Has US Drug Policy Changed so Little over 30 Years?' (2013) 42 *Crime and Justice* 75.

3 Leo Beletsky and Corey S Davis, 'Today's Fentanyl Crisis: Prohibition's Iron Law, Revisited' (2017) 46 *International Journal of Drug Policy* 156.; Csete et al (n 1).; David F Musto, *The American Disease: Origins of Narcotic Control* (Oxford University Press, 1999).

4 Ayden I Scheim, et al, 'Impact Evaluations of Drug Decriminalisation and Legal Regulation on Drug Use, Health and Social Harms: A Systematic Review' (2020) 10 *BMJ Open* e035148.

5 Rosalie Liccardo Pacula, et al, 'Developing Public Health Regulations for Marijuana: Lessons from Alcohol and Tobacco' (2014) 104 *American Journal of Public Health* 1021.; Scott Burris and Evan Anderson, 'Legal Regulation of Health-Related Behavior: A Half Century of Public Health Law Research' (2013) 9 *Annual Review of Law and Social Science* 95.

6 Tara Ramanathan, et al, 'Legal Epidemiology: The Science of Law' (2017) 45 *The Journal of Law, Medicine & Ethics* 69.
7 Scott Burris, et al, 'Policy Surveillance: A Vital Public Health Practice Comes of Age' (2016) 41 *Journal of Health Politics, Policy and Law* 1151.
8 Scott Burris, et al, 'Making the Case for Laws that Improve Health: A Framework for Public Health Law Research' (2010) 88 *Milbank Quarterly* 169.; Scott Burris and Evan Anderson, 'Making the Case for Laws that Improve Health: The Work of the Public Health Law Research National Program Office' (2011) 39 Suppl. 1 *Journal of Law, Medicine & Ethics* 15.; Scott Burris, et al, 'A Transdisciplinary Approach to Public Health Law: The Emerging Practice of Legal Epidemiology' (2016) 37 *Annual Review of Public Health* 135; Scott Burris, Lindsay K Cloud & Matthew Penn, 'The Growing Field of Legal Epidemiology' (2020) 26 *Journal of Public Health Management and Practice* S4.
9 Scott Burris, Ichiro Kawachi & Austin Sarat, 'Integrating Law and Social Epidemiology' (2002) 30 *Journal of Law, Medicine & Ethics* 510.
10 Scott Burris, Evan D Anderson & Alexander C Wagenaar, 'The "Legal Epidemiology" of Pandemic Control' (2021) 384 *New England Journal of Medicine* 1973.
11 Alison Ritter, et al, 'Comparative Policy Analysis for Alcohol and Drugs: Current State of the Field' (2016) 31 *International Journal of Drug Policy* 39.; Scott Burris, 'Theory and Methods in Comparative Drug and Alcohol Policy Research: Response to a Review of the Literature' (2017) 41 *International Journal of Drug Policy* 126.
12 Rosanna Smart, Bryce Pardo & Corey S Davis, 'Systematic Review of the Emerging Literature on the Effectiveness of Naloxone Access Laws in the United States' (2021) 116 *Addiction* 6.
13 Steven J Hoffman, et al, 'Impact of the WHO Framework Convention on Tobacco Control on Global Cigarette Consumption: Quasi-experimental Evaluations Using Interrupted time Series Analysis and In-sample Forecast Event Modelling' (2019) 365 *BMJ* l2287.
14 Alexander C Wagenaar and Kelli A Komro, 'Natural Experiments: Research Design Elements for Optimal Causal Inference without Randomization' in Alexander Wagenaar and Scott Burris (eds.), *Public Health Law Research: Theory and Methods* (Jossey-Bass, 2013).
15 Alcohol Policy Information System, 'Peer-Reviewed Publications Using APIS Data' 2017 <https://alcoholpolicy.niaaa.nih.gov/resource/peer-reviewed-publications-using-apis-data/22> accessed 30 April 2022.; Scott Burris and Evan Anderson (n 5).
16 Matthew M Kavanagh, et al, 'Global Policy Surveillance: Creating and Using Comparative National Data on Health Law and Policy' (2020) 110 *American Journal of Public Health* 1805.
17 Matthew JP Poirier, et al, 'Principles and Methods of Global Legal Epidemiology' (2022) 76 *Journal of Epidemiology & Community Health* 828.; Steven J Hoffman, et al, 'Impact of the WHO Framework Convention on Tobacco Control on Global Cigarette Consumption: Quasi-experimental Evaluations Using Interrupted Time Series Analysis And In-sample Forecast Event Modelling' (2019) 365 *BMJ* 12287.
18 Matthew M Kavanagh, et al, 'Law, Criminalisation and HIV in the World: Have Countries that Criminalise Achieved More or Less Successful Pandemic Response?' (2021) 6 BMJ *Global Health* e006315.
19 Wagenaar and Komro (n 14).
20 Evan Anderson, et al, 'Measuring Statutory Law and Regulations for Empirical Research' in Alexander Wagenaar and Scott Burris (eds.), *Public Health Law Research: Theory and Methods* (John Wiley & Sons, 2013).; Burris (n 11).

21 James W Buehler, 'Surveillance' in Kenneth J Rothman, Sander Greenland & Timothy L Lash (eds.), *Modern Epidemiology*, 3rd ed (Wolters Kluwer Health/Lippincott Williams & Wilkins, 2008).
22 Scott Burris, et al (n 7).
23 Alcohol Policy Information System, 'Peer-Reviewed Publications Using APIS Data'. <https://alcoholpolicy.niaaa.nih.gov/resource/peer-reviewed-publications-using-apis-data/22> accessed April 30.
24 Center for Public Health Law Research, 'LawAtlas: The Policy Surveillance Portal' (The Policy Surveillance Program of the Robert Wood Johnson Foundation, 2023) <www.LawAtlas.org> accessed 9 March 2022.; Center for Public Health Law Research, 'Prescription Drug Abuse Policy System (PDAPS' 2023) <www.PDAPS.org> accessed 9 March 2022.
25 Kavanagh, et al (n 16).; Benjamin Mason Meier, et al, 'Examining National Public Health Law to Realize the Global Health Security Agenda' (2017) 25 *Medical Law Review* 240.
26 Anderson, et al (n 20).
27 Ray Pawson, 'Evidence-Based Medicine & Evidence-Based Policy: The World's Most Perfectly Developed Method & the 79-Pound Weakling?' (2017) <https://torontoevaluation.ca/centre/wp-content/uploads/2017/03/Pawson-1-EBMEBPLEEDS.pdf> accesses 12 March 2023.
28 Anderson, et al (n 20).
29 Abraham Gutman, et al, 'Law as Data: Using Policy Surveillance to Advance Housing Studies' (2019) 21 *Cityscape: A Journal of Policy Development and Research* 183.
30 Scott Burris and Alexander Wagenaar, 'Integrating Diverse Theories for Public Health Law Evaluation' in Alexander Wagenaar and Scott Burris (eds.), *Public Health Law Research: Theory and Methods* (John Wiley & Sons, 2013).
31 For an example of this error, see Jennifer L Doleac and Anita Mukherjee, *The Moral Hazard of Lifesaving Innovations: Naloxone Access, Opioid Abuse, and Crime* (Discussion Paper Series, 2018).
32 Evan Anderson and Scott Burris, 'Researchers and Research Knowledge in Evidence-Informed Policy Innovation', in Tania Voon, Andrew D Mitchell & Jonathan Liberman (eds.), *Regulating Tobacco, Alcohol and Unhealthy Foods: The Legal Issues* (Routledge, 2016).
33 Kavanagh, et al (n 18).
34 O'Neill Institute for National and Global Health Law, 'HIV Policy Lab' (2023) <www.hivpolicylab.org/> accessed 9 March 2023.
35 <www.cityhealth.org/> accessed 9 March 2023.
36 Policy surveillance is the ongoing systematic, scientific collection and analysis of laws of public health significance. See, for example, Scott Burris, et al (n 7).
37 Policy surveillance is conducted at the Center for Public Health Law Research at Temple University Beasley School of Law https://phlr.org/content/policy-surveillance-program accessed 9 March 2023.
38 For more information on specific criteria for each policy see www.cityhealth.org accessed 9 March 2023.
39 Burris, et al (n 7).
40 Kavanagh, et al (n 16).
41 Jennifer K Ibrahim, et al, 'Supporting a Culture of Evidence-Based Policy: Federal Funding for Public Health Law Evaluation Research, 1985–2014' (2017) 23 *Journal of Public Health Management & Practice* 658.

42 European Monitoring Centre for Drugs and Drug Addiction, *Strategies and Coordination in the Field of Drugs in the European Union: A Descriptive Review* (2002).; European Monitoring Centre for Drugs and Drug Addiction, *Illicit Drug Use in the EU: Legislative Approaches* (EMCDDA Thematic Papers, 2005).

43 M Meacham, et al, 'Review of Methodologies of Evaluating Effects of Drug-Related Legal Changes' (EMCDDA, 2010).; Paula Vale de Andrade and Ludmila Carapinha, 'Drug Decriminalisation in Portugal' (2010) 341 *BMJ* c4554.

44 Ambros Uchtenhagen, 'Heroin-Assisted Treatment in Switzerland: A Case Study in Policy Change' (2010) 105 *Addiction* 29.

45 Cate Kelly and Katherine M Conigrave, 'The Sydney Medically Supervised Injecting Centre: A Controversial Public Health Measure' (2002) 26 *Australian and New Zealand Journal of Public Health* 552.

46 Vale de Andrade and Carapinha (n 43).; Ximene Rêgo, et al, '20 Years of Portuguese Drug Policy—Developments, Challenges and the Quest for Human Rights' (2021) 16(1) *Substance Abuse Treatment, Prevention and Policy* 59.

47 Burris, et al (n 7).

48 Amir Attaran, et al, 'Healthy by Law: The Missed Opportunity to Use Laws for Public Health' (2012) 379 *Lancet* 283

49 United Nations Office on Drugs and Crime, 'Sharing Electronic Resources and Laws on Crime (SHERLOC' 2015) <https://sherloc.unodc.org/cld/en/st/home.html> accessed 1 August 2022.

50 Kavanagh, et al (n 16).

51 Ibid.

52 Lindsey Sanner, et al, 'The Challenges of Conducting Intrastate Policy Surveillance: A Methods Note on County and City Laws in Indiana' (2021) 111 *American Journal of Public Health* 1095.

53 Warren A Kaplan, 'Global Policy Surveillance and Legal Epidemiology: Next Steps?' (2020) 110 *American Journal of Public Health* 1726.

Part III

Harm Reduction in the Changing Landscape

7 Harm Reduction Post-Prohibition

Naomi Burke-Shyne and Ajeng Larasati

Introduction

Harm reduction, a non-judgmental approach to drug use grounded in evidence, pragmatism, justice and compassion, has played a key role in protecting the health, rights and lives of people who use drugs under prohibition. Harm reduction has also established and expanded zones of *de facto* decriminalisation and exceptions which have normatively supported efforts to erode components of prohibition. While many of the potential harms associated with drug use are consequences of the punitive law and policy environment (including law enforcement practices and incarceration), the legal environment is not the sole driver of potential harms. Harms can also arise from the potency of a substance, the adulterants present in a substance and the modes of consumption of a substance. All of these potential harms are worsened by structural and socio-economic factors, including poverty, gender, ethnicity and race. In light of this – —and the fact that the end of prohibition would not guarantee well-regulated drug markets, preclude the existence of a parallel illicit market, nor address the structural or social factors that exacerbate risk – —there will remain a critical role for harm reduction even if currently illicit drugs were legally regulated. Post-prohibition, harm reduction will be vital in addressing the potential harms of drug use in new markets, in mitigating the impact of structural and social factors and in safeguarding the rights of people who use drugs. Central to the effectiveness of harm reduction and health in the post-prohibition era is the leadership of people who use drugs and expanded recognition of community expertise[1] and agency.

This chapter will focus on the relevance of harm reduction in the post-prohibition era across the axes of health and rights. First, the harm reduction approach and harm reduction commodities will remain central to the effective implementation of preventative health interventions, dissemination of information and exercise of choice in a post-prohibition era. Second, the harm reduction approach offers a conceptual framework which balances the need for access to controlled medicines with the prerogative to challenge paternalistic approaches and unnecessary medical expansion. Third and final, reform of prohibition laws (which have been used to police poor and marginalised groups and justify racist policing practices) will not eliminate stigma or discrimination or prevent excessive use of policing of people

DOI: 10.4324/9781003169765-11

who use drugs under the auspices of other laws, policies and practices. In this context, legal services and human rights advocacy – indispensable elements of harm reduction – will remain critical in upholding and protecting the rights of people who use drugs in the post-prohibition era.

For the purposes of this chapter, there are two presumptions made about a post-prohibition era:

1 A post-prohibition era will involve the decriminalisation and regulation of currently illicit drugs. However, illicit markets are likely to continue in parallel to some degree.
2 The reforms necessary to dismantle prohibition will occur in a staggered manner globally and are likely to benefit those with power and privilege first (this presumption contemplates power and privilege both *within* countries and *between* countries).

The Harm Reduction Approach

Harm reduction refers to policies, programmes and practices that aim to minimise negative health, social and legal impacts associated with drug use, drug policies and drug laws. It is grounded in justice and human rights and prioritises the dignity, leadership and agency of people who use drugs.[2] At a practical level, harm reduction encompasses a range of health and social services which mitigate the harms of drug use. These include, but are not limited to, needle and syringe programmes, opioid agonist therapy, the provision of information on safer drug use, drug checking, overdose prevention and reversal, drug consumption rooms, psychosocial support, legal services and non-abstinence-based housing. Of the 179 governments around the world reporting injecting drug use, approximately half have put in place one or more of the above-mentioned interventions to mitigate the harms of drug use.[3] There are currently 105 countries with explicit reference to harm reduction in their national policies,[4] up from 70 countries in 2008.[5] This points to a gradual uptake of the concept of harm reduction, although coverage, implementation and scale remain insufficient – just 2% of people who inject drugs live in countries with high coverage of both needle and syringe programmes and opioid agonist therapy.[6]

The core commitment of harm reduction – to work with people without judgment, coercion and discrimination – stands in sharp distinction to the notions of shame and punishment which underpin prohibition. In addition, it is the fact that the harm reduction approach does not require a person to stop using drugs as a precondition to support that attracts attention. The dismissal of an abstinence-only approach has generated significant normative debate and tension at both national and international levels. While the international drug control conventions do not explicitly prohibit interventions or approaches which aim to reduce the harms of drug use, in the broadly hostile environment of prohibition, commentators have described harm reduction as a normative deviation from the prohibitive ethos of the conventions.[7]

In corollary to this normative deviation, harm reduction has played a central role in establishing and expanding zones of de facto decriminalisation and exceptions to prohibition. Drug consumption rooms and drug checking services are clear examples of harm reduction interventions with this impact.

The establishment of state-sanctioned drug consumption rooms (also referred to as overdose prevention sites) create decriminalised zones in which staff and people who use drugs are exempt from prosecution for drug possession on the premises. These exemptions are often established through agreements between local law enforcement and service providers, with a view to providing services to some of the most vulnerable people in society. More than 120 drug consumption rooms are now lawfully operating in 17 countries around the world.[8] In practice, the functioning of a drug consumption room means that a person is able to travel to and enter a facility with illicit substances, with the intention of consuming the substances in a safer environment. This necessitates agreement between local law enforcement, service users and service providers not only in relation to the facility but also clients approaching the facility. This has the practical effect of extending a (fragile) halo of decriminalisation around client pathways.

Drug checking services have also established and expanded exceptions to prohibition. Staff working at drug checking services take possession of a small amount of illicit substances for the purpose of checking it for potency or adulterants. The legality of this has been articulated in the interpretation of law and via agreement with government authorities. For example, in Switzerland, two legal scholars (Stefan Seiler and Peter Albrecht) concluded in separate legal opinions that testing MDMA pills, and communicating the results, was not prohibited under Swiss law. In Switzerland, drugs can be checked in laboratories in possession of a government-issued license for handling controlled substances.[9] In the Netherlands, specific arrangements have been made with national and subnational authorities to provide for drug checking, including an official agreement with the Public Prosecution Service which ensures that anyone possessing illicit drugs attending a drug checking service will not be arrested or prosecuted. Services involved in drug checking are required to request and hold a waiver of the Dutch Opium Act.[10] In Wales, the WEDINOS anonymous drug checking service has been operating for ten years with the support of Welsh Government and Public Health Wales.[11]

The definition of harm reduction and the role it has played during prohibition point to the role of harm reduction in the post-prohibition era. Harm Reduction International sets out four principles of harm reduction which will have deep relevance throughout reform processes:

1 Respecting the rights of people who use drugs – treating people who use drugs – along with their families and communities – with compassion and dignity.
2 A commitment to evidence – harm reduction policies and practices are informed by a strong body of evidence that shows interventions to be practical, feasible, effective, safe and cost-effective in diverse social, cultural and economic settings.

3 A commitment to social justice and collaborating with networks of people who use drugs – harm reduction is rooted in a commitment to addressing discrimination and ensuring that nobody is excluded from the health and social services they may need and the leadership and meaningful involvement of people who use drugs.
4 The avoidance of stigma – harm reduction practitioners are committed to meeting people who use drugs 'where they are' in their lives, without judgment, and to employing respectful language.[12]

As global consensus around prohibition continues to fracture in the face of more effective, humane and just solutions,[13] harm reduction approaches and interventions will continue to mitigate the potential harms of drug use and drug policy and safeguard the rights of people who use drugs. It is the inclusive, holistic and pragmatic nature of harm reduction, and its emphasis on community leadership, that ensures its continued relevance. These factors are all particularly pertinent in a staggered global process of reforming prohibitionist laws and policies.

Post-Prohibition – Harm Reduction and Health Interventions

In a post-prohibition era, harm reduction will continue to play a critical role protecting health in the context of drug use. This role can be broken down into three interconnected and overlapping components: securing access to health interventions and support to reduce the potential risks of drug use; providing evidence-based information; and supporting people who use drugs to make informed choices around their health and safety. Central to these efforts is improved recognition of the expertise, capabilities and agency of people who use drugs.[14] In a rapid review of literature on peer involvement in services, Chang et al collate evidence and conclude peer involvement reduces HIV incidence and prevalence; increases service access, acceptability and quality; changes risk behaviours; and reduces stigma and discrimination.[15] Going forward, people who use drugs must lead in the design, planning, implementation and evaluation of interventions and must be appropriately funded or remunerated to take on this work.[16]

- **Access to Health Interventions and Support**

Post-prohibition, people who use drugs will still need access to non-judgmental services and support to protect their health. This includes providing sterile commodities to avoid skin and soft tissue infections and prevent transmission of communicable diseases (e.g. needles and syringes, safer smoking kits, alcohol swabs) as well as naloxone to reverse opioid overdoses. An example of work to strengthen access to health interventions and support which is likely to translate particularly effectively to a post-prohibition environment is the self-care model led by É de Lei in São Paolo, Brazil. É de Lei's *Centro de Convivencia* is grounded in peer involvement and offers a safe space for social interactions that promote harm reduction, mutual respect, autonomy and citizenship.

É de Lei runs outreach programmes to distribute harm reduction materials, has tailored programmes to reach women and gender non-conforming people, provides referrals and accompanies clients to appointments for physical and mental health services under the national health system, and holds conversation circles to grapple with complex issues – including stigma and prejudice. Honing in on the specific needs of their clients and modes of drug consumption in the local area (i.e. smoking), É de Lei and service users co-designed and developed silicone tubes with different diameters for use with improvised pipes. These silicone tubes reduce damage to lips and lungs, reduce the likelihood of sharing pipes and reduce the health risks associated with sharing consumption equipment.[17]

- **Evidence-Based Information**

Evidence-based harm reduction information will also remain vitally important to mitigating the potential harms of drug use in a post-prohibition environment. People with fewer resources and/or more complex needs are likely to continue to access harm reduction information via in-person services and outreach, while other people may increasingly turn to online sources for harm reduction information and support. Literature and case reports have reported online harm reduction services to be effective in offering verified harm reduction information, responding to minor issues and offering general support.[18]

Online platforms and cryptomarkets are also likely to build up their current approaches to providing (and utilising) harm reduction information in a post-prohibition environment.[19] Cryptomarkets rely on information to reduce harms in two broad categories: offering consumers the information they need to support their choices and, at a broader level, reducing harms to consumers by responding to warnings of adulterated substances.[20] In relation to the former category, in addition to providing a platform for vendors to offer information and space for user feedback, cryptomarkets strengthen access to harm reduction information by creating space for sharing knowledge around potential drug risks and practice between vendors and users.[21] In the latter category, a Spanish nonprofit project called Energy Control notes administrators of cryptomarkets have responded to the results of Energy Control drug checking services, including taking down listings and the removal of vendors selling adulterated products.[22] There is also the example of the Alphabay market which encourages vendors to provide naloxone with purchases by waiving the vendor bond for those who do.[23]

Cryptomarkets have the capacity to separate drug distribution from other environments in a post-prohibition era and, in this way, further reduce some potential harms. For example, separating a buyer from the potential violence associated with drug trade, or the harms that may arise from nightclub environments or sexual exchange. As a mitigating force this is useful, though not a holistic disruption of the unequal power dynamics that exist in the offline drug market.[24]

- **Informed Choices around Health and Safety**

Geopolitical uncertainties – from border closures linked to COVID-19[25] to the 2022 Taliban prohibition of the cultivation of poppy[26] – tend to influence the availability of traditional opiates and the use of new psychoactive (or synthetic) substances (NPS). These changes and uncertainties require monitoring as well as tailored harm reduction responses to support informed choices. The changes associated with the end of prohibition will further compound any existing uncertainties in drug markets and increase demand for verification of the substances sold via the regulated market (in order to establish trust between new regulated vendors and buyers), on top of the ongoing need to check substances sold via illicit markets. Data from the Canadian government following the legalisation of cannabis indicate that licit markets do not rapidly push out illicit vendors, and that some people retain a preference for accessing drugs via their existing pathways and/or illicit sources.[27] It follows that drug checking such as those described above will be a critical harm reduction tool for supporting informed choices in the future.

A 2021 systematic review of drug checking services found that while concerns about drug contents and negative health consequences were a primary driver for people using the services, uncertainty related to drug market changes and distrust in drug markets and sellers were also significant.[28] The review highlighted European studies which indicated increased detection of NPS by drug checking services over time and reported that many drug checking services aim to prevent harms from NPS, including synthetic opioids.[29] A qualitative study on NPS in Eastern Europe similarly notes evidence of increased NPS use in the region and reports some respondents would not choose to use NPS if traditional opiates were available or affordable.[30] That study emphasises the need for enhanced and expanded harm reduction services, including more information on NPS and drug checking services. These studies and findings offer further insights into the importance of harm reduction and drug checking in a post-prohibition environment.

Broader Challenges for Health and Harm Reduction

Another urgent challenge for a post-prohibition landscape is the need for sustainable funding for implementing harm reduction services at scale. In low- and middle-income countries, harm reduction currently relies heavily on international donors and is significantly underfunded.[31] This is notwithstanding the substantial evidence demonstrating that harm reduction interventions are cost-effective and can be cost-saving in the long term.[32] Services tailored to women, young people, rural populations and Indigenous communities are particularly under-resourced.[33] Future drug policy reform processes represent an opportunity to challenge societal acceptance of massive State investment in law enforcement and call for accountability around State expenditure. It is critical that during reform processes, advocates seize the moment and urge governments to repurpose criminal justice budgets, divest from drug law enforcement and invest in harm reduction, health and community initiatives.

Post-Prohibition – Access to Controlled Medicines, Paternalism and Unnecessary Medical Expansion

In a post-prohibition era, harm reduction will continue to offer a conceptual framework which balances the need for access to controlled medicines with the prerogative to challenge paternalistic approaches and unnecessary medical expansion.[34] A stronger recognition of the space for both these concepts will support the evolution of thinking around drug use, offering a foundation for a more nuanced approach.

It is worth noting that a key catalyst for harm reduction in the prohibition era has been the HIV response. Global political commitments related to HIV and related investments over multiple decades have driven a pragmatic approach to drug use and established evidence-based health interventions designed to prevent HIV transmission among people who inject drugs. While the HIV framing has yielded positive public health outcomes, it also has its limits. The HIV response has enabled advocates to challenge criminalisation and punitive approaches in the name of better health outcomes, yet this advocacy is just one step towards a more nuanced comprehension of the drivers of drug use, and, in many ways, is a simplification which offers an engagement point on a highly stigmatised issue. In a post-prohibition era, harm reduction approaches and interventions will build upon the significant gains of the HIV movement while moving beyond the dichotomy of health versus criminal justice. This will support the recognition of drug use as a diverse phenomenon made more complex by structural and socio-economic factors such as poverty, gender, ethnicity and race, and place bodily autonomy as a principal consideration.

The issue of access to controlled medicines within harm reduction relates to the prescription of controlled medicines in the form of opioid agonist therapy (OAT) for opioid dependence (primarily via the medicines methadone and buprenorphine).[35] OAT is considered to be a harm reduction intervention because it reduces the frequency of injecting, reduces illicit opioid use (and thus reliance on potentially adulterated street supply) and reduces the sharing of injecting equipment.[36] OAT has also been demonstrated to have a positive impact in many aspects of participants' lives.[37] Methadone and buprenorphine can be characterised as drug treatment as well as harm reduction, as a person may elect to use OAT as a means of supporting a journey to reduce or cease drug use. Critically, a harm reduction approach recognises the choice of the person receiving the medicine is key.

A 2023 systematic review demonstrated global coverage of OAT is low, with an average of only 18% of people who inject drugs receiving OAT.[38] This is significantly below the World Health Organization recommendation that 40 out of 100 people with opioid dependence receive OAT.[39] Low coverage rates for OAT are consistent with the broader global deficit in controlled medicines – 50% of the global population (3.6 billion people who reside in the poorest countries) receive less than 1% of the morphine distributed worldwide.[40] The dismantling of prohibitionist frameworks is likely to reduce some of the legal barriers to controlled medicines for drug dependence, predominantly those created by overly strict or bureaucratic national and international controls. Further reforms will be required to ensure robust, non-judgmental, equitable access to controlled medicines, and to put in place normative standards for decision-making frameworks supporting administration of controlled medicines.[41]

The rapid evolution of new controlled medicines for drug dependence in the form of long-acting OAT formulations and subdermal implants raise important questions related to access to controlled medicines and paternalistic approaches. Long-acting formulations tend to reduce points of engagement with health services and, therefore, represent the preferred approach for some people who use drugs.[42] For other people, the availability of low-engagement pharmaceutical solutions may be detrimental to health, rights and bodily autonomy, or represent a significant risk of a coercive use.[43] Long-acting formulations promoted for provider and client convenience produce a subtle but critical shift in control and bodily autonomy because the nature of these formulations mean that clients are locked in for the period set by the particular formulation and particular provider. This means a client cannot choose to cease receiving the medicine and is tied to the medical regime. Wolfe and Saucier describe this as 'drug control dressed in the sheep's clothing of medicine'.[44]

In a post-prohibition era, there remains a real risk that controls previously rolled out via drug laws will be reworked as controls exerted in the medical sphere. In this context, long-acting OAT formulations may double up as a means of enforcing morally driven ideas of abstinence and reducing the choices available to individuals with drug dependence. In this context, it will be essential that harm reductionists (in particular community leaders) advocate for controlled medicines to be employed to support people to self-regulate their drug use and manage health symptoms, and not for the pursuit of enforced abstinence.

Finally, in a post-prohibition era, the harm reduction approach will also be useful as a framework for challenging paternalistic approaches and unnecessary medical expansion, and advocating for bodily autonomy. Advancing a less paternalistic (and harm reducing) approach to drug use is the concept of safe supply (or safer supply). Safe supply is defined by the Canadian Association of People who Use Drugs as a legal and regulated supply of drugs with mind/body altering properties that traditionally have been accessible only through the illicit drug market. A key aim of safe supply is to address the life-threatening risks of the illicit market by providing pharmaceutical-grade substances as an alternative to highly toxic street drugs.[45]

Safe supply strategies were implemented in a number of Canadian cities in 2020–2021 as part of an urgent response to the dual pandemics of COVID-19 and opioid overdose. Strategies were explicitly intended to provide pharmaceutical-grade drugs to people with drug dependency to 'support a reduced risk of withdrawal, exposure to COVID-19, and exposure to a limited and toxic drug supply'.[46] By way of specific example, the provincial government of British Columbia provided guidance to clinicians, enabling them to facilitate access to prescription opioids, stimulants and benzodiazepines for people otherwise reliant on the illicit drug market.[47] Although these safe supply options only reached a small percentage of the people in British Columbia experiencing dependency on drugs, people who accessed the no-cost prescription substances reported the approach allowed them to take back control over their drug use.[48] Others reported it enabled them to establish more stable drug use patterns with broader positive effects on their lives.[49]

It is also worth noting that under safe supply models in Canada, people may take away their substances. In other words, people are not required to consume their safe supply substance under supervision, although prescribers often encourage the use of supervised consumption sites as a complementary harm reduction intervention.[50] These approaches, though underdeveloped, represent a significant shift towards a less paternalistic approach to drug use and are a robust example of practical approaches likely to remain relevant post-prohibition.

Post-Prohibition – Harm Reduction, Legal Services and Human Rights Advocacy

In a post-prohibition era, harm reduction will continue to play an essential role in upholding and protecting the rights of people who use drugs. Drug criminalisation has been used to justify police violence and special law enforcement operations, violated human rights,[51] fuelled mass incarceration and impacted poor and marginalised groups, including Black, Brown, Indigenous and ethnic minority individuals, hardest.[52] Reinforcing these points, in 2019, the UN Working Group of Experts on People of African Descent described the war on drugs as operating 'more effectively as a system of racial control than as a mechanism for combating the use and trafficking of narcotics'.[53] Echoing this, in 2021, the UN Working Group on Arbitrary Detention reported that 'the war on drugs may be understood to a significant extent as a war on people. Its impact is often greatest on those who are poor, but also frequently overlaps with discrimination in law enforcement directed at vulnerable groups'.[54]

The reforms involved in ending prohibition are unlikely to comprehensively address the entrenched practices targeting poor or marginalised groups, the structural and socio-economic factors that contribute to intersectional vulnerability or the grotesque excesses of prohibition (a notable example being the use of the death penalty for drug offences, in violation of international law).[55] In this context, legal services and human rights advocacy will be critical harm reduction tools in the post-prohibition environment. Legal services – including paralegal services – will defend and uphold the rights of people who use drugs and empower people with the skills to navigate legal systems.[56] In complement, human rights advocacy will be important in documenting rights violations and trends, challenging residual punitive approaches, holding governments to account and establishing the way forward in repairing the harms of the war on drugs.

- **Legal and Paralegal Services**

Post-prohibition, over time, there is likely to be a reduction in need for legal defence against *drug-related* offences. However, people who use drugs, their families and communities, are still likely to face stigma, discrimination, prejudice and/or paternalistic interventions. Legal and paralegal services will be critical in actively defending people who use drugs against the application of laws and policies disproportionately targeting poor and vulnerable people. Punitive practices, which enable people to be discriminated against, have the capacity to negatively impact people or exclude people from opportunities on the basis of their drug use. Such practices may include urine testing for drugs to disqualify people from employment, welfare assistance or social housing,[57] as well as the exclusion of children and young people from education.[58] Past criminal records will continue to create barriers to full participation in society,[59] as expungement of records will take time and political will, and responding to an evolving national and international legal and policy environment (as decriminalisation and regulation gather pace) will require legal advice.

Street lawyers and community paralegals are practical ways to effectively uphold the rights of people who use drugs in a post-prohibition environment. In Indonesia, LBH Masyarakat established a cadre of community paralegals. The paralegals, some are individuals with experience of drug use, are equipped with the knowledge and skills that enable them to provide basic legal and human rights information and to engage strategically with law enforcement at the point of arrest and in pretrial detention.[60] In Denmark, Philippines and Russia, street lawyers make themselves available in public spaces and via outreach to offer information, support and sterile harm reduction commodities, as well as advice on rights.[61]

In the Netherlands and Portugal, lawyers have worked to link social housing services to harm reduction services and vice versa, as marginalised people who use drugs may be vulnerable to both homelessness and greater health risks due to poor access to sterile drug use paraphernalia.[62] Many lawyers and paralegals working for people who use drugs and other criminalised groups are part of a global network offering legal support and international solidarity, named Lawyering on the Margins.[63]

The prohibition era has caused mass incarceration and prison overcrowding. It is estimated that 2.2 million people are imprisoned for drug offences and that 22% of this group are imprisoned for drug possession for personal use.[64] At least 3,000 people are on death row for drug offences.[65] Addressing drug war-related mass incarceration in a post-prohibition time will require both legal services and human rights advocacy. Legal and paralegal services will be necessary to secure the release of people convicted and imprisoned for activities which are no longer criminalised, and to offer defence to those recently detained and in pretrial detention. Accompanying advocacy will be critical in monitoring the implementation of large-scale reforms. In the Philippines, StreetLawPH runs paralegal seminars for women detained for low-level offences, including drug offences, while also engaging in human rights advocacy related to prison overcrowding and the war on drugs. Low-threshold paralegal services will be particularly important in the transition to decriminalisation and regulation, to defend people in the context of related poverty and status-related offences.

- **Human Rights Advocacy**

Human rights advocacy will be important in a post-prohibition era in three ways: (a) documenting the changing human rights landscape, including rights violations and good practice and bad practice trends; (b) challenging residual approaches which seek to carry on punitive approaches to drugs; and (c) clarifying a rights-based path forward and repairing the harms of the war on drugs.

Human rights documentation will support monitoring of the implementation of decriminalisation and regulation, ensuring accountability for implementation of changes (including law enforcement practice) after law reform. Of particular importance will be advocacy for the prompt cessation of special law enforcement operations and arrests.

The pervasive nature of the war on drugs means the punitive framework of drug control extends significantly beyond the pure criminalisation of drugs. Human rights advocacy at multiple levels (national, regional and international) will be key in identifying and challenging the laws, policies and practices which extend the reach of prohibition in insidious ways beyond the criminal justice system, such as via administrative penalties, exclusion from social services or employment or through paternalistic treatment.[66] It will take decades to begin to dismantle the vast architecture which has upheld these punitive policies. Human rights advocacy will be essential in sustaining engagement and centring principles of justice and equity.

Advocacy to clarify a rights-based path forward and repair the harms of the war on drugs will be the most challenging new territory in a post-prohibition era. Defining a rights-based way forward requires careful development of new laws or policies, guided by the leadership and unique perspectives of the communities of people who use drugs and people most impacted by the drug war. New laws and policies need to end the impact of the criminal justice system on lives, ensure the formal and effective expungement of millions of convictions and put in place new mechanisms to explicitly protect human rights, as a first step towards beginning to repair the harms of prohibition. This will be even more complex in countries where prohibition has disproportionately impacted on one group, such as in the United States where drug law enforcement has targeted Black, Brown and Indigenous individuals and communities. As Michelle Alexander concludes 'mass incarceration in the United States [has], in fact, emerged as a stunningly comprehensive and well-disguised system of racialized social control that functions in a manner strikingly similar to Jim Crow'.[67] Rebuilding and repairing the harms of the drug war will require governments to commit to restitution, to divest from law enforcement and invest in community projects,[68] to listen to communities who have been harmed by decades of violence and exclusion, and a radical commitment – by both the State and society – to find ways to heal.

Conclusion

The vast, pervasive and violent impact of the war on drugs will only become more apparent in retrospect. It may never be possible to convey its total damage across the decades, from health harms and overdose deaths to egregious rights violations and families torn apart by incarceration. The practical examples showcased in this chapter serve to demonstrate the critical importance of harm reduction post-prohibition. This is evident in three forms: harm reduction in its capacity to promote access to healthcare and information; harm reduction in its capacity to strengthen access to medicines while challenging paternalistic approaches and unnecessary medical expansion; and harm reduction via legal services and human rights advocacy – safeguarding the rights of people who use drugs and addressing the complex stretch of the war on drugs beyond the criminal justice system. The harm reduction approach – grounded in evidence, pragmatism, justice and compassion – provides a framework for a post-prohibition era which will enable community, civil society and states to navigate the challenges associated with staggered global reforms, while challenging power and privilege and bringing intersectional vulnerability to light.

Notes

1 Unless otherwise specified, 'community' refers to the community of people who use drugs, linked to the definition of 'community-led' agreed by UNAIDS and communities in 2020: Community-led organizations, groups and networks, whether formally or informally organized, are entities for which the majority of governance, leadership, staff, spokespeople, membership and volunteers, reflect and represent the experiences, perspectives and voices of their constituencies and who have transparent mechanisms of accountability to their constituencies. Community-led organisations, groups and networks are self-determining and autonomous, and not influenced by government, commercial or donor agendas. See UNAIDS, *Progress report of the multi-stakeholder task team on community-led AIDS responses* (19 November 2020) UNAIDS Programme Coordinating Board, UNAIDS/PCB (47)/20.30 Agenda Item 6, para 32.

2 Harm Reduction International, 'What Is Harm Reduction?' <www.hri.global/what-is-harm-reduction> accessed 31 January 2022.

3 Harm Reduction International, *Global State of Harm Reduction 2020* (Harm Reduction International, 2020) 18.

4 Harm Reduction International, *Global State of Harm Reduction 2022* (Harm Reduction International, 2022) 19.

5 Harm Reduction International, *Global State of Harm Reduction 2008* (Harm Reduction International, 2008) 14.

6 Samantha Colledge-Frisby, et al 'Global Coverage of Interventions to Prevent and Manage Drug Related Harms among People who Inject Drugs: A Systematic Review' (2023) 11 *The Lancet Global Health* 673

7 David Bewley-Taylor, *International Drug Control: Consensus Fractured* (Cambridge University Press, 2012).; David Bewley-Taylor and Martin Jelsma, 'The UN Drug Control Conventions: The Limits of Latitude' (International Drug Policy Consortium and Transform Series on Legislative Reform of Drug Policies Nr. 18, 2012).

8 Harm Reduction International (n 4) 23.; Brian Mann and Caroline Lewis, 'New York City Allows the Nation's 1st Supervised Consumption Sites for Illegal Drugs', *National Public Radio* (30 November 2021).

9 InfoDrug, 'Factsheet Drug Checking' (InfoDrug, 2017).

10 Trimbos Institute, 'The Drugs Information and Monitoring System (DIMS): Factsheet on Drug Checking in the Netherlands' (Trimbos Institute, 2019).

11 WEDINOS, 'Annual Report 2021/2022' (Public Health Wales, 2022).

12 Harm Reduction International (n 2).

13 Bewley-Taylor (n 7).; Katherine McLean, 'A Kind of Peace: Tracking the Reflexive and Resilient Drug War' (2018) 51 *International Journal of Drug Policy* 117.

14 United Nations Office on Drugs and Crime, International Network of People Who Use Drugs, Joint United Nations Programme on HIV/AIDS, United Nations Development Programme, United Nations Population Fund, World Health Organization, United

States Agency for International Development, 'Implementing Comprehensive HIV and HCV Programmes with People Who Inject Drugs: Practical Guidance for Collaborative Interventions' (2017).

15 Judy Chang, et al, 'Peer Driven or Driven Peers? A Rapid Review of Peer Involvement of People Who Use Drugs in HIV and Harm Reduction Services in Low- and Middle-Income Countries' (2021) 18 *Harm Reduction Journal* 15.

16 International Network of People who Use Drugs, 'Consensus Statement on Drug Use under Prohibition' (International Network of People who Use Drugs, 2015).

17 Harm Reduction International, 'Integrated and Person-Centred Harm Reduction Services' (Harm Reduction International, 2021).

18 Arsen Davitadze, et al, 'Harm Reduction via Online Platforms for People Who Use Drugs in Russia: A Qualitative Analysis of Web Outreach Work' (2020) 17 *Harm Reduction Journal* 98.; Harm Reduction International, *The Impact of COVID-19 on Harm Reduction in Seven Asian countries* (Harm Reduction International, 2020.; Harm Reduction International (n 3) chap 1.2.

19 See Chapter 8, 'Can Darknet Drug Markets Be Harm Reducing?'

20 Angus Bancroft, 'Responsible Use to Responsible Harm: Illicit Drug Use and Peer Harm Reduction in a Darknet Cryptomarket' (2017) 19 *Health, Risk & Society* 336.; Martin Horton-Eddison, et al, 'Drug Cryptomarkets in the 2020s: Policy, Enforcement, Harm, and Resilience' (Global Drug Policy Observatory, the University of Manchester, Swansea University, Policy Brief 16, June 2021).; Fernando Caudevilla, 'The Emergence of Deep Web Marketplaces: A Health Perspective' in European Monitoring Centre for Drugs and Drug Addiction (ed.), *The Internet and Drug Markets* (EMCDDA Insights 21, 2016).

21 Bancroft (n 20).; Caudevilla (n 20).

22 Horton-Eddison, et al (n 20).

23 Michael Gilbert and Nabarun Dasgupta, 'Silicon to Syringe: Cryptomarkets and Disruptive Innovation in Opioid Supply Chains' (2017) 46 *International Journal of Drug Policy* 160.

24 Monica J Barratt, Jason A Ferris & Adam R Winstock, 'Safer Scoring? Cryptomarkets, Social Supply and Drug Market Violence' (2016) 35 *The International Journal on Drug Policy* 24.; Bancroft (n 20).

25 EMCDDA and EUROPOL, 'EU Drug Markets: Impact of COVID-19' (May 2020).

26 'Taliban Bans Drug Cultivation, Including Lucrative Opium', *Reuters* (3 April 2022).

27 Public Safety Canada, 'Cannabis Black Market' (Parliamentary Committee Notes, June 2020).

28 Nazlee Maghsoudi, et al, 'Drug Checking Services for People Who Use Drugs: A Systematic Review' (2022) 117 *Addiction* 532.

29 Ibid.

30 Eliza Kurcevič and Rick Lines, 'New Psychoactive Substances in Eurasia: A Qualitative Study of People Who Use Drugs and Harm Reduction Services in Six Countries' (2020) 17 *Harm Reduction Journal* 94.

31 Research indicates combined budgets committed by international donors and national donors amount to just 5% of the level required for an adequate HIV response for people who use drugs by 2025; Harm Reduction International, 'Failure to Fund: The Continued Crisis for Harm Reduction Funding in Low- and Middle-Income Countries' (Harm Reduction International, 2021).

32 Harm Reduction International, 'Making the Investment Case: Cost-Effectiveness Evidence for Harm Reduction' (Harm Reduction International, 2020).

33 Harm Reduction International (n 3) 18.

34 See Chapter 9, 'Prisoner to Patient. The Pathologisation of People Who Use Drugs'.

35 Methadone and buprenorphine are on the World Health Organization's Essential Medicines List and scheduled under the international drug control conventions.

36 Linda Gowing, et al, 'Oral Substitution Treatment of Injecting Opioid Users for Prevention of HIV Infection' (2011) *The Cochrane Database of Systematic Reviews 8*.

37 Pramila Karki, et al, 'The Impact of Methadone Maintenance Treatment on HIV Risk Behaviors among High-Risk Injection Drug Users: A Systematic Review' (2016) *Evidence-Based Medicine & Public Health* 2.

38 Colledge-Frisby, et al (n 6).

39 *WHO, UNODC, UNAIDS Technical Guide for Countries to Set Targets for Universal Access to HIV Prevention, Treatment and Care for Injecting Drug Users* (2012 revision) 43.

40 Felicia M Knaul, et al, 'The Lancet Commission on Palliative Care and Pain Relief – Findings, Recommendations, and Future Directions' (2018) *The Lancet Global Health,* Vol. 6 Special Issue.

41 Diederik Lohman and Damon Barrett, 'Scheduling Medicines as Controlled Substances: Addressing Normative and Democratic Gaps through Human Rights-Based Analysis' (2021) 20 *BMC International Health and Human Rights* 10.

42 Anthony Barnett, et al, 'Tracing the Affordances of Long-Acting Injectable Depot Buprenorphine: A Qualitative Study of Patients' Experiences in Australia' (2021) 227 *Drug and Alcohol Dependence* 108959.

43 International Network of People who Use Drugs, 'Extended-Release Opioid Agonist Products: A Community Position Statement' (International Network of People who Use Drugs, 2019).

44 Daniel Wolfe and Roxanne Saucier, 'Biotechnologies and the Future of Opioid Addiction Treatments' (2021) 88 *International Journal of Drug Policy* 103041.

45 Canadian Association of People who Use Drugs, 'Safe Supply Concept Document' (Canadian Association of People who Use Drugs, 2019). CAPUD excludes agonist treatments, such as methadone, buprenorphine from the definition of safe supply, as these therapies do not contain the mind/body altering properties that people seek in recreational drugs.

46 British Columbia Centre on Substance Use, 'Risk Mitigation in the Context of Dual Public Health Emergencies: Interim Clinical Guidance' (British Columbia Centre on Substance Use, 2020).

47 Prescription opioids include hydromorphone and sustained-release oral morphine; prescription stimulants include dextroamphetamine, methylphenidate; and prescription benzodiazepines include clonazepam, diazepam.

48 Ryan McNeil, et al, 'Implementation of Safe Supply Alternatives during Intersecting COVID-19 and Overdose Health Emergencies in British Columbia, Canada, 2021' (2022) 112 *American Journal of Public Health* 151.

49 Ibid.

50 Dafna Izenberg and Seema Marwaha, 'Safe Supply: The Debate around Prescribing Opioids to People Who Use Drugs' (15 August 2019) *Healthy Debate* <https://healthydebate.ca/2019/08/topic/safe-supply> accessed 29 April 2022.; Ontario HIV Treatment Network, 'Possible Benefits of Providing Safe Supply of Substances to People Who Use Drugs during Public Health Emergencies Such as the COVID-19 Pandemic' (April 2020) Ontario HIV Treatment Network Rapid Response Service #147.

51 International Network of People who Use Drugs, 'Drug User Peace Initiative: A War on the Health of People who Use Drugs' (International Network of People who Use Drugs, 2015).

52 Office of the United Nations High Commissioner for Human Rights, 'Promotion and Protection of the Human Rights and Fundamental Freedoms of Africans and of People of African Descent against Excessive Use of Force and Other Human Rights Violations by Law Enforcement Officers' (9 July 2021) A/HRC/47/53.

53 Office of the United Nations High Commissioner for Human Rights, Media Statement: 'Fight against World Drug Problem Must Address Unjust Impact on People of African Descent, Say UN Experts' (14 March 2019) <www.ohchr.org/en/news/2019/03/fight-against-world-drug-problem-must-address-unjust-impact-people-african-descent-say> accessed 29 April 2022.

54 UN Working Group on Arbitrary Detention, 'Arbitrary Detention Relating to Drug Policies Study of the Working Group on Arbitrary Detention' (18 May 2021) A/HRC/47/40, para 51.

55 Gen Sander and Giada Girelli, 'The Death Penalty for Drug Offences: Global Overview 2019' (Harm Reduction International, 2020).

56 David Scamell, Tatyana Margolin & Constantin Cojocariupage, 'Lawyering on the Margins: How Lawyers Are Becoming Important Tools for Advancing Health and Human Rights of the Most Marginalised' (2013) 17 *Interights Bulletin* 106.

57 Harm Reduction International and the International Network of People who Use Drugs, 'Written Comments for the Special Rapporteur on the Right to Adequate Housing on the Draft Guidelines for the Implementation of the Right to Adequate Housing' (18 November 2019) <www.hri.global/files/2019/11/26/Written_comments_on_draft_Guidelines_for_the_implementation_of_the_right_to_adequate_housing_HRI_INPUD_2019.pdf> accessed 29 April 2022.

58 Adam Fletcher, 'Drug Testing in Schools: A Case Study in Doing More Harm than Good' in Damon Barrett (ed.), *Children of the Drug War: Perspectives on the Impact of Drug Policies on Young People* (The International Debate Education Association, 2011).

59 Human Rights Watch and American Civil Liberties Union, 'Every 25 Seconds: The Human Toll of Criminalizing Drug Use in the United States' (Human Rights Watch, 2016).

60 Albert Wirya, et al, 'Expanding the Role of Paralegals: Supporting Realization of the Right to Health for Vulnerable Communities' (2020) 20 *BMC International Health and Human Rights* 8.

61 Open Society Foundations, *Justice Programs for Public Health: A Good Practice Guide* (Open Society Foundations, 2015).

62 Ruth Kasper, 'Integrating Harm Reduction in Homeless Services, Resource Hub & Good Practice Collection' (Erasmus/HR4Homelessness, 2021) 3.

63 The Lawyering on the Margins Network: www.lotmnetwork.org

64 Penal Reform International, 'Global Prison Trends 2023' (Thailand Institute of Justice, 2021) 18.

65 Giada Girelli and Ajeng Larasati, 'The Death Penalty for Drug Offences: Global Overview 2021' (Harm Reduction International 2022) 16–17.

66 For example, https://uprootingthedrugwar.org/

67 Michelle Alexander 'The New Jim Crow: How Mass Incarceration Turns People of Color into Permanent Second-Class Citizens' (6 December 2010) *The American Prospect* < https://prospect.org/special-report/new-jim-crow/> accessed 26 May 2022.

68 Harm Reduction International, 'Redirection' (2021) <www.hri.global/redirect> accessed 29 April 2022.

8 Can Darknet Drug Markets Be Harm Reducing?

Building Decriminalised Spaces in Central and Eastern Europe and Central Asia

Eliza Kurcevič

Introduction

In Central and Eastern Europe and Central Asia (CEECA), as in many other regions of the world, psychoactive substances have been consumed for various purposes for centuries. However, crucial changes in the perception of drug use in the region started in the 20th century. At the beginning of the century, drugs such as opium, cocaine and morphine were legal and available in most of the pharmacies in the region. In Central Asia, opium and hashish were used and traded in the teahouses as part of the local culture. All that started to change when the Soviet ideological constructs began to be introduced to these societies. A new narrative emerged that was based around the 'importance of elimination of "social evils" like drug use, social control approach to prevent "social evils", changing culture in the name of "enlightenment" and defining drug use as foreign, Western issue while placing drugs under the taboo topics'.[1]

When the Soviet Union dissolved in the early 1990s, countries in the region saw increases in drug use, which was related to the new economic and social challenges that emerged. The last 30 years have been a drug policy roller coaster for former Soviet bloc States, trying to find a balance between law enforcement measures and health and social supports for people who use drugs. In this process, two different directions emerged among the countries of the former Soviet Union.

In countries in the Central and South-Eastern Europe and the Baltic regions, governments focused on the development of more pragmatic and balanced policies (a process also later influenced by their membership in the European Union). Countries such as Czechia and Estonia chose a health-oriented approach by decriminalising the use and possession of small amounts of drugs, as well as introducing evidence-based health services for people who use drugs. Others such as Moldova, Ukraine, Georgia, Kyrgyzstan and Tajikistan implemented *de jure* decriminalisation of use and possession of small amounts of drugs and are also trying to introduce and maintain evidence-based harm reduction interventions – such as needle and syringe exchange, opioid agonist therapy and naloxone – in the face of stigmatised perceptions about drug use. Other countries such as Lithuania and Poland are struggling to position themselves in the international drug policy

DOI: 10.4324/9781003169765-12

arena, maintaining criminalisation of possession while at the same time working to improve harm reduction programmes and introduce new approaches such as drug checking services and naloxone.

On the other hand, Russia and the countries of the Central Asia and Caucasus region focused on punitive policies and promotion of the anti-drug propaganda narratives. In this group, Russia maintains a significant influence. Even though Russia has *de jure* decriminalisation, in which the possession of drugs in small amounts is an administrative rather than a criminal offence, in reality this is just a veil.

Russia is well known for gross human rights violations against people who use drugs, and almost non-existent health services for this population.[2] For example, opioid agonist therapy is banned by the law, and Russia also banned methadone therapy in occupied Crimea (Ukraine territory).[3] In 2021, the government introduced a 'drug propaganda' bill, which restricts sharing of information on drugs, drug dependence and evidence-based health approaches such as harm reduction, drug treatment and prevention.[4] The government also introduced a 'foreign agent' law,[5] which essentially criminalises civil society work. This law bans organisations, individuals and even journalists from being involved in political activities while receiving money from abroad, and from expressing opinions regarding State policies if the government thinks these opinions are in the interests of a foreign entity. Since the law was enacted in 2012, the government has sanctioned over 200 civil society organisations as being 'foreign agents'.[6]

Repressive laws affect the types of drugs people consume, and the manner in which they consume them. Punitive laws also affect the shape of the market itself. In the case of CEECA, the extremely punitive legal environment has inspired drug sellers and consumers to develop alternative spaces for the drug trade – darknet markets. For both sellers and customers, the darknet offers a reliable and easily accessible place to sell or purchase drugs while minimising risk of police attention. For harm reduction service providers, particularly those working in a context where the sharing of information on safer drug use is a crime, the darknet creates a new niche for providing services to hard-to-reach groups and a safer space for users to share peer support.

This chapter will explore the development and use of these markets in the region, and their significance as a response to punitive drug policy environments. In a context where progressive drug policy reform is difficult to imagine in many countries, the entrenched nature of punitive prohibitionist laws has empowered consumers and sellers to create their own decriminalised spaces online. While the increase in darknet markets has created concern among politicians and law enforcement in the EECA, who have often responded by introducing punitive responses, for others there is a recognition that darknet drug markets can in fact be harm reducing.

The Darknet Markets in EECA

Research from the EECA region shows that in recent years punitive and prohibitionist drug laws have had the effect of changing patterns of drug use.[7] Because of harsh drug policies, traditional drugs such as heroin slowly began to disappear from the market, to be replaced by new psychoactive substances.[8] When these substances first appeared in the local drug markets, most were not included in national drug laws. Thus, people were able to avoid criminal liability because the substances were technically not illegal. Even today, dozens of new substances appear on the market each month, making it difficult, if not impossible, for the State to impose controls on them.

Patients in receipt of opioid agonist therapy also found new psychoactive substances appealing. People on agonist programmes must undergo occasional urine tests to screen for illegal drugs. If illegal drugs are detected, patients may face punitive sanctions, such as a reduction in their dosage, losing access to take-home prescriptions or even being thrown out of the programme altogether. However, people learned that urine drug tests could not, and in some countries still cannot, detect the presence of these new psychoactive substances. Here again, punitive drug policies were the driver for people making choices about drug use they might not have otherwise made.[9]

Developments in digital interconnectivity also played a role in this process of change. Over the past ten years, our understanding of how drug markets operate in the region has vanished in a puff of smoke, and the development of information technology has led to a proliferation of new ways to access drugs online.

The first attempts to sell drugs online were in the early 1970s,[10] and the modern approach of trading drugs through the darknet markets started in 2010.[11] One of the first major darknet markets, the Silk Road, began operation in 2011 and was shut down by law enforcement in 2013. After it closed, a new version (Silk Road 2.0) started up. The number of marketplaces increased each year, and by 2019 up to 118 markets were known to be in operation.[12] While each year individual darknet forums close, there are always new ones to replace them. Today it is estimated that about two-thirds of the illicit goods and services on darknet markets are drug related.[13] Interestingly, most darknet closures are not a result of a 'war on online drug market'[14] but rather because of scamming customers or based on the mutual consent of seller and customer.[15]

Despite the high volatility of darknet markets, there was an overall increase in darknet drug sales between 2011 and 2020, 'with the annual minimum doubling and the average estimated total increasing almost fourfold'.[16] Global data on people who use drugs show that an increasing number of people are purchasing drugs online, and over a seven-year period that number tripled. In 2014, 4.7% of people who use drugs were purchasing drugs via darknet markets. By 2021, that number had reached 14.5%.[17]

Within EECA region, the most popular online spaces to sell and buy drugs are messenger applications (Telegram, VIPole, Wickr, VKontakte) and market spaces (Hydra, Union,[18] Legalizer, PsyLab). Although there is little research on the number of people using darknet platforms in EECA region, analysis conducted by DrugStat provides some interesting data on the Hydra and Union markets.

Kazakhstan and Belarus are two examples that illustrate the popularity and relevance of the darknet drug markets in the region. The Hydra drug market in

Kazakhstan started in 2016. In that year there were only a few online reviews left by customers purchasing substances through the platform. However, by January 2020, it was receiving 2,900 reviews per month from consumers. In total, approximately 42,000 reviews were left by consumers between 2016 and 2020, of which almost one-third were left in the first five months of 2020. The most commonly purchased drug through Hydra was mephedrone, which had more than 17,600 customer reviews, 42% of the total number of transactions made on Hydra in Kazakhstan.

Hydra also started in 2016 in Belarus. Between 2016 and 2020, approximately 216,000 online reviews were left by customers, 35% of which (80,000) were left in the first five months of 2020. As in Kazakhstan, the most popular drug purchased on Hydra in Belarus was mephedrone. In the first five months of 2020, more than 23,000 reviews were left by mephedrone customers, more than one-third of all sales. Since it opened in 2016, over 58,000 reviews have been left on Hydra in Belarus by purchasers of mephedrone.[19]

The Darknet and Harm Reduction

There are a range of reasons why people use darknet drug markets. Research conducted among Silk Road customers from Australia, United Kingdom and the United States found the most common reasons for purchasing from Silk Road was the wider range of products (75–89%), better quality (72–77%), greater convenience (67–69%) and use of vendor review systems (60–65%).[20] In the EECA, the virtual location of the market and the ability to remain anonymous are particularly attractive features in the context of harsh punitive drugs laws. When using these markets, there is no need to meet a seller or a consumer face-to-face, which increases safety and minimises the risk of violence or arrest. Anonymity also changes the nature of the experience of purchasing drugs, shifting the perception of power from the seller to the consumer. In the world of darknet drug markets, power is not based on physical size or strength but instead on online rating systems. Here consumers leave feedback for others to see, and sellers can be rewarded for providing good products and services or penalised for supplying poor product.

The darknet also allows people who use drugs, who are harshly criminalised in many EECA countries, to access support and to share life-saving information in the safety of online chat rooms and discussion forums. In addition to this peer support, for some it can be an entry point to health services, bridging the barriers between people who use drugs and professionals. Online forums create the possibility to engage specialists (i.e. doctors, nurses, social workers, harm reduction workers) with health-related questions without meeting them in person.

Within EECA, darknet drug markets empower the creation of safe spaces by consumers, sellers and service providers to engage with each other. The anonymity provided by the platforms, as well as the unique nature of the markets themselves, create an important opportunity for providing peer support and sharing harm reduction information in places where it is otherwise repressed by the State.

- **Reporting Dangerous Substances to Vendors**

Darknet drug markets provide a non-judgmental and anonymous environment in which buyers can share their experiences without fear or stigmatisation. For consumers, these markets enable people who use drugs to evaluate the quality and potency of substances bought online through the rating systems and inform other customers of potentially dangerous substances.

In a traditional drug market, imagine a situation in which an individual decides to report the low quality of a substance to their drug seller. How many of those sellers would take that feedback into account and remove a possibly dangerous substance from the market? How can the individual customer be assured that drug seller is not selling that substance to others? In a conventional drug market this situation is possible, but very unlikely. However, in online markets, drug sellers are interested in building trust with their customers while customers are interested in making informed decisions about what they purchase. Darknet drug markets employ customer feedback systems, which encourage customers to review the drugs they purchase and their experience with the seller. These systems are similar to those found on eBay, or Amazon or Uber. After the customer receives drug, they are encouraged to leave a star rating from one to five. They may also comment on the quality of drug, the speed of the transaction and delivery, the seller's safety procedures (or their 'stealth)[21] and give a subjective opinion whether the price was fair for the product received.

In a study conducted among Silk Road customers in Australia, United Kingdom and the United States, 60–65% of respondents said that existence of review systems is motivating them to use darknet markets for purchasing drugs. Statements such as, 'I feel more comfortable buying from sellers with high ratings' were common.[22] The term 'comfortable' referred to various elements of the transaction–reduction or elimination of violence, reduced discrimination, reduced risk of scams, more informed decision-making – based on the previous reviews and feedback.

However, reviews about the quality or potency of drugs are typically the subjective opinion of customer, who usually evaluates this based on their own experience. Only rarely do reviews reflect data received as a result of testing the substance through a drug checking service. Because the feedback is subjective, there is no guarantee that a substance will not contain adulterants that are potentially dangerous, or might have a higher potency than expected. Despite these risks, the review system still provides useful information to customers, allowing them to adjust their use or moderate their dosing based on peer experiences and feedback, which can help reduce overdose.

Darknet drug markets also utilise a 'reputation system' for sellers, which can also contribute to reducing risk.[23] In this system, vendors who have low ratings or feedback on their products, or who provide low-quality services, are less visible in the marketplace than are vendors with high feedback scores. This system advantages reputable sellers, highlighting such sellers more visibly in the marketplaces and, therefore, keeping vendors accountable for what they are selling.

- **Sharing Living Experience in the Darknet Discussion Forums**

Pragmatic information about drug use and harm reduction is largely invisible, or even actively censored, in media and educational institutions in the EECA region. In the traditional media, drug-related information is mainly focused on 'just say no' messages, picturing drugs as 'evil' and stigmatising people who use drugs. As a result, harm reduction information initially gained popularity on the internet via harm reduction websites, discussion forums and social media. But this did not last long as censorship also reached social media, and harm reduction-related content started being banned, as a 'violation of community standards on Facebook'.[24]

In the case of *SIN v. Facebook*, the Polish non-profit organisation Civil Society Drug Policy Initiative (SIN) filed a strategic litigation case because Facebook removed a fan page and a group run by SIN. Later one of SIN's accounts on Instagram was also removed because of alleged 'violation of community standards'.[25] Countries known for repressive drug laws, such as Russia, also started to introduce 'drug propaganda laws' in order to restrict information on drugs, drug dependence and humane and science/evidence-based methods of drug dependence treatment and harm reduction.[26] As a result, harm reduction activists in the region started to feel excluded not only from the mainstream media but from social media as well. However, with the emergence of global online drug cultures, new opportunities for provision of harm reduction services and information appeared. The darknet became a meeting point for people in the region to document personal experiences of drug use and share information and knowledge about drugs. In the context of suppression of public discussions of drug use and harm reduction, the darknet became an important source for sharing drug-related information, especially from the perspective of people who use drugs.

Almost all darknet platforms provide chat rooms or discussion forums where customers can anonymously share knowledge and experiences, ask questions and feel connected to a virtual community that shares similar interests.[27] Because of the anonymous nature and non-judgmental environment of these forums, consumers tend to be more open to discuss a broad range of issues related to drug use. This platform therefore provides a safer space for users who are otherwise isolated from mainstream services due to stigma and concerns over identifying themselves as a drug user.

Online drug forums have subsections dedicated to different topics: 'trip reports', reviews on payments and shipments, quality of drugs, legal issues, etc. Most, if not all, of the forums have subsections dedicated to health issues, where customers discuss safer use and strategies to reduce risk. Darknet 'users are a source of lay expertise for others', 'develop and share protective strategies' and 'provide care and support. Users are producers of knowledge about harm reduction that can augment, run ahead of, and challenge that of experts.'[28]

Despite the positive user-driven side of the forums, in most cases people are sharing personal experiences and subjective information. In some cases this may lead to sharing of incomplete information or even incorrect information, which may have negative health consequences for others. Therefore, in order to facilitate evidence-based information and provide an entry point for support services, peers working in the harm reduction organisations in the EECA region became involved in the forums. Trained peers participate in discussions and provide evidence-based information on harm reduction or treatment. Based on the needs identified by forum participants, peers can also create new content. This activity not only provided accurate information to forum participants about safer drug use but can also create a contact with harder-to-reach groups. In a literature, this process is called 'web outreach', 'online outreach' or 'netreach' work.[29] Exchanging peer knowledge and experience in the darknet, and building connection and trust, can benefit not only to individuals but also enable harm reduction services to access isolated users and extend harm reduction services into virtual platforms.

In EECA, there are numerous examples of good practice of peer-based harm reduction in the darknet forums. In 2019, the Russian-based charitable organisation, Humanitarian Action, started to provide harm reduction information on the Hydra drug forum,[30] at that time the largest darknet market in the country.[31] Before starting the project, the organisation assessed what kinds of content were lacking in the discussion forum. Following this background research, the organisation launched three discussion threads on the forum: harm reduction services available in St. Petersburg, HIV and hepatitis C. A few months later, the organisation also started using Telegram instant messenger. Telegram is one of the most secure messenger systems, with end-to-end encryption, and is a popular social media platform in Eastern Europe and Central Asia both for connecting people and for selling drugs. Humanitarian Action opened Telegram instant messenger to interact online with people who use drugs and build a trust and create an entry point for services. As a result of these new activities, the organisation had 89% increase in requests for harm reduction services in comparison with the time when only offline services were provided.[32]

- **Bridging the Gap between Peers and Professionals**

Many studies have found that people who use drugs and experience stigmatising incidents in health care settings are less likely to access services in future.[33] There are also countries in which evidence-based health services for people who use drugs are simply not available, and those programmes that are available are unattractive or stigmatising. In response, many people who use drugs seek to access alternative, non-judgmental environments for information or support. Darknet forums are a place where people can engage with others on drug use issues without prejudice or stigma.

The involvement of professionals in darknet forums not only provides opportunity to save lives and assist consumers in making informed decisions but also offers a way to build connections and trust in the online environment and, if needed, to provide support to individuals in real life. As discussed in the previous section, while people might access information on darknet forums and share their knowledge with peers, there are still situations when professional knowledge or expert advice might be needed (i.e. discussions about wounds, overdose, poisoning, mental health issues, etc.). However, unlike support accessed in a health care setting, providing support in a darknet discussion forum reaches people who use drugs in their own private environment. This can not only make accessing information faster and more anonymous but also allows professionals to reach out to contact with otherwise isolated and harder-to-reach populations. However, to keep harm reduction workers safe from criminalisation, agreements with governmental institutions should ensure that health service providers and peers can safely provide information and support for people who use drugs in the darknet platforms.

One of the most publicised and successful examples on the darknet of bridging the gap between consumers and health experts was the 'Doctor X' threads in the darknet forums, called 'Ask a Drug Expert Physician about Drugs and Health'. Doctor X provided information on the Silk Road, Silk Road 2.0 and Evolution marketplaces. In 22 months of running this service, people visited his threads 136,407 times and a total 1,146 questions were answered by a health professional (approximately 81% were answered in public discussion forums and another 19% privately).[34] The nature of questions asked by users shows the need to integrate harm reduction and health specialists into these platforms. The most frequently asked questions included those on drug effects, dosage, adverse effects, medical contraindications, interaction with other legal and illegal drugs, detoxification and neurotoxicity.[35] This initiative received positive feedback not only from users of forums but also from vendors and moderators of these forums.

Looking Forward: Opportunities for Further Development of Harm Reduction in Darknet Markets

Fixed-site harm reduction services and street outreach are the traditional options to provide safer injecting equipment to people who use drugs. In different countries of the world, these services operate in various ways but the principle is the same – an individual who needs clean paraphernalia comes to the drop-in centre and takes it, or orders it via a home-delivery service. But what about using the darknet as a way to distribute drug paraphernalia?

Eastern Europe and Central Asia have a unique model of online drug delivery through the use of hidden packages, or so-called 'zakladki'.[36] In short, the customer orders the drugs via an online or social media platform, and after the payment is made via an ATM, the person receives GPS coordination where the hidden package can be collected. It may be buried under a tree in a forest, attached with a magnet to an iron object or simply hidden under a bench in a public park. This unique method of transaction is therefore completely anonymous, minimising risk from law enforcement. It also creates the possibility for harm reduction interventions.

Delivery of drug paraphernalia kits could be organised using similar method to the selling of drugs. As discussed earlier, one of the easiest options to integrate harm reduction services into darknet markets is to involve trained peers and web-outreach workers in discussion forums. Trained peers or web-outreach workers can create a thread in the darknet forum dedicated to the delivery of free safer drug use paraphernalia kits. The thread should clearly describe what is included in the kits, how people can receive it and where people can receive more information or support (if needed) from health specialists. Safer drug use kits could be delivered to people in hidden packages using GPS coordinates. This kind of approach was tested by activists in Ukraine.[37] After safer use kits were delivered to people, the 'trip reports', or feedback about kits, started to come back from consumers. In five days of work on the darknet platform 'Legalizer.info', 299 people posted reviews. Activists received 18 messages and 12 people undertook rapid HIV and hepatitis tests which were included in the kits.

Another option of delivering safer use equipment is through the drug vendors themselves while they are delivering the drugs in hidden packages. Given the importance of positive customer feedback in the darknet marketplaces, vendors have an incentive to include safer drug use paraphernalia in their 'hidden packages' to encourage positive customer reviews. There are examples of individual vendors providing reagents tests or smoking pipes when a customer buys drugs. However, this is most often intended as a 'bonus' or marketing strategy rather than specifically as a harm reduction intervention. However, even though the aim might be to attract more customers by providing safer use kits, it is still promoting harm reduction, particularly in countries where access is otherwise difficult.

Another important step in ensuring public health is to develop direct contact with online shops selling drugs and inform them about dangerous substances which are being sold. This action can be taken by the government forensic laboratories or drug checking service providers if they exist in the country. Not all vendors know the exact composition of the substances they are selling, and most do not have an intent to sell life-threatening psychoactive substance. Thus, national forensic laboratories and drug checking services could take initiative and start work with vendors in darknet channels. This would ensure not only public health safety but also safer supply in the alternative online spaces.

Conclusion

Initially conceived as a novel approach of selling illegal drugs, darknet drug markets are slowly becoming a place where global online drug cultures are discussed and where individuals develop a sense of belonging to community they could not find in the real life. Darknet markets can also be used as a platform to provide harm reduction services and connecting with hard-to-reach populations by reporting dangerous substances to vendors, sharing living experiences in the darknet discussion forums, seeking out health information from professionals and extending the provision of information into provision of drug paraphernalia.

In most countries of EECA region, decriminalisation may sound like an unattainable fantasy. However, alternative drug policies are already functioning in the darknet markets in the region. As this chapter shows, repressive laws are not a barrier for resilient communities to create alternative decriminalised spaces, reaching consumers in their private settings and building secure connections with professionals.

Notes

1 Raminta Stuikyte, 'Perception of Drugs in Central and Eastern Europe and Central Asia: Overhaul Needed' (Eastern and Central European and Central Asian Commission on Drug Policy, 2021).

2 Russian Civil Society Mechanism for Monitoring of Drug Policy Reforms in Russia, 'Report to the UN Human Rights Committee for the List of Issues in Relation to the Review of the 8th Periodic Report of the Russian Federation CCPR/C/RUS/8' (May 2020).

3 Jennifer J Carroll, 'Sovereign Rules and Rearrangements: Banning Methadone in Occupied Crimea' (2019) 38 *Medical Anthropology* 508.

4 Russian Civil Society Mechanism for Monitoring of Drug Policy Reforms, et al, 'Submission on Russia to the Special Rapporteur on the Right of Everyone to the Enjoyment of the Highest Attainable Standard of Physical and Mental Health and to the Special Rapporteur on the Promotion and Protection of the Right to Freedom of Opinion and Expression' (17 June 2020).

5 Eurasian Harm Reduction Association, 'Submission to the Special Rapporteur on the Rights to Freedom of Peaceful Assembly and of Association (30 January 2021).

6 European Parliament, 'Foreign Agents' and 'Undesirables' – Russian Civil Society in Danger of Extinction?' *European Parliamentary Research Service* (8 March 2022).

7 Eliza Kurcevič and Rick Lines, 'New Psychoactive Substances in Eurasia: A Qualitative Study of People Who Use Drugs and Harm Reduction Services in Six Countries' (2020) 17 *Harm Reduction Journal* 94.; Eurasian Harm Reduction Association, 'New Psychoactive Substance Use in Eastern Europe and Central Asia: Regional Report' (Eurasian Harm Reduction Association, 2021).

8 Ibid. Such as carfentanyl (synthetic opioids group), alpha-PVP, mephedrone, methylone (synthetic cathinones group) and JWH and spice (synthetic cannabinoids group).

9 Kurcevič and Lines (n 7).

10 European Monitoring Centre on Drugs and Drug Addiction, 'Drugs and the Darknet: Perspectives for Enforcement, Research and Policy' (EMCDDA/Europol, 2017).

11 Ibid.

12 United Nations Office on Drugs and Crime, *World Drug Report 2021* (United Nations, 2021).

13 European Monitoring Centre on Drugs and Drug Addiction (n 10).

14 Europol, 'Global Law Enforcement Action against Vendors and Buyers on the Dark Web: Buying in the Dark Web? You Are on the Menu!' (26 March 2019) <www.europol.europa.eu/media-press/newsroom/news/global-law-enforcement-action-against-vendors-and-buyers-dark-web> accessed 11 April 2023.

15 See European Monitoring Centre on Drugs and Drug Addiction (n 10).

16 See United Nations Office on Drugs and Crime (n 12).

17 Ibid.

18 The 'Union' drug market was doing active advertising campaigns on billboards in several cities in Kazakhstan in the autumn of 2019.

19 DrugStat, 'Investigation of the Impact of COVID-19 on Internet Drug Trading in the EECA Region' (2020).

20 Monica J Barratt, Jason A Ferris & Adan R Winstock, 'Use of Silk Road, the Online Drug Marketplace, in the United Kingdom, Australia and the United States' (2014) 109 *Addiction* 774.

21 Rachel Botsman, 'Who Can You Trust? How Technology Brought Us Together and Why It Might Drive Us Apart', *Nautilus* (14 December 2017) <https://nautil.us/how-darknet-sellers-build-trust-6901/?_sp=e5f6cc97-2f59-4a9f-9dfd-f3de14d01d41.1649858041702#!> accessed 13 April 2023.
22 See Barratt, et al (n 20).
23 Joseph Cox, 'Reputation Is Everything: The Role of Ratings, Feedback and Reviews in Cryptomarkets' in Jane Mounteney, Alessandra Bo & Alberto Oteo (eds.), *The Internet and Drug Markets* (European Monitoring Centre for Drugs and Drug Addiction, 2016).
24 Maia Szalavitz, 'Facebook Is Censoring Posts That Could Save Opioid Users' Lives', *VICE* (2 July 2019).
25 Panoptykon Foundation, 'SIN v Facebook: Tech Giant Sued over Censorship in Landmark Case', *EDRI* (8 May 2019) <https://edri.org/our-work/sin-v-facebook/> accessed 14 April 2023.
26 See Russian Civil Society Mechanism for Monitoring of Drug Policy Reforms, et al (n 4).
27 Fernando Caudevilla, 'The Emergence of Deep Web Marketplaces: A Health Perspectives' in Jane Mounteney, Alessandra Bo & Alberto Oteo (eds.), *The Internet and Drug Markets* (European Monitoring Centre for Drugs and Drug Addiction, 2016). (www.emcdda.europa.eu/publications/insights/internet-drug-markets_en)
28 Angus Bancroft, 'Responsible Use to Responsible Harm: Illicit Drug Use and Peer Harm Reduction in a Darknet Cryptomarket' (2017) 19 *Health, Risk & Society* 336.
29 Arsen Davitadze, et al, 'Harm Reduction via Online Platforms for People Who Use Drugs in Russia: A Qualitative Analysis of Web Outreach Work' (2020) 17 *Harm Reduction Journal* 98.
30 Ibid.
31 'Hydra' was the largest and longest-running darknet market in the world. It was also the largest cryptomarket in Russia. It was shut down in April 2022. 'Justice Department Investigation Leads to Shutdown of Largest Online Darknet Marketplace', Department of Justice, U.S. Attorney's Office, Northern District of California (5 April 2022).
32 See Davitadze, et al (n 29).
33 Brandon Muncan, et al, '"They Look at us Like Junkies": Influences of Drug Use Stigma on the Healthcare Engagement of People Who Inject Drugs in New York City' (2020) 17 *Harm Reduction Journal* 53. https://doi.org/10.1186/s12954-020-00399-8; Kaitlin Ellis, et al, 'Breaching Trust: A Qualitative Study of Healthcare Experiences of People Who Use Drugs in a Rural Setting' (2020) 5 *Frontiers in Sociology* 593925.
34 Cristiana Vale Pires, F Caudevilla Gálligo & Helena Valente, 'Netreach Work: Implementing Web-Based Harm Reduction Interventions with Online Drug Users (2016) 2 *Addictology Journal* 182.
35 See Caudevilla (n 27).
36 Kurcevič and Lines (n 7).; Eurasian Harm Reduction Association (n 7).
37 See 'Harm Reduction 2.0' (June 2018) <www.youtube.com/watch?v=zr8CGc3G_tg&t=878s> accessed 15 March 2023.

9 Prisoner to Patient

The Pathologisation of People Who Use Drugs

Shaun Shelly

Introduction

As calls for new approaches such as decriminalisation and legal regulation of drugs increase, there are shared concerns about how best to deal with those who become 'addicted' to drugs and how to limit the perceived harmful effects of drugs. The effectiveness and mainstreaming of harm reduction, high levels of drug-related morbidity, the failure of the criminal justice approach and the call for scientific evidence and human rights-informed policies have led many to frame the world drug problem as a health issue, rather than a law enforcement issue.[1] Many stakeholders across a wide range of sectors now believe that people who are 'addicted' need treatment, not punishment.[2] Some argue that the binary option of prisoner or patient is a false dichotomy.[3]

In this chapter, I suggest that criminalisation and pathologisation are not a dichotomy. Rather, they are two sides of the same coin. There is a danger that while prisoners are labelled as patients, patients could soon become de facto prisoners. I argue that seeing all people dependent on drugs as sick, diseased or otherwise in need of medical intervention and treatment to restore them to a non-addicted state is an insidious form of prohibition that will continue to exploit and control people and holds a range of harms that, even if unintended, are easily foreseen.

This chapter intentionally focuses on data and examples from the United States. The United States dominates, influences and often dictates drug research, interventions and policy globally. Given the history of the United States of using economic incentives and disincentives to ensure sovereign nations align drug policies with US policies and the significant influence the United States has on the Commission on Narcotic Drugs and other UN agencies, I believe focusing on US policies and examples is appropriate as an illustration of wider common concerns.

Prohibition, Policing, Power and Profit

The war on drugs, prohibition and the criminal justice response to drugs serve a political, financial, moral and power agenda.[4] Framed by the UN Single Convention as a fight against 'evil',[5] the war on drugs has been used to justify military operations in independent nations, eliminate political opposition, restrict movement across

DOI: 10.4324/9781003169765-13

borders and disproportionally incarcerate certain people.[6] The drug policies of the United States, exported to all corners of the globe and forced upon some countries, have created a prison industrial complex worth billions of dollars and increased the size, powers and resources of militarised police forces.[7] Prohibition has created a criminal economy that benefits political campaigns, financial institutions and entire countries.[8] The prevalence of drug use and dependence in communities is a politically expedient distraction from government failures, disparities in power, education and wealth and lack of economic opportunity.[9] For some, the war on drugs has been and continues to be a financial, political and social success.[10]

The over-reliance on law enforcement to address people who use drugs or have mental health issues inevitably escalates confrontation and violence. Jack Cole, the Executive Director of Law Enforcement Action Partnership, is widely referenced as saying, 'When you train your police to go to war, they've got to have an enemy'.[11] The inappropriate and heavy-handed responses can often create a problem rather than solve it.

Mental health issues are an example. Where there is a lack of residential care and community-based outreach, the police are often the first responders to suicidal or psychotic people. Because police are not mental health professionals, they often escalate the event because of their training. The over-reliance on the police to respond to mental health issues and the resultant aggressive responses have increased the phenomenon known as 'suicide by cop'.[12] Miller suggests that

> the aggressively assertive, forthright cognitive style, temperament, and action-orientation of most cops allows them to unconsciously identify with the resolve to 'do whatever it takes' to survive and overcome a situation, even if they consciously repudiate the actual criminal motives and agenda of the offender.[13]

After a century of prohibition and 50 years of the 'war on drugs', the last decade has seen an increasing number of stakeholders calling for a different response to the drug 'problem' and the people who use them.[14] There is significant evidence and growing recognition that some people and communities have disproportionally suffered because of criminal justice-focused drug policies. Prohibitionist policies have been exposed as servicing a racist and colonial agenda intent on oppressing specific populations.[15] Prohibition has cost trillions of dollars and has not reduced the supply or consumption of drugs. As this evidence mounts, it is becoming increasingly difficult to justify the war on drugs and the financial, political and human costs of mass incarceration that results from it. Unable to ignore the evidence, many policymakers, UN bodies and governments have begun (often somewhat reluctantly) to acknowledge the need for alternatives to the criminal justice response to drugs and the people who use them.[16]

People who use drugs suffer significantly from more health issues than the general population, particularly when drug use intersects with other forms of social or economic marginalisation.[17] Considering the multiple morbidities marginalised people who use drugs experience, medicalising services may seem logical. However, as with limiting the response to the criminal justice system, the focus is on the individual. By seeing social problems through a single lens, there is a significant risk of focusing on the individual and ignoring the context and circumstances that narrow choices and outcomes.

In reality, many social determinants impact health and behaviours. The World Health Organization describes the social determinants of health 'as the circumstances in which people are born, grow up, live, work and age, and the systems put in place to deal with illness. These circumstances are shaped by a wider set of forces: economics, social policies, and politics'.[18] For people who use drugs, many vulnerabilities are due to economic and social exclusion, limited access to sterile injecting equipment and sanitary products, living on the street, poor nutrition and criminalisation.[19] Unless there is a significant shift in resources to address the social determinants of dependent drug use and the related health risks, the shift from the criminal justice to health system response will still target the individual and discount the impact of the context and circumstances that narrow choices and health outcomes.

Among drug policy reformers, there is the hope that the end of the war on drugs will stop drug policy-related racism, oppression, marginalisation and the abuse of the rights of people who use drugs and their communities. However, the political need to control people, exert influence, demonstrate power, the economic exploitation of communities, the need for scapegoats and profiting off the labour of others will not die with prohibition.

The Paradox of Harm Reduction

One alternative to the prohibitionist approach could be to focus on reducing the harm associated with drug use rather than futile attempts to stop drug use. People who inject drugs are particularly vulnerable to contracting HIV, viral hepatitis, infective endocarditis and other infections. In the 1980s, HIV spread rapidly among people who inject, and increasing numbers of people died horrific deaths. To reduce the spread of HIV, people who use drugs, anarchists, renegade doctors, social workers and nurses formed unlikely collaborations to reduce the risks of injecting drug use. The harm reduction movement was born, and many HIV infections were prevented and lives saved.

The success of harm reduction interventions in reducing HIV transmission quickly became apparent.[20] The mainstreaming of harm reduction smoothed off the anarchist edges and narrowed the focus to people who inject drugs and use opioids. Harm reduction is now synonymous with the supply of sterile injecting equipment and opioid agonists, partial agonists and, recently, long-acting antagonists. Internationally, many harm reduction services have morphed from peer and activist-led, clinician-supported organisations into health and medical services run by professionals, often at the exclusion of peers.[21] Harm reduction services save lives, and in medical settings their principles include humanism, individualism and autonomy. Yet, it can often operate in a policy and clinical space that ensures the social control of people on opioid substitution treatment and prevents people from integrating into the community. What was originally a programme of community and peer empowerment and a rejection of prohibitionist thinking and State control has become, in some settings, another form of social control.[22]

The implementation of methadone programmes in the United States exemplifies how harm reduction can become a paradox: both a life-saving and a life-limiting intervention. In the United States, opioid substitution treatment programmes must comply with Federal Guidelines for Opioid Treatment Programs.[23] The standards require special licensing for doctors, and additional training and record keeping. Programmes must perform at least eight random drug tests annually on people receiving opioid substitution therapy. Agonist medications like methadone are initially only available as observed daily doses. The maximum take-home dose is one day per week during the first 90 days of entering the programme, two doses per week in the second 90-day period, increasing to six doses per week during the next six months. Only after two years of treatment can a person be given a 30-day supply of medication. People must attend the same clinic and cannot transfer to another except under 'exceptional circumstances'. In contrast, people who want to access methadone as an analgesic can go to their doctor, receive a prescription and collect a 30-day supply of methadone at the pharmacy.[24] The US domestic guidelines and policies are replicated in many global settings, spread through extensive training programmes and policy guidance through the many organisations globally representing US interests or dependent on US funding.

During COVID-19, these restrictions were relaxed in the United States, and take-home doses increased by more than 200% without an increase in overdose or concurrent heroin use.[25] Despite the evidence of no increased risk and increased uptake of services due to fewer restrictions, the relaxation of the restrictions is being reversed. Similarly, in other parts of the world, COVID-19 resulted in lower thresholds for people accessing methadone, and the literature suggests that there were few increases in adverse events. Yet, many of the pre-COVID restrictions have been reintroduced. The reinstated restrictions are unnecessary, prejudicial and aimed at controlling people who use drugs. The general public can access products with far more potential for harm than methadone. The current restrictions on access to opioid agonists indicate the level of the inherent stigma the medical field has towards people who use drugs.

Drug Use as a Disease

The idea that drug dependence is a medical issue is not new. However, in the 20th century, dependent drug use became widely referred to as a 'disease' and, more recently, a 'brain disease'. Alcoholics Anonymous refers to 'alcoholism' as an 'illness',[26] and Narcotics Anonymous describes 'addiction' as a 'disease'.[27] Both organisations claim that total abstinence is essential for recovery, and the recovery process is lifelong. In 1997, Alan Leshner, then head of National Institute of Drug Abuse (NIDA) in the United States, described addiction as a chronic disease of the brain.[28] Replacing Leshner as head of NIDA, Nora Volkow went a step further.

> [I]t is not enough to say that addiction is a chronic brain disease. What we mean by that is something very specific and profound: that because of drug

> use, take[ing] a drug – a person's brain is no longer able to produce something needed for our functioning and that healthy people take for granted, free will.[29]

Despite claims that the disease model reduces stigma and is a more scientific approach, the stigma and language that 'others' people who use drugs are central to the disease model of drug use. 'The Big Book' of Alcoholics Anonymous proclaims that 'alcoholics' 'are constitutionally incapable of being honest with themselves'.[30] Narcotics Anonymous literature labels people as 'clean' or 'dirty' and discourages using any medications to treat the disease of addiction and other mental health issues.[31] The repeated claims that the use of drugs leads to a disordered, dysfunctional and irrational brain that renders the drug user incapable of acting in their and others' best interests feeds into the image of a dangerous person with no ability to moderate their behaviour.

The overarching image of a person who uses drugs is that of a person who is either dangerous, or likely to become dangerous, to themselves and society. The disease model does nothing to dispel this negative image. Whether it is the demon drug, the inherent deviance of the individual or the pathology of a disordered, damaged and dysfunctional brain, people who use drugs are 'othered'. The dominant approaches to resolving drug dependence promote the need for spiritual exorcism, criminal sanction or treatment to save people who use drugs from themselves and to protect society from them. As Davies has written,

> the more we treat drug problems as if they were the domain of inadequate, sick or helpless people, the more people will present themselves within that framework, and the more we will produce and encounter drug users who fit that description.[32]

Considering the moral and medical panic about drug use, it is perhaps surprising that extensive population size studies show that most people who use drugs do not develop an addiction.[33] Those who do are most likely to mature out of dependence, and 75% of people who resolve their addiction do so without formal treatment.[34] Many factors mediate or moderate the resolution of drug dependence, and several variables outside the drug itself contribute to a potential increase in the harm and duration of drug dependence.[35,36]

People with good support structures, who develop secure relationships, find employment and housing and are otherwise healthy are more likely to resolve their dependence. People with mental health issues, without housing and social support, who are unemployed with low education, are single, have more stress, have histories of trauma, are from marginalised communities and have been incarcerated are likely to suffer significantly more consequences from their drug use over prolonged periods, and are less likely to resolve their drug dependence. The data would suggest that context and exogenous factors, the previously described social determinants, play a critical role in drug dependence development, duration and resolution.

NIDA acknowledges that 'We will never be able to address addiction without being able to talk about and address the myriad factors that contribute to it – biological, psychological, behavioural, societal, economic, etc.'[37] Yet it continues to promote the belief that dependent drug use is a pathology, rooted in the individual, one that needs curing. As NIDA Director Nora Volkow explains,

> ...viewing it [addiction] as a treatable medical problem from which people can and do recover is crucial for enabling a public-health–focused response that ensures access to effective treatments and lessens the stigma surrounding a condition that afflicts nearly 10 percent of Americans at some point in their lives... .
>
> What the brain disorder model, within the larger biopsychosocial, captures better than other models – such as those that focus on addiction as a learned behavior – is the crucial dimension of interindividual biological variability that makes some people more susceptible than others to this hijacking.[38]

Continuing to see addiction as a brain or other form of primary disease will keep the focus on the individual. Regarding drug dependence, the social determinants that place specific communities at risk of health and drug issues will stay unaddressed.

NIDA, the World Health Organization and other stakeholders claim that 'treatment works', but there is little consensus about what constitutes evidence-based addiction treatment, or even if addiction treatment as a separate entity is needed. The phrase 'treatment as usual' is used in many studies, yet 'usual treatment' is seldom defined or described in detail. Programmes based on the 12-Steps of Alcoholics Anonymous are ubiquitous, dominating both peer-led and inpatient rehab interventions. Narcotics Anonymous has over 70,000 meetings in 144 countries.[39] The abstinence-focussed 'Minnesota Model' of treatment is the default response and is widely used in residential rehabs worldwide.[40] The model relies on 12-step facilitation, an appropriation of the 12-step approach developed in the 1950s.[41] Interventions can be diverse and include equine or canine therapy, rapid detoxification under general anaesthetic, untreated withdrawals, forced confinement, confrontational approaches, forced labour and long-term isolation from family and friends. Some approaches use medication (including psychedelics), while others forbid any medication.

Even the desired outcomes of treatment are contested, with two divergent philosophical views informing treatment approaches. The prohibitionist philosophy includes moral, criminal or medical (including many harm reduction) models of treatment that consider abstinence as the ultimate and the only acceptable goal of treatment. Harm reduction focuses on identifying and reducing potential risks such as blood-borne infections and drug poisoning. Programmes that apply the original harm reduction philosophies have a humanist and rights-based focus on what the individual wants and accepts: moderation or intentional use with reduced harms as a successful outcome. However, several programmes that include harm reduction interventions will often see these as part of the journey towards abstinence. The pharmacological, psychotherapeutic and social and peer-led interventions, typically provided as an in-patient or outpatient services, are reflected in the catch-all phrase, which is often used to describe addiction, 'bio-psycho-social treatment'.[42]

The 'bio' in bio-psychosocial refers to the pharmacological approaches to addressing dependence. Pharmaceutical interventions fall primarily into four categories: agonist (e.g. methadone) and partial agonist-type (e.g. buprenorphine) analogues of unregulated drugs, antagonists (e.g. naltrexone) and aversive medications (e.g. disulfiram). In broad strokes, agonists act in similar ways to the targeted drug and prevent withdrawal (by maintaining a dependence) and reduce cravings. Partial agonists reduce withdrawal and craving and block or limit the effect of simultaneous drug use antagonists block the drug receptor or displace existing drugs attached to the receptor and stop the drug from having the desired effect. Aversive medications make the person sick if they take the targeted drug. None of these medications focuses on the as-yet-unidentified biological 'source' of the disease of addiction.

Despite their different mechanisms of action, most of the medications used in addiction medicine potentially have one thing in common: They can reduce the chaos, cost, stress, uncertainty, morbidity and risk of being punished, prosecuted or poisoned by the use of unregulated drugs. The medications can create the time, space and interactions for people to get the support and health, social, financial, housing and other services they need to improve their circumstances. If the resources and services are available, then life, with its commitments and responsibilities and relationships, over time, will usually help people resolve their drug dependence. For people who cannot or do not want to stop using drugs, prescription agonists relieve cravings, reduce the use of unregulated drugs and reduce the potential risks and possible harms of using unregulated drugs.

Psychotherapeutic interventions for drug use are the most common intervention used in treatment settings.[43] While psychodynamic and other therapies can assist people in addressing their dependence and the issues that underlie the addiction, specialist addiction-focused approaches often deviate from, ignore or contradict standard good practice based on the assumption that the 'addict' is an addict first and a person second.

For example, in psychology, Rogerian non-directive approaches are often considered inappropriate for addiction treatment.[44] Overt and subtle confrontations regarded as unacceptable in other medical or supportive settings are especially evident in residential rehab programmes.[45] Combining psychotherapeutic and social interventions, therapeutic communities (long-term residential rehabilitation) are getting renewed attention.[46] Undoubtedly, the idea of a socially supportive community and ongoing support as people seek to resolve their dependent drug use is attractive and can avoid the incarceration or treatment dichotomy. However, troubling allegations of abuse in therapeutic communities, which started with Synanonin in the sixties and seventies,[47] continues to persist today with programmes such as San Patrignano. San Patrignano, a therapeutic community in Italy that accommodates more than 1,500 people, receives funding from both corporate and international donors[48] and is often lauded by UN officials as a model of good practice.[49] The community members are a captive source of labour for the commercial ventures run at the facility, and their labour raises half of the funds needed to sustain the project. There have been consistent reports of human rights violations, and concerns have been raised about the 'cult-like' status and murder trial of San Patrignano's founder and leader, Vincenzo Muccioli.[50]

A further type of social intervention, self-help and peer-support programmes are widely recommended and used, with the various 'anonymous' 12-step programmes dominating this space. It is reasonable to assume peer-led programmes to be more sensitive, less stigmatising and empowering. However, the 12-step literature, written in the mid-20th century, as well as later editions, retain many confrontational, offensive, arrogant and privileged views and descriptions that are, at best, unhelpful, and possibly harmful.[51] Harm reduction programmes have shown how peer-led programmes and interventions can broaden the type of response needed to address drug use in communities and increase engagement.[52] In either case, there is a risk that peer-led programmes can also ignore the data and academic and expert input required to understand complex systems.

Emerging Treatment

More recently, there has been a focus on the neuroscience of addiction. The observation of brain activity and changes in people using drugs has given rise to a new approach to treatment – directly targeting the brain to change how people experience drugs. There have been several attempts to change the brain through invasive interventions, including ablation and direct electrical stimulation through implants. For example, a Chinese programme targeted heroin-dependent people, and more than 1,000 people reportedly underwent ablative surgery targeting the nucleus accumbens.[53] One analysis reports that 50% of 'patients gradually recovered more than five years after surgery'.[54] The mean age of people receiving this treatment was 36.96 years ± 5.33. Considering that most people will resolve their dependence as they mature, it is highly possible that these patients would have spontaneously remitted from their dependence within the five years after the study.

Even more concerning, in multiple studies, side effects experienced by patients receiving ablative surgery included short-term intracranial haemorrhage, memory loss, personality changes, decreased motivation, hypomania, insomnia and decreased sexual desire.[55] Building on the ablation studies, some researchers and clinicians are experimenting with direct brain stimulation to change addictive behaviours.[56] Research on pharmacological approaches targeting the dopamine system and other neural pathways has regularly been described as promising.[57] Yet, despite years of research, there have been no effective treatments. Significant potential harms could also arise,[58] and some attempts to dampen motivation or limit responses to certain chemicals could be considered a form of chemical ablation.

The net of addiction treatment is continually widening. Three of the leading voices in the addiction research field, McLellan, Koob and Volkow, published a paper on their concept of 'preaddiction'.[59] The authors repeat the assertion that people who use drugs, a far broader category than those 'addicted' to drugs, cause significant harm to society. They propose that a new category of 'preaddiction' should be used to intervene before someone meets the diagnostic criteria for addiction treatment. They suggest that an approach similar to type 2 diabetes, where prediabetes can now be treated pre-emptively, could be a model for addiction medicine. The obvious fault in comparing diabetes and addiction is that there are definitive lab tests that can identify the dysregulation related to diabetes. No such empirical tests exist for substance use, and subjective opinions based on false beliefs and fears will guide pre-addiction diagnosis. If the term is accepted into the mainstream, pre-addiction will significantly increase the potential to label, stigmatise, profit from and exert control over people who use drugs or are considered vulnerable to drug use and dependence.

Pathologisation in the Pursuit of Power and Profit

In Brave New World, Huxley writes, 'People are comfortable handing over freedom to people in power in exchange for safety and stability. In this exchange, people learn to love their servitude, choosing it over any dreams of revolution.'[60] Of course, people must be afraid of something to make this work. The fear of drugs has systematically been instilled in society for so long that many patently inaccurate claims are considered incontestable facts. A recent example of fear-mongering is the numerous reports about police officers and emergency personnel being poisoned by trace amounts of fentanyl, an outcome disproven by many scientists and people who use fentanyl.[61]

A significant proportion of the addiction treatment industry has long exploited the fear of drugs by offering expensive, unproven and sometimes abusive treatments. Treatment services use 'strong-arm tactics' to exert control over poorer communities. In 2012 Gowan and Whetstone wrote:

> We understand the 'medicalization' represented by strong-arm rehab not as a reprieve from judgment, but instead as a process of translation and amplification. Translated by staff into therapeutic, moral, and finally cultural versions, the biochemical 'diagnosis' of pathology comes to serve as a neutral, medicalized front behind which the systemic injuries of race and class disappear. Instead, the strongarm process amplifies the taint of addiction into a new biologization of poverty and race.[62]

The Biden administration's drug policy emphasises closing the treatment gap.[63] However, 95% of people who met the criteria for a substance use disorder and did not seek treatment reported that they did not think they needed treatment.[64] The Biden plan aims to increase treatment admissions for people vulnerable to overdose by 100% using case-finding, increased screening and making treatment more accessible and attractive. In 2020, 40.5 million people in the United States had a substance use disorder, yet only 6.5% accessed specialist substance use disorder treatment.[65] According to the diagnostic criteria, a massive market of untreated people exists. With the medicalisation and pathologisation of drug use and dependence and the extensive neuroscience research, the role of psychiatry and specialised clinicians is considered central to treating addiction. Because addiction is described as chronic and many people who meet the diagnostic criteria are not accessing any

Table 9.1 The common outcomes of prohibition or pathologisation of drug use

Behaviour or activity	*Prohibitionist view*	*Medical view*	*Resulting outcome or belief*
The non-prescription use of drugs	A criminal act that must be prevented or punished.	Is harmful to self (and others) and must be controlled by medical professionals.	Drug use is abnormal and deviates from acceptable behaviour.
A person dependent ('addicted') on drugs	A criminal	Has a disease.	The person is different and places the rest of society at risk.
The person needs	Punishment	Treatment	The individual must change and is the target of interventions.
Risk to self and others	Incarcerated and removed from the community	In rehab away from the community	Removal from community support and societal norms. Increased contact with excluded people and increased psychosocial dislocation.
The person needs to be rehabilitated through	Criminal sanction	Treatment	They are unable to resolve any problems themselves. Need extrinsic motivation.
If not rehabilitated or in recovery they	Will harm others. They are irresponsible and will return to jail.	Will harm themselves and others. They are not recovered and need ongoing treatment.	They need to abstain from all drugs, and drug testing is to help them remain that way.
They cannot be trusted because they	Are devious by nature	Have a disease and have lost free will	They cannot be trusted to make 'good' decisions and should have limited autonomy.
Cannot be allowed to use drugs again	Will be monitored and drug tested	Will be monitored and drug tested	Will be sanctioned through exclusion from the community

treatment, there is an opportunity for businesses that capture the market to earn a sustained revenue stream over the span of decades.

In 2020, the US treatment industry was worth $42 billion annually and was predicted to reach $53 billion by 2025.[66] Unethical practices and marketing are common, with patient brokers receiving referral payments[67] and facilities agreeing to admissions without any assessment apart from the ability to pay the upfront costs that average around $17,434.[68] Despite the limitations of drug testing, many treatment providers and independent testing companies are making excessive profits of up to 3,000 times the actual cost. Some consultants specialise in helping service providers maximise their earnings and coverage.[69]

In 2014, the testing industry was reported to be worth more than $8 billion.[70] This is a lot of money being spent on enforcing the imposed ideal of abstinence and there is no evidence that testing is effective. The evidence base for many treatment approaches widely used in the addiction rehab industry is, at best, weak, and some commonly used practices are harmful to the clients. As Dr Mark Willenbring, former director of treatment and recovery research at the National Institute on Alcohol Abuse and Alcoholism, has said, 'There's no such thing as an evidence-based rehab. That's because no matter what you do, the whole concept of rehab is flawed and unsupported by evidence.'[71]

A Change in Name but More of the Same

The increase in drug courts has foretold the shift from the incarceration and criminal sentencing of people towards a more health-system approach to drug use. However, the power of control over the individual's non-medical use of drugs continues unabated: only the language has changed.[72] Without deconstructing the myths, preconceptions and stigma related to drugs and the people who use them, the medicalisation of drug use will lead to over-pathologising people who use drugs. Even in a regulated or decriminalised policy space, if addiction is considered a pathology, a disease of the brain, treatment is justified as the compassionate and appropriate response for people who use drugs in certain ways. Ultimately the outcomes could be similar to incarceration.

A Brave New World

The use of drugs exists over a broad spectrum of purposes, and trying to force the use of drugs into the framework of either medical or pathological use is short-sighted and potentially harmful. The binary division fails to recognise that once drug use is decriminalised and supplies are not contaminated, many drugs currently considered illegal to use can play a constructive and meaningful role for many people, both as formalised medicines and as non-medical tools for a variety of social, creative and personal developmental uses among adults.[73] We do not expect people to drink beer in a closely supervised clinical space reserved for beer drinkers only. Who would want to attend their MDMA-enhanced social or creative activities in a clinical setting and under a psychiatrist's supervision? And who could afford it? Yet this is what the future holds for people who use drugs – supervised consumption facilities, prescription-only access to drugs with psychiatrists as gatekeepers to the social, creative, euphoric and mystical effects of drug use by adults. By ignoring and not accepting and planning for the use of drugs outside of the medical context, choices will again be limited, and over-regulation will result in many of the current prohibition-related harms continuing. Perhaps the use of unregulated drugs in unregulated ways will be even more highly stigmatised and penalised in an overly regulated future unless the person accepts a diagnosis.

With the blind acceptance of addiction as a disease, medical systems and specialised medical professionals will hold influence and power over people who use drugs. As the net widens, people will be caught and trapped in a system of treatment that will dominate and dictate their life trajectory and restrict their autonomy.

Many hotly contested issues will emerge as the 'war on drugs' ends. Decriminalisation and legal regulation in its many forms will bring new problems to be debated. Many of these issues will be inconsequential and serve as distractions, diverting attention away from uncontested areas that will escape critical examination. I believe that the pathologisation of drug use and related social issues will be one of those potentially uncontested areas. It is important to remember that although a ceasefire in the war on drugs is imminent, the vast majority of society has been indoctrinated over decades to believe that rational people must never consume certain drugs, and their use can only cause harm, and society must be protected from the people that use certain drugs. Political structures will still want to keep chemical euphoria, enlightenment and mystical experiences under the control of the State, church and related structures. Increasingly, the medical field and treatment industrial complex will replace the criminal justice system and police as the defence against drugs. Treatment will be the accepted, seemingly compassionate response to drug dependence. The prisoners will become patients. Patients will need rehabilitation and treatment for a lifelong disorder of the brain that compromises free will.

A standard narrative in addiction is that treatment only fails if the individual fails to comply. Without treatment, with an impaired brain, people who use drugs will not be considered suitable for employment and social or political inclusion. But unlike prisoners, people who use drugs will be expected to pay for treatment. Treatment which, at best, may shorten their drug dependence. Mostly treatment will be unneeded, financially debilitating and potentially iatrogenic. Treatment may leave people medicated with drugs that provide no comfort or benefit and possibly leave them unmotivated and anhedonic. At worst, treatment may change who they are. We will no longer have a war on drugs. But we will have patients who must follow medical advice or be treated until, or to, death.

Notes

1 Aliza Cohen, et al, 'How the War on Drugs Impacts Social Determinants of Health beyond the Criminal Legal System' (2022) 54 *Annals of Medicine* 2024.

2 Nora D Volkow, et al, 'Drug Use Disorders: Impact of a Public Health rather than a Criminal Justice Approach' (2017) 12 *World Psychiatry* 213.
3 Stephen J Morse, 'Addiction, Choice, and Criminal Law' in Nick Heather and Gabriel Segal (eds.), *Addiction and Choice* (Oxford University Press, 2016).
4 Antony Loewenstein, *Pills, Powder, and Smoke: Inside the Bloody War on Drugs* (Scribe Publications, 2020).; Eric Blumensont and Eva Nilsentt, 'Policing for Profit: The Drug War's Hidden Economic Agenda' (1998) 65/1 *University of Chicago Law Review 35.*
5 Rick Lines, 'Deliver Us from Evil? – The Single Convention on Narcotic Drugs, 50 Years On' (2011) 1 *International Journal on Human Rights and Drug Policy* 3.
6 Neil Woods and JS Rafaeli, *Drug Wars: The Terrifying Inside Story of Britain's Drug Trade* (Random House, 2018).
7 Ibid.
8 Nathan Jones. 'Review of Tom Wainwright's *Narconomics: How to Run a Drug Cartel*' (2017) 18/*1 Georgetown Journal of International Affairs* 83.
9 Stuart Taylor, Julian Buchanan & Tammy Ayres, 'Prohibition, Privilege and the Drug Apartheid: The Failure of Drug Policy Reform to Address the Underlying Fallacies of Drug Prohibition' (2016) 16 *Criminology & Criminal Justice* 391.
10 HR Hutson, et al, 'Suicide by Cop' (1998) 32 *Annals of Emergency Medicine* 665.
11 For example, see Forest Hylton, 'A Different Sort of Blowback', *The Brooklyn Rail* (5 November 2009).
12 Hutson, et al (n 10).
13 Laurence Miller, 'Suicide by Cop: Causes, Reactions, and Practical Intervention Strategies' (2006) 8/3 *International Journal of Emergency Mental Health* 165.
14 The Lancet, 'The Time to End the War on Drugs Is Long Overdue' (2021) 8(7) *The Lancet HIV* e387.
15 Kojo Koram, *The War on Drugs and the Global Colour Line* (Pluto Press, 2019).; Colleen Daniels, et al, 'Decolonizing Drug Policy' (2021) 18 *Harm Reduction Journal* 120.
16 United Nations systems Chief Executives Board for Coordination, 'Summary of Deliberations: Segment 2: Common United Nations System Position on Drug Policy' (18 January 2019) CEB/2018/2.
17 Louisa Degenhardt, et al, 'The Global Burden of Disease Attributable to Alcohol and Drug Use in 195 Countries and Territories, 1990–2016: A Systematic Analysis for the Global Burden of Disease Study 2016' (2018) 5 *The Lancet Psychiatry* 987.
18 World Health Organization, 'Social Determinants of Health: Key Concepts' <www.who.int/news-room/questions-and-answers/item/social-determinants-of-health-key-concepts> accessed 22 April 2023.
19 Josie Watson, Jamie Crawley & D Kane, 'Social Exclusion, Health and Hidden Homelessness' (2016) 139 *Public Health* 96.
20 Alex Wodak, 'Harm Reduction Is Now the Mainstream Global Drug Policy' (2009) 104 *Addiction* 343.
21 Teresa Gowan, Sarah Whetstone & Tanja Andic, 'Addiction, Agency, and the Politics of Self-Control: Doing Harm Reduction in a Heroin Users' Group' (2012) 74 *Social Science & Medicine* 1251.
22 Christopher Smith, 'Harm Reduction as Anarchist Practice: A User's Guide to Capitalism and Addiction in North America' (Critical Public Health, 2023).
23 Substance Abuse and Mental Health Services Administration, 'Federal Guidelines for Opioid Treatment Programs' (2015) HHS Publication No. (SMA) PEP15-FEDGUIDEOTP.
24 Deborah Dowell, et al, 'CDC Clinical Practice Guideline for Prescribing Opioids for Pain – United States, 2022' (2022) 71/3 *Morbidity and Mortality Weekly Report* 1.

25 Ofer Amran, et al, 'The Impact of Relaxation of Methadone Take-Home Protocols on Treatment Outcomes in the COVID-19 Era' (2021) 47 *American Journal of Drug and Alcohol Abuse* 722.
26 Alcoholics Anonymous, *The Big Book* (AA World Services, 1983) 40.
27 Narcotics Anonymous, *Narcotics Anonymous*, 6th ed (NA World Services, 2008) preface.
28 Al Leshner, 'Addiction Is a Brain Disease, and It Matters' (1997) 278 *Science* 45.
29 Nora Volkow, 'Addiction Is a Disease of Free Will' (2015) Addiction Education Society https://addictioneducationsociety.org/addiction-is-a-disease-of-free-will accessed 22 March 2023.
30 Alcoholics Anonymous (n 26) 58.
31 Narcotics Anonymous, 'NA Groups and Medication' (NA World Services, 2007).; Narcotics Anonymous,, 'Narcotics Anonymous and Persons Receiving Medication Assisted Treatment' (NA World Services, 2016).
32 John Booth Davies, *The Myth of Addiction* (Routledge, 1998) 23.
33 William L White, 'Recovery/Remission Recovery/Remission from Substance Use Disorders from Substance Use Disorders: An Analysis of Reported Outcomes in 415 Scientific Reports, 1868 in 415 Scientific Reports, 1868–2011' (Philadelphia Department of Behavioral Health and Intellectual disAbility Service, 2012).
34 Ibid.
35 Norman Zinberg, *Drug, Set, and Setting*, (Yale University Press, 1986).
36 Bruce K Alexander, *The Globalisation of Addiction: A Study in Poverty of the Spirit* (Oxford University Press, 2008).
37 Nora Volkow, 'What Does It Mean When We Call Addiction a Brain Disorder?' (2018), Scientific American Blog Network <https://blogs.scientificamerican.com/observations/what-does-it-mean-when-we-call-addiction-a-brain-disorder/> accessed 28 January 2023.
38 Ibid.
39 Narcotics Anonymous, 'Information about NA' (NA World Services, 2006–2018).
40 Anne M Fletcher, *Inside Rehab: The Surprising Truth about Addiction Treatment – and How to Get Help That Works* (Penguin, 2013).; See also Kenneth Andersons's series of books, *The Untold History of Addiction Treatment in the United States*.
41 Damian McElrath, 'The Minnesota Model' (1997) 29 *Journal of Psychoactive Drugs* 141.
42 Daniel Z Buchman, Wayne Skinner & Judy Illes, 'Negotiating the Relationship between Addiction, Ethics, and Brain Science' (2010) 1 *AJOB Neuroscience* 36.
43 Fletcher (n 40).
44 William Lee White W and William R Miller, 'The Use of Confrontation in Addiction Treatment: History, Science and Time for Change' (2007) 8(4) *Counsellor* 12.
45 Fletcher (n 40).
46 KA Kast, G Manella & J Avery, 'Community as Treatment: The Therapeutic Community Model in The Era of The Opioid Crisis' (2019) 8 *Journal of Addictive Behaviors, Therapy & Rehabilitation* 2.
47 Richard Ofshe, et al, 'Social Structure and Social Control in Synanon' (1974) 3 *Nonprofit and Voluntary Sector Quarterly* 67.
48 World Federation Against Drugs, 'San Patrignano' <https://wfad.se/user/322/#:~:text=San%20Patrignano%20does%20not%20accept,following%20a%20principle%20of%20autonomy> accessed 14 May 2023.
49 See, for example, United Nations Information Service, '"Rainbow" Anti-Drug Association and United Nations To Map Drug Abuse Trends, Review Global Strategy' (25 October 2000) UN Doc UNIS/NAR/703; United Nations Secretary General,

'Secretary-General's Remarks at Special Event on the International Day against Drug Abuse and illicit Trafficking 26 June 2013' <www.un.org/sg/en/content/sg/statement/2013-06-26/secretary-generals-remarks-special-event-international-day-against> accessed 1 May 2023.

50 Susanna Ronconi, 'SanPa: Where Did We Leave Off? Where Are We Now?', Drugreporter (23 January 2021).; Gabriele Cruciata 'Behind the Notorious Italian Rehab Community in Netflix's "SanPa" ', *Filter* (25 February 2021); Netflix, 'SANPA: Sins of the Saviour' <www.netflix.com/title/81010965> accessed 14 May 2023.

51 David Frank, 'The Trouble with Morality: The Effects of 12-Step Discourse on Addicts' Decision-Making' (2011) 43 *Journal of Psychoactive Drugs* 245.

52 Sam Friedman, et al, 'Harm Reduction Theory: Users' Culture, Micro-Social Indigenous Harm Reduction, and the Self-Organization and Outside-Organizing of Users' Groups' (2007) 18 *International Journal of Drug Policy* 107.

53 Nan Li, et al, 'Nucleus Accumbens Surgery for Addiction' (2013) 80 *World Neurosurgery* S28.e9–19.

54 Ibid.

55 Shuo Ma, et al, 'Neurosurgical Treatment for Addiction: Lessons from an Untold Story in China and a Path Forward' (2019) 7 *National Science Review* 702.

56 Rui Chang, et al, 'Deep Brain Stimulation in Drug Addiction Treatment: Research Progress and Perspective' (2022) 13 *Frontiers in Psychiatry* 858638.; Tony R Wang, et al, 'Deep Brain Stimulation for the Treatment of Drug Addiction' (2018) 45 *Neurosurgical Focus* E11.

57 See, for example, M Heval Ozgen and Stuart Blume, 'The Continuing Search for an Addiction Vaccine' (2019) 37 *Vaccine* 5485.

58 Kathleen M Kantak 'Vaccines against Drugs of Abuse' (2003) 63 *Drugs* 341.

59 A Thomas McLellan, George F Koob GF & Nora D Volkow, 'Preaddiction – a Missing Concept for Treating Substance Use Disorders' (2022) *79 JAMA Psychiatry* 749.

60 Aldous Huxley, *Brave New World* (Harper Brothers, 1932).

61 Brandon del Pozo, et al, 'Can Touch This: Training to Correct Police Officer Beliefs about Overdose from Incidental Contact with Fentanyl' (2021) 9 *Health & Justice* 34.; See also Scott Shackford, 'Don't Let Police, Media Mislead You about Fentanyl Exposure Overdoses', Reason (15 December 2022).

62 Teresa Gowan and Sarah Whetstone, 'Making the Criminal Addict: Subjectivity and Social Control in a Strong-Arm Rehab' (2012) 14 *Punishment & Society* 69..

63 White House Executive Office of the President Office of National Drug Control Policy, 'National Drug Control Strategy' (2022).

64 Substance Abuse and Mental Health Services Administration, 'Key Substance Use and Mental Health Indicators in the United States: Results from the 2020 National Survey on Drug Use and Health' (Department of Health and Human Service, 2021).

65 Ibid.

66 MarketResearch.com, 'The U.S. Addiction Rehab Industry' (Marketdata LLC, 2020).

67 US House of Representatives Committee on Energy and Commerce, 'Hearing Entitled "Examining Concerns of Patient Brokering and Addiction Treatment Fraud (8 December 2017) <www.congress.gov/115/meeting/house/106716/documents/HHRG-115-IF02-20171212-SD002.pdf> accessed 11 January 2023.

68 Tamara Beetham, et al, 'Admission Practices and Cost of Care for Opioid Use Disorder at Residential Addiction Treatment Programs in the US' (2021) 40 *Health Affairs Journal* 2.

69 See, for example, Joe Reilly and Associates, Inc, 'How to Sell Drug Testing' (11 February 2021) <www.joereilly.com/how-to-sell-drug-testing/> accessed 12 May 2023.
70 PBS NewsHour, 'Urine Screens Cost $8.5 Billion a Year – More than the Entire EPA Budget' (7 November 2017) <www.pbs.org/newshour/health/urine-screens-cost-8-5-billion-a-year-more-than-the-entire-epa-budget> accessed 10 January 2023.
71 The Influence, 'The Rehab Industry Needs to Clean up Its Act. Here's How', *Huffington Post* (16 February 2016).
72 Robin Mackenzie, 'Feeling Good: The Ethopolitics of Pleasure; Psychoactive Substance Use and Public Health and Criminal Justice Governance: Therapeutic Jurisprudence and the Drug Courts in the USA' (2008) 17 *Social & Legal Studies* 513.
73 The re-emerging evidence around the clinical and therapeutic use of psychedelics.

Part IV

Emerging Rights Issues at the Supply Side

10 Peasants' Rights after the War on Drugs

The Case for Transformative Cannabis Regulation

Alejandro Rodríguez-Llach, Isabel Pereira-Arana and Luis Felipe Cruz-Olivera

Introduction

The peasant population, the war on drugs and the armed conflict in Colombia have been tragically intertwined. In the late 1980s, armed members of the insurgency[1] got involved in the drug business to finance their operations, which prompted a marked increase in the scale of the internal armed conflict. Paramilitary groups later followed suit, and the disputes in the late 1990s and early 2000s were mediated by an international war on drugs that was waged in Colombia's fields. Throughout it all, peasants were there, in a dangerous middle ground, stigmatised by the State and its drug policy, stuck in the crossfire of illegal and legal armed groups, and engaging in the cultivation of illicit plants facilitated by the historical precariousness of the rural environment.

As both drug policy and drug trafficking were being consolidated in Colombia, the peasant population became a political player, having mobilised against inequality in access to land – an aspect that lies at the very origin of the armed conflict. These struggles continue today, and they are manifested in identity-related and redistributive demands. If peasants are recognised as historically disadvantaged actors who became involved in illegal economies due to the shortcomings of rural development, any attempt at legal regulation must guarantee their participation (in their capacity as a subject with special constitutional protection[2]) in the legal cannabis market as a way of repairing the damage they have suffered due to drug trafficking and anti-drug efforts.

Any scheme for the regulation of cannabis must include reparation measures for the populations most affected by marijuana prohibition. In this chapter we address exclusively the case of peasants,[3] focusing on how the fiscal policy behind a regulatory scheme should finance such measures.

Context: Peasants, Marijuana Crops and the Illegal Market

Any regulation of cannabis for adult use in the Colombian context must take into account discussions regarding the toll of drug policy as part of the implementation

DOI: 10.4324/9781003169765-15

of the Final Peace Agreement signed by the Colombian government and the Revolutionary Armed Forces of Colombia-People's Army (FARC-EP) in 2016.[4] The country is a key piece in the international prohibition regime and in drug trafficking. As of 2019, 87% and 68% of the cocaine that entered the United States and Europe, respectively, was of Colombian.[5] Because of this, the international community – and the United States in particular – has wielded diplomatic and economic pressure to ensure that the country acts as an ally in the war on drugs. For more than 40 years, Colombian governments have applied anti-drug strategies as if they were a foolproof recipe, and they have facilitated an 'intervention by invitation', especially since the implementation of Plan Colombia.[6]

According to figures from the Colombian Drug Information System, between 1994 and 2015 the country fumigated more than 1.8 million hectares of coca using the herbicide glyphosate. Since 1999, about 5,000 tonnes of cocaine have been seized, along with over 14,000 tonnes of coca leaf. However, Colombia currently has around 230,000 hectares planted with coca. The war on drugs has also had consequences for people who use drugs.[7] Uprimny et al. have shown that between 2005 and 2014 the police made nearly 2.4 million arrests – or nine arrests per hour – of which 29% (727,091) were for drug offenses, correlating to an increase in the population incarcerated for such crimes. As of 2015, 20 out of every 100 detainees were being held on drug-related offenses.[8]

The persecution of marijuana and its users has been a characteristic trait of drug policy throughout its history. According to data from the Criminality Information Group,[9] records on seizures from 2015 to April 2019 show that 46% of cases were for cannabis, and within those cases 76% involved quantities of less than 100 grams.[10] All of these institutional efforts – which entailed human rights-related costs – have not managed to achieve the goals of prohibition, since neither drug availability nor drug use has declined, nor has the illegal market shrunk in size. In Colombia, more than one million people use cannabis, constituting a domestic market with a value estimated at between 2.2 and 4.4 trillion pesos in 2015,[11] according to the National Planning Department.[12]

Thus, Colombia was repeating the recipes and failures of prohibition with a certain degree of inertia until debate on drug policy reform began under the presidency of Juan Manuel Santos, who even stressed the need to regulate drugs – cocaine included – in the framework of the UNGASS[13] process.[14] In this way, international debates interacted with the internal dynamics of the Colombian peace process, which had included the issue of illicit crops on the agenda as a stand-alone topic. That is why the context in which a regulation scheme may be forged includes the implementation of the Final Peace Agreement, particularly Chapter 1 on 'Comprehensive Rural Reform' and Chapter 4 on the 'Solution to the Illicit Drugs Problem'.

The Final Peace Agreement[15] recognised that the link between peasant families and illicit economies was based on factors such as the existence of an agricultural frontier, of settlements forgotten by the elite, high levels of unemployment, precarious family income and control by illegal groups.[16] Rural violence in the mid-20th century displaced large peasant populations, which moved into more isolated territories, and plants that had been declared illicit served to finance the population's stabilisation in these new areas.[17]

Although cannabis and coca have different histories, they share this context of 'State abandonment' of populations that ended up being criminalised by drug policies. The *bonanza marimbera*[18] that occurred between the 1960s and mid-1980s began when US agronomists brought seeds and technical assistance to La Guajira department of Colombia, in order to produce mythical marijuana strains such as 'Santa Marta Gold'. Although at the beginning, the *marimbera* economy used historical smuggling routes to transport the cannabis that was cultivated in other regions of the country, the needs of the business led to the creation of productive enclaves.[19] In 1980, the National Association of Financial Institutions reported that more than 40,000 families in the region were living off the crop, accumulating the earnings derived from this business.[20] The end of the bonanza resulted from the repression of marijuana trafficking and from the criminal transformation, which entailed moving into other regions and other drug markets, specifically cocaine.[21] While the United States and Colombia enforced the war on drugs on cannabis producers and traffickers, criminal networks in the United States chose to develop local production of the plant, thereby minimising transaction costs and risks.[22]

Cannabis crops became of secondary importance as of the mid-1980s as coca crops began to expand in Colombian territory.[23] Starting in the late 1970s, the department of Caquetá became the epicentre of the air bridge landing area for coca leaf and cocaine base paste being moved between Bolivia, Perú and Colombia. The drug cartels of that time were slowly able to set up laboratories and *cristalizaderos,*[24] extending to the areas reached by buyers from the Valle del Cauca and Antioquia, who later smuggled the drugs out for export to the United States. However, due to US cooperation, the governments of Bolivia, Perú and Colombia initiated the interdiction and shooting down of the planes loaded with cocaine base paste that were heading to Caquetá department.[25] The intervention of the Peruvian Air Bridge Denial Program in the first half of the 1990s was 'so successful' that coca crops were shifted to Caquetá and Putumayo, in Colombia.[26] By the end of that decade, the country was already facing the consequences of disputes between the FARC-EP and other actors in the drug trafficking chain, in addition to a resurgence of the armed conflict.

The relationship between armed groups, specifically FARC-EP, and drug trafficking made it necessary for drug policy to be included in the negotiations that led to the Final Peace Agreement. After overcoming the difficulties to have the Agreement and its regulatory mechanisms for implementation enter into force, in 2017 the Colombian government and the FARC-EP announced the start of implementation of Chapter 4, specifically of the National Comprehensive Program for the Substitution of Crops Used for Illicit Purposes.[27] The PNIS contemplated a payment of approximately 36 million pesos[28] to each family that registered with the Program, along with agreements on territorial development plans that would transform the conditions that were keeping peasant families economically dependent on coca and marijuana. However, this strategy's implementation has encountered administrative and budgetary problems, which created delays and a loss of trust among the peasant population that chose to abandon coca cultivation. According to the most recent report by the *Procuraduría General de la Nación* (PGN),[29] the PNIS is facing very serious budget limitations due to the cutbacks made to the programme each year. In 2019, the PNIS had a budget of 300.8 billion pesos,[30] whereas in 2020 that amount dropped to 191.0 billion pesos,[31] marking a 36% reduction in resources.[32] Meanwhile, the PGN affirms that from 2017 to 2021, 1.4 trillion pesos were invested in the PNIS, and 2.3 trillion pesos must still be allocated to fully implement the Program.[33]

The implementation of this programme requires a bigger budget and more institutional effort than crop eradication, a fact that influences the government's decision to prioritise the latter. The integration of families in economic circuits that would enable them to obtain similar or higher incomes to what they get from coca leaf or marijuana will not be possible if there is no land titling or clarification of property rights to the land, no means to transport products or no improvement in access to social rights.[34] That is the fabled 'territorial transformation' that has not been defined, or projected in the budget, to date.

Any cannabis regulation scheme that seeks to include peasants must learn from the processes that have been carried out before to include such populations in areas that rely on illegal economies. The epicentre of marijuana production for the illegal market is located in the Northern Cauca subregion, home to 55% of the light emission alerts recorded by the National Police in 2016.[35] The challenges centre around the lack of socio-economic conditions that would enable rural cannabis growers to produce marijuana using the quality standards required for the legal market. The five municipalities with the largest marijuana tracts have a high index of unmet basic needs, higher illiteracy rates and lower public services coverage.[36] The big question is whether in a scenario of regulating cannabis for adult recreational use, small-scale cannabis growers will be relegated again due to red tape and requirements they cannot fulfil, such as paying for costly licenses.[37] This was the situation that occurred in the process of regulating medical cannabis, which evolved in a way that favoured the interests of big companies. In fact, that regulatory framework tentatively included small growers, small manufacturers and patients/relatives. However, the main implementation challenge for peasants who cultivate marijuana lies in the high cost of legality, which has become a significant barrier to making the expensive leap to the regulated medical marijuana market.

Elements for Any Regulation: Fiscal Policy, Human Rights and Reparations

The regulation of marijuana Colombia-style cannot take place outside the context in which the war on this plant has occurred. Nor can it be decoupled from the past that peasant communities have inherited. We start with a simple premise: the pillars of cannabis regulation in Colombia must include reparations and social justice. That is the only way to promote the most affected populations' inclusion in the market, with human rights guarantees, and to create mechanisms for providing reparations to the victims of the war.

The regulatory process is organised based on the State's participation, to a greater or lesser extent, in defining the rules of the market, including the fiscal framework. It is there, in the rules to be established, that officials can design a regulatory model focused on reparations for the peasants who suffered under the war. This is not a new approach. Some jurisdictions that have regulated the cannabis market for adult use in the United States, such as Massachusetts or Illinois,[38] have used their regulations' fiscal policy as an opportunity to provide reparations to the African-American population, which was the most affected by the persecution and criminalisation stemming from prohibition.[39]

Fiscal policy, in addition to being a key instrument for guaranteeing rights through the provision of resources to finance them, is also subject to States' human rights-related commitments and obligations. This is understandable since human rights norms are recognised as a legal framework with which all State actions, including taxation and public spending, should comply.[40]

The reference point for this chapter is the *Principles for Human Rights in Fiscal Policy*.[41] This compendium of principles and guidelines, developed by experts in both fields, 'offers a clear framework, based on normative sources and other complementary documents, to design, implement and monitor fiscal policy' so that 'public and private economic actors can comply with their fiscal obligations and responsibilities'.[42] The principles are the result of a three-year process involving experts from the Americas with the aim of grouping a set of guidelines derived from human rights standards in the public expenditure field. The principles were launched in May 2021.

The content of these general principles could potentially be applied in a forthcoming regulation process to guide the rules for a post-prohibition world in which peasants are no longer stigmatised and persecuted, but instead receive reparations and are included in the new market. Out of all the principles set forth, we have chosen three that we consider applicable to designing fiscal policy in a scenario of regulating the cannabis market for adult use in Colombia[43].

Principle 3 talks about designing fiscal policy using principles of equality, equity and non-discrimination, so that taxes and public spending can be socially just. This principle can be understood as a call to the role of the State as the regulatory body for ending the structural discrimination that Colombian peasants have experienced, especially those who for decades depended on plants that had been declared illicit, in contexts of violence and material deprivation. Meanwhile, Principle 10 deepens this perspective by underscoring that it is the State's obligation to ensure, through tax levies, that it has the maximum amount of resources available to guarantee economic, social, cultural and environmental rights, particularly the rights of historically marginalised populations, such as Colombian peasants. In other words, any regulatory parameters or measures – such as the peasant population being subject to special protection, or the regulation of cannabis involving affirmative action for traditional growers – will be useless unless they are backed up with resources to enable their effective realisation in people's lives. Thus, under the guidance of

Principle 10, expenditure allocations must be aimed at ensuring the progressive realisation of the rights of peasants, which involves elements such as the construction and improvement of road infrastructure, conditions that facilitate commerce, the provision of public goods and decent health and educational services, among others.

Based on the principles above, talking about peasants' rights in a regulation scheme thus forces us to develop a framework of prioritised taxes and expenditures for contributing to closing the socio-economic gaps between Colombia's rural and urban areas. It also demands a remedy for the peasant and grower population's stigmatisation, criminalisation and socio-economic marginalisation in the country's distinct producer regions, seeking to promote equality – or level the playing field, if you will – in accordance with Principle 5.[44] In addition, affirmative action in the fiscal policies associated with marijuana regulation will enable peasants, with their knowledge and abilities, to be the protagonists of this nascent market and the beneficiaries of the fruit it bears.

The fiscal policy elements we have set forth acquire meaning as a function of the regulation's goals. Which is to say, the fiscal framework – taxes and expenditure allocations – must be geared towards achieving the regulation's goals. From our perspective, and as adapted to the Colombian context, we contend that a Colombian regulatory scheme should have at least four goals: (i) to reduce marijuana's comparative impact in illegal economies and drug trafficking networks; (ii) to protect public health; (iii) to promote rural development in priority areas; and (iv) to promote reparation measures financed with the resources raised through regulation.

In Colombia, the coexistence of various illicit economies and organised crime disputes over their profits and territories will continue to be a problem, particularly affecting the security and integrity of the peasants who live in the regions where these economies operate. A regulated market must wrest users and clients away from illegality, aspiring to have an impact on reducing the size of the illegal market, which will siphon off resources from a sector of organised crime. This, in turn, will have effects on peasants' daily lives. Again, this goal must be treated in a nuanced way given the complexity of the local situation, and in that sense, managing expectations is crucial.

Furthermore, any regulation in Colombia must strive to promote rural development in certain regions, especially the ones negatively affected by marijuana prohibition due to their historical context. Cannabis is a plant that has a particular historical significance. What we know today as drug trafficking developed out of the first *bonanza marimbera* of the 1970s, and in some sense, the war on this plant served to cut off the places where illicit crops were cultivated from rural and institutional development. As mentioned in the previous section, the gaps in socio-economic conditions are dramatic, and one of the goals of cannabis regulation must be to close these gaps through specific budgetary allocations and the creation of incentives for rural development in these regions.

Finally, any regulation scheme should have a focus on reparations, and to that end must generate income and revenue to finance such measures. This also requires identifying the victims of prohibition in a precise way, particularly the peasant populations whose territories were militarised in a scenario of violence between distinct armed groups. This regulation with a focus on reparations should therefore pursue measures and affirmative action to ensure that the victims who want to enter the market have the guarantees they need to do so, and also to collectively repair the damage that was caused. These reparation measures, under the overarching goal of social justice, should be financed with the revenue raised under the new regulation scheme, and that is where the principles of fiscal justice and human rights provide the necessary signposts.

Final Reflections

Striving for a regulation that would transform structural conditions of marginalisation and poverty is both ambitious and necessary. Its design will also require striking a delicate balance between the need to fund social policy and the need to invite users to the legal market, thus, to prevent the emergence of parallel markets, or a widening of gaps for the peasant population. The following is needed to achieve these goals: (i) mobilising resources through taxes on the regulated cannabis market and (ii) allocating resources in a prioritised and progressive fashion, as proposed by the principles for human rights in fiscal policy.

The market's regulatory rules, and their fiscal policies in particular, set the tone for the regulation scheme because they define the type of expenditures and their redistributive orientation. In a country that is implementing a Peace Agreement today, with various illegal armed groups still disputing drug trafficking profits and routes, and with peasants who are fighting for a fairer world in their territories, marijuana regulation cannot replicate the errors of prohibition and treat these farmers as simply suppliers of raw material. It is precisely fiscal policy that can gear the regulation scheme towards including peasants as key actors in the nascent market.

In the case of Colombia, we suggest that direct taxes should be applied to this market (income tax on the companies that operate in any of the phases of the market's value chain) along with indirect taxes on the sale or consumption of cannabis products. The indirect taxes in the Colombian Tax Code (*Estatuto Tributario*) that could be applied to such products include the value-added tax (VAT) and sales tax. Taking into account that the latter levy applies to the consumption of goods that are not considered to be part of the basic needs basket, its rate varies between 4%, 8% and 16% and is applied in addition to the VAT. Policymakers could also exact specific taxes on the consumption of this type of product, echoing what is done with other products that can be harmful to people's health, such as tobacco and alcohol.

However, it is important to consider the Colombian context, where the cost of cannabis production for the illegal market is very low. If numerous indirect taxes are applied, it will be very difficult to compete with the prices in the illegal market, and therefore, the displacement of this market will be ineffective. That is why we propose that the application of indirect taxes – such as the VAT and a specific tax on consumption – be carried out gradually, in accordance with how implementation of the regulation scheme progresses and the extent to which production costs decline.[45] That way, there will be time and the capacity to capture the market that is currently in the hands of illicit economies.

The opportunity for reparation in a post-prohibition world lies precisely in collecting these taxes and allocating expenditures. This is not just about providing raisable funds from the taxes collected by the nascent industry offering marijuana for adult use. On the contrary, it entails a paradigm shift in Colombia's relationship to cannabis, and to other drugs that have been declared illicit. In that sense, an end to the war on drugs is needed in the country in order to move towards a different relationship with substances. The actions that would help achieve this shift must be seen as symbolic reparation, and an acknowledgement of the errors and harmful undertakings of the State as it implemented public policy.

A focus on reparations in cannabis regulation should take into account the difficulty of repairing the damage, considering the scope of drug policy impact, as well as personal, community-wide, regional or collective harms. In the case of peasants, we can affirm that the effects were both individual and community wide. This population was harassed, their income capacity was reduced, and at the same time their communities suffered collective impacts, living for years in the crossfire as a result of the wars on drug traffickers and on plants.

This focus on reparations could be developed in coordination with the funding of the Development Programs with a Territorial-Based Focus (*Programas de Desarrollo con enfoque territorial* or PDETs)[46] in areas that produce cannabis, and even with the presence of the coca economy, so as to deepen territorial transformation and support the regulation's progress along the path taken to implement Chapters 1 and 4 of the Final Peace Agreement.[47] This financing could also include technical assistance to improve cannabis production practices in rural areas, through support for associative schemes and investment subsidies for small-scale producers. The inclusion of cannabis growers with small plots should entail differentiated fees for licenses of any kind, so that costs are not a barrier to entering the market.

Finally, the transition from war to peace in Colombia is a critical source of hope with regard to both the armed conflict and the violence associated with prohibition, so that imagining a world of regulation is to imagine and give substance to that world along with the peasants who sustain production of these plants.

Notes

1 From the 1960s onwards, Colombia lived through an internal armed conflict, with a number of insurgent guerrillas, such as FARC-EP, ELN, EPL and M-19.

2 Colombia's Constitutional Court (*Corte Constitucional*) affirms that a subject of special Constitutional protection is one that in collective terms deserves special treatment by public authorities due to historical and structural conditions of inequality. This concept arises from an interpretation of Article 13 of the Constitution, which establishes that the State must promote 'the conditions so that equality can be real and effective and will adopt measures in favor of discriminated or marginalized groups'.

3 This is not the only population in Colombia that has been affected negatively by drug policies. Women have been incarcerated at an alarming rate, poor people who use drugs are targeted heavily by the police, among many differentiated impacts of Colombia's war on drugs.

4 This Agreement was signed after four years of negotiations in Havana, putting an end to the conflict between the Colombian State and the longest-standing guerrilla group on the continent. The Agreement has six chapters, one of which focuses exclusively on the issue of illicit drugs, including a national programme for the substitution of illicit crops.

5 United Nations Office on Drugs and Crime, *World Drug Report 2021: Booklet 4 – Drug Market Trends: Cocaine, Amphetamine-Type Stimulants* (United Nations, 2021) 103.

6 Juan Gabriel Tokatlian, 'El plan Colombia: ¿un modelo de intervención?' (2001) 54–55 *Revista CIDOB d'Afers Internacionals* 203, 209.

7 Ministerio de Justicia y del Derecho, *Sistema de información de Drogas de Colombia* (SIDCO) <www.minjusticia.gov.co/programas-co/ODC/Paginas/SIDCO.aspx> accessed 16 January 2023.

8 Rodrigo Uprimny Yepes, Sergio Chaparro Hernández & Luis Felipe Cruz Oliveria, 'Delitos de drogas y sobredosis carcelaria en Colombia' (Dejusticia, 2017) 34, 50.

9 *Grupo Información de Criminalidad* (GICRI) de la Policía Nacional.

10 Luis Felipe Cruz and Isabel Pereira Arana,'Laberintos de prohibición y regulación: Los grises de la marihuana en Colombia' (Dejusticia, 2021) 106.

11 This assumes that marijuana seizures represent 5% and 10%, respectively. The amount of pesos involved is equivalent to between USD $583.1 million and USD $1.17 billion, using the official Colombian exchange rate (known as TRM) from October 2021.

12 Departamento Nacional de Planeación, 'Narcomenudeo en Colombia: Una transformación de la economía criminal' (Departamento Nacional de Planeación, 2017) 116.

13 The United Nations General Assembly Special Session (UNGASS) is the main policy-making space at the UN level and holds thematic meetings periodically. The 2016 edition was the special session on the world drug problem, promoted by the governments of Colombia, Mexico and Guatemala in an attempt to reform existing drug policies.

14 John Mullholland, 'Juan Manuel Santos: "It Is Time to Think Again about the War on Drugs"', *The Observer* (12 November 2011).

15 Government of the Republic of Colombia and FARC-EP (Fuerzas Armadas Revolucionarias de Colombia – Ejército del Pueblo), *Final Agreement to End the Armed Conflict and Build a Stable and Lasting Peace* (2016).

16 Jorge Giraldo-Ramírez, Marcela Barón, Gustavo Duncan, Ana Maria Jaramillo & Alberto Naranjo, *Economía criminal en Antioquia y Valle de Aburrá: Una aproximación* (2010) 17.

17 Luis Felipe Cruz Olivera and Sergio Chaparro Hernández, 'Coca, instituciones y desarrollo: Los retos de los municipios productores en el posacuerdo' (Dejusticia, 2017) 45.

18 'Marimbera' is an adjective used to describe things related to marijuana, which is known in local slang as "marimba". The *bonanza marimbera* refers to the boom period for this economy in Colombia between the 1960s and 1980s.

19 Lina M Britto, 'A Trafficker's Paradise: The "War on Drugs" and the New Cold War in Colombia' (2010) 1 *Contemporánea: Historia y Problemas Del Siglo* 159, 166.

20 Asociación Nacional de Instituciones Financieras, 'La legalización de la marihuana (Serie Estudios ANIF)' (Asociación Nacional de Instituciones Financieras, 1980) 22.

21 Eduardo Rovner Sáenz, *Conexión Colombia: Una historia del narcotráfico entre los años 30 y los años 90* (Editorial Planeta, 2021) 66–70.

22 Cruz and Pereira (n 10) 48.
23 Sáenz (n 21) 81–83.
24 A *cristalizadero* is a makeshift laboratory used to transform cocaine base paste into cocaine hydrochloride.
25 Theo Roncken, 'The Drug War in the Skies. The US "Air Bridge Denial" Strategy: The Success of a Failure' (Transnational Institute, 1999).
26 Darren C Huskisson, 'The Air Bridge Denial Program and the Shootdown of Civil Aircraft under International Law' (LLM thesis, McGill University, 2004) 14.
27 *Programa Nacional Integral de Sustitución de Cultivos de Uso Ilícito*, PNIS.
28 USD $9,500 using the TRM from October 2021.
29 The PGN is an autonomous body of the Colombian government charged with overseeing compliance with public functions and exercising disciplinary control over state officials.
30 USD $79.8 million using the TRM from October 2021.
31 USD $50.6 million using the TRM from October 2021.
32 Procuraduría General de la Nación, 'Tercer informe al Congreso sobre el estado de avance de la implementación del Acuerdo de paz' (Procuraduría General de la Nación, 2021) 718.
33 Ibid.
34 Maria Clara Torres Bustamante, 'La coca campesina en Colombia: Un desafío para el posconflicto' (Desarrollo y paz territorial con dignidad, participación, solidaridad. Sabemos cómo, 2017).
35 United Nations Office on Drugs and Crime (n 5) 116.
36 Alejandro Rodríguez-Llach, Luis Felipe Cruz-Olivera & Isabel Pereira-Arana, 'Fiscal Policy in the Regulation of Adult-Use Cannabis in Colombia' (Dejusticia, 2022) 6.
37 Cruz and Pereira (n 10) 136.
38 See Chapter 1, 'Towards Transformative Drug Policy Reform', and Chapter 4, 'Lessons Learned from Legal Regulation of Cannabis'.
39 Harvey Slade, 'Altered States: Cannabis Regulation in the US' (Transform Drug Policy Foundation, 2020) 21–26.
40 D Blanco, et al, *Principles for Human Rights in Fiscal Policy* (Initiative for Human Rights Principles in Fiscal Policy, 2021) 4.
41 Ibid.
42 Ibid, 6.
43 There are other principles that are pertinent to the debate on regulation, particularly in reference to the reduction of externalities and the need to manage, via taxes, the possible public health consequences of consumption. We do not mention these in this text because they are unrelated to the rights of the peasant population.
44 Principle No. 5, in the same vein as Principle No. 3, alludes to the State's responsibility to use fiscal measures that would contribute to eliminating structural inequalities and discrimination in all its forms, utilising a differentiated approach.
45 Beau Kilmer, 'How Will Cannabis Legalization Affect Health, Safety, and Social Equity Outcomes? It Largely Depends on the 14 Ps' (2019) 45 *The American Journal of Drug and Alcohol Abuse* 664.; Slade (n 39) 10.
46 The Development Programs with a Territorial-Based Focus (*Programas de Desarrollo con enfoque territorial*, PDET) are one of the components of Chapter 1 on Comprehensive Rural Reform in the Final Peace Agreement signed by the Government of Colombia and the FARC-EP in 2016. They seek to close the development gap that persists in many rural

areas of the country due to the armed conflict, using various rural development measures that are adapted to the needs of each region.

47 Chapter 4 of the Agreement is entitled 'Solution to the Illicit Drugs Problem', and it includes the National Comprehensive Program for the substitution of illicit crops. It is worth noting that its implementation has been centred on the coca-growing population and has not covered the peasants who cultivate marijuana.

11 Are Coca Crops Causing Deforestation in Colombia?

Would a Future Regulated Market Impact the Environment?*

María Alejandra Vélez

Introduction

The impact of illicit drug production, in particular cocaine, has been mostly studied and debated as a security problem with social and development consequences.[1] This has also been the case for the potential benefits of a new regulated market. Expected benefits have been discussed in terms of human rights, reduction of violence and public health, among others. However, in this debate, less attention has been devoted to the interaction between illicit drug production and the environment,[2] and the potential benefits or risks of a new regulated market.[3]

From an environmental standpoint, illicit drug production and drug policy can lead to a broad array of negative impacts, with complex interactions. Environmental impacts of cocaine production include deforestation[4] or land grabbing[5] due to production and commercialisation of illicit crops, and water and soil pollution due to cultivation of illicit crops and production of synthetic drugs,[6] among others. In this chapter the focus is the forest impacts of coca crops used to produce cocaine in Colombia, a global illegal commodity with a market estimated at 20 million consumers worldwide.[7]

Ninety per cent of the cocaine consumed in the world is produced from coca crops in Colombia, one of the most biodiverse countries on the planet. In 2020, there was an estimated 143,000 hectares of coca crops with more than 120,000 households in the country directly associated with crop cultivation. Twenty-nine per cent of coca crops in the country are located in strategic and protected environmental areas[8]: 4.4% of coca crops are in National Parks; 9% in collective property of indigenous communities; and 16% in collective property of Afro-Colombian Communities. Thus, the potential effect of coca crops on the environment is not a minor issue, based on the importance of these areas for biodiversity and forest conservation. Deforestation and water and soil pollution due to the chemicals[9] and products used to produce cocaine are some of the potential problems associated with this activity.[10]

However, there is a complex relationship between coca and deforestation, and according to the academic literature coca crops are not always a direct driver.[11] Furthermore, it is not the most important driver of deforestation at the national

DOI: 10.4324/9781003169765-16

level, and there are regional heterogeneities. Punitive drug policy itself could be causing more deforestation than does coca cultivation.[12] One example is the impact of aerial spraying with herbicides to eradicate coca crops, which has negative effects on soil and water sources, is toxic to macro- and microorganisms and has consequences on the health of plants and animals.[13] It also causes crop displacement,[14] pressuring farmers to move their planting activity to more remote locations, thus expanding logging further into the forest or upstream.[15]

Forced aerial eradication in the Colombian case exposed farmers to respiratory and dermatological problems and to a greater risk of miscarriage in women.[16] Also, recent studies report direct and indirect effects of aerial fumigation and armed conflict on coca crops and deforestation. Davalos and co-authors report that aerial fumigation is positively correlated with conflict which in turn explains part of the observed deforestation.[17]

In this chapter I provide a review of recent scientific literature that explores the relationship between coca cultivation and deforestation in Colombia and discuss the potential benefits or risks of an eventual new regulated market on the environment. Historically, coca crops are not the main driver of deforestation in Colombia and the relationship between coca cultivation and deforestation is mainly indirect. Nevertheless, I will show how coca crops are expanding into environmental strategic areas which require a reoriented drug policy that considers the environmental dimension. However, any effort to include environmental requirements under a prohibitionist framework would fall short. I discussed how a regulated market, if design properly with social and environmental requirements, could solve some of the environmental impacts of coca crops including the expansion in protected areas.

Deforestation in Colombia: What Do the Official Figures Show? What Is the Relation with Coca Crops?

According to a study conducted by the Institute of Hydrology, Meteorology and Environmental Studies (IDEAM), the Ministry of Environment and Sustainable Development and the UN-REDD Colombia Program which examines the main causes and agents of deforestation in the country, it was estimated that approximately 1.5 million hectares of forest, the equivalent to more than 2.1 million soccer fields, had been lost in Colombia between 2005 and 2015. During this period, the country's forest cover was reduced by 1.4%, with the Caribbean and the Andes being the regions with the highest degree of absolute losses. In terms of total area, the regions that lost the most forest during this period were the Pacific, the Amazon and the Caribbean. The report also indicates that between 2005 and 2012 the forest cover was converted mostly into grasslands (50% of the territory), followed by shrublands (28%), crops (7%) and pastures (5%).[18] In 2018, Colombia's deforested area measured 197,159 hectares, 10% less than in 2017 (219,973 hectares).[19] By 2020, deforestation was measured in 171.685 hectares, 7.5% directly associated to coca cultivation and 22% indirectly associated with coca crops.[20]

When discussing the effect of coca crops, it is worth differentiating the ways to quantify the forest damage that they cause: deforestation, degradation, forest affectation and deforestation associated indirectly with coca cultivation.[21] The first refers to the direct conversion of natural forest cover into coca crops in a given period; the second is the continuous reduction of forest's capacities due to the establishment of coca crops; the third is the total loss of forest cover and the continuous reduction of the forest's capacities due to the establishment of coca cultivation (a combination of the two previously described); and lastly, the loss of forest cover in areas surrounding the forest that has already been affected by coca cultivation (at a distance of 1 km), due to the presence of anthropogenic activities prompted by the appearance of this crop.

The cultivation of illicit crops, mainly coca crops, is considered a direct driver when it leads to the logging of forest cover (generally primary forests) and indiscriminate burning. Coca crops also have an indirect impact on forest destruction because they allow the arrival of other productive activities that exert a greater direct impact. For example, the construction of clandestine roads and airstrips, and the accelerated transformation of the forest into agriculture and/or livestock farming land, in order to launder assets.[22] According to the German Corporation for International Cooperation (GIZ), although the direct effect is rather low in Colombia, coca indeed acts as a 'spearhead' because it spurs surrounding areas towards other activities that result in significant forest cover loss.[23]

Visually, it is possible to establish that the presence of deforestation and coca cultivation is concentrated in specific areas of the territory, with clear spatial heterogeneities within the departments. Maps 11.1 and 11.2 compare the presence of coca and/or deforestation by highlighting Colombia's special management zones between 2016 and 2018.[24] These maps show a complex relationship between coca and deforestation. In some regions, both phenomena are concentrated in the same area. In others, coca is concentrated in formerly deforested sites. In others still, deforestation is not associated with coca cultivation. For the most part, it would seem that the special management zones set limits to the expansion of these phenomena.

The academic literature has used different statistical tools to ponder and establish significance between multiple variables (e.g. presence of coca crops, distance to roads, distance to municipal capitals, presence of illegal armed groups, among others) in order to explain deforestation and thus determine its direct causes and underlying mechanisms in the Colombian context.

A study conducted at municipal level concluded that between 1990 and 2005 coca cultivation was not significant enough to explain deforestation at the national level, yet it was significant, at the regional level, for the Caribbean and Orinoco.[25] Likewise, another study uses grid-level data and discriminates by region to show that proximity to new coca fields and a higher density of coca crops increased the probability of deforestation in southern Colombia only between 2002 and 2007.[26] However, for the total number of municipalities and during this same period, neither eradication nor coca cultivation predicted the country's deforestation rates. This shows that the deforestation process in Colombia is not homogeneous. It depends on regional differences and different stages of socio-economic development.

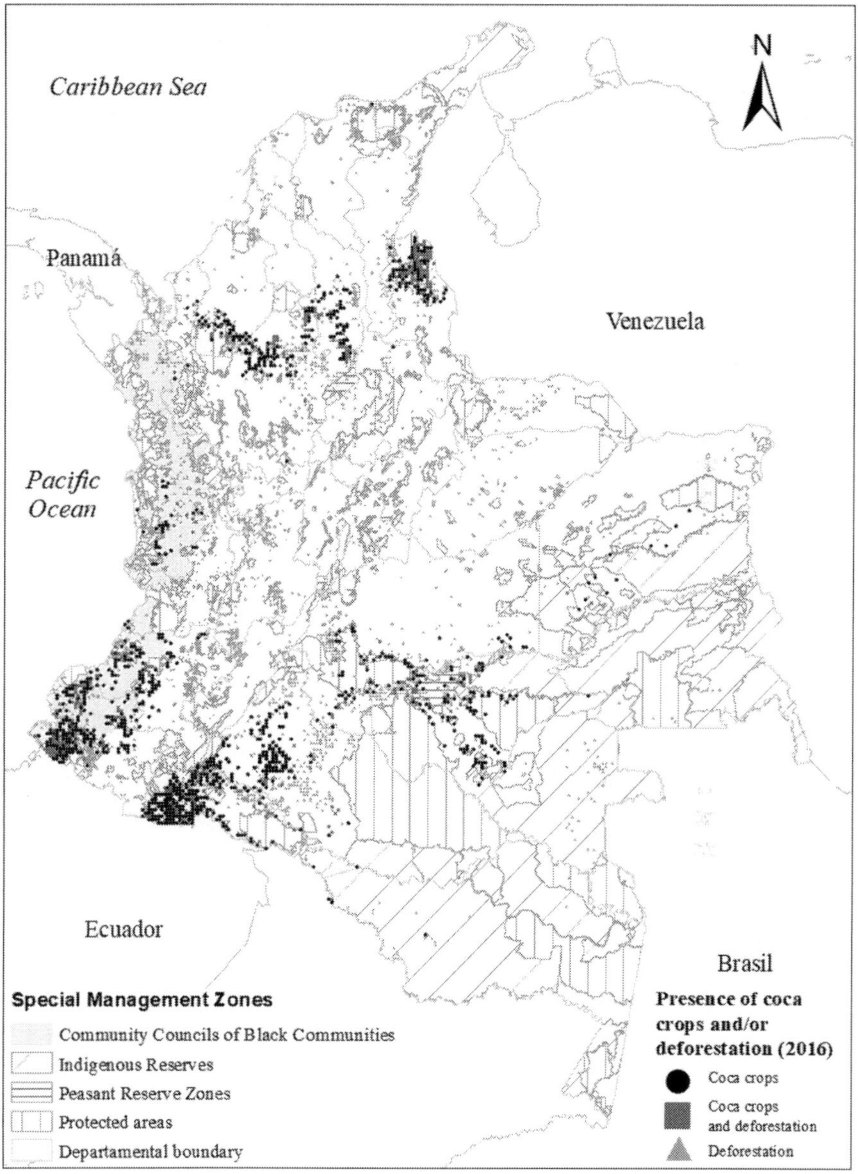

Map 11.1 Presence of coca and/or deforestation according to special management zones in Colombia, 2016.

Source: Based on data from the Forest and Carbon Monitoring System (SMBYC-IDEAM) and the Integrated Illicit Crop Monitoring System (SIMCI-UNODC).

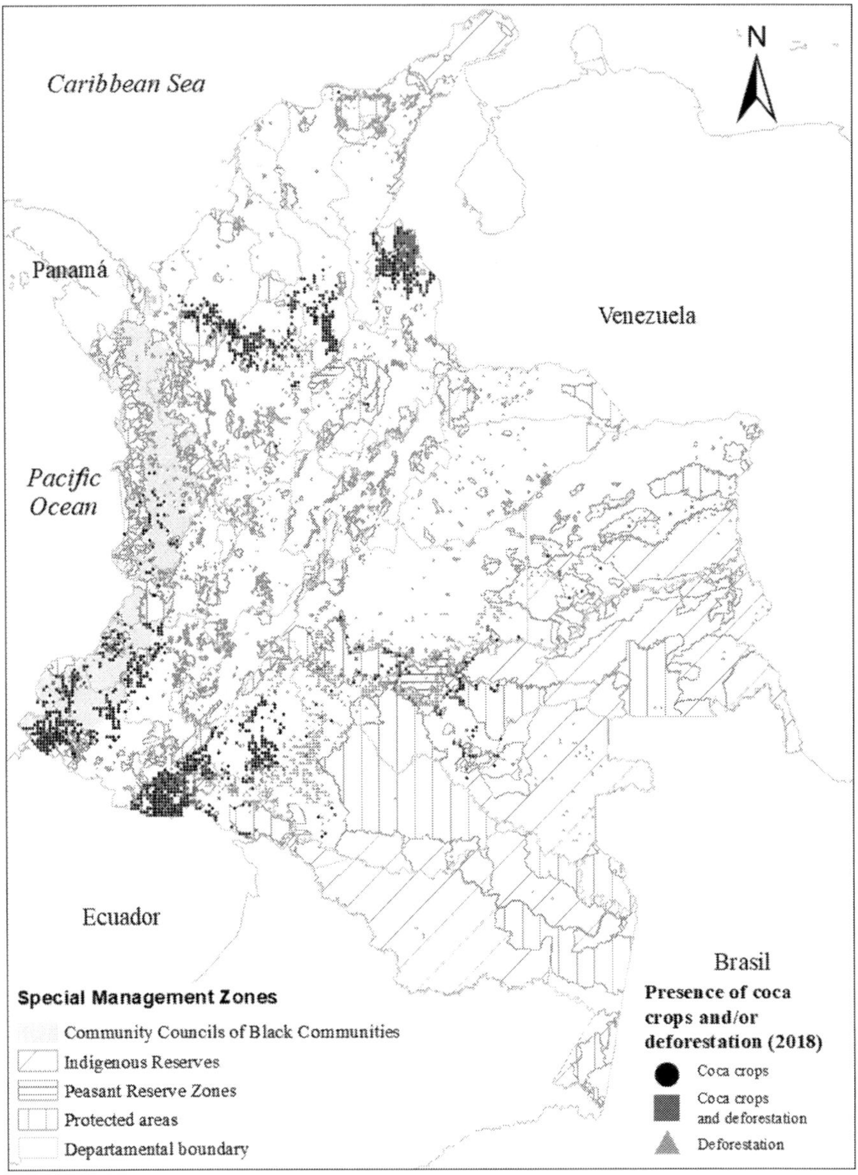

Map 11.2 Presence of coca and/or deforestation according to special management zones in Colombia, 2018.

Source: Based on data from the Forest and Carbon Monitoring System (SMBYC-IDEAM) and the Integrated Illicit Crop Monitoring System (SIMCI-UNODC).

On the other hand, through spatial statistical analysis conducted at the municipal level, Rincón-Ruiz and co-authors point to an inverse relationship between the percentage area of coca crops within a municipality, and the percentage of primary forest areas in the departments of Putumayo and Caquetá in 2001.[27] Furthermore, in 2008 this relationship was also found in Nariño, Cauca, Córdoba, Antioquia, Norte de Santander and Bolívar, due to possible effects of the spraying policy applied to Putumayo and Caquetá, which displaced the crops to these new zones. These results are consistent with the findings of Dávalos and co-authors.[28]

In a more recent period of 2011–2017, using a proxy for coca cultivation (climatic and coca soil suitability), Prem, Saavedra and Vargas found no differential effect of this crop to explain higher deforestation in municipalities in which the Revolutionary Armed Forces of Colombia (FARC) were present, after the ceasefire agreed during the government of Juan Manuel Santos.[29] Finally, Negret and co-authors assert that, although proximity to coca plantations exhibited a positive relationship with deforestation between 2000 and 2010 at grid level, its explanatory power upon excluding this variable and any other related to the armed conflict only generated a 3% loss in the predictive capacity of the full model (78% accuracy), which indicates its low level of relevance.[30]

Recent analysis explores the frontier dynamics of forests, coca and conflict as key variables to understand the deforestation of the Colombian Amazon area.[31] The authors show that illicit coca cultivation is directly associated with grassland grow and both illicit coca cultivation and eradication by aerial fumigation (but not manual eradication) are directly associated with the proliferation of armed conflict, which, in turn, is correlated with deforestation. Thus, the relationship between coca cultivation and deforestation is indirect and secondary to the overall push of the agricultural frontier into pristine forest. Thus, as Dávalos and co-authors rightly point out, the expansion of coca itself is an indication of an agricultural frontier: coca seems to be a symptom, not the ultimate cause of deforestation.[32]

However, as shown by recent data, the expansion of these crops into areas of environmental importance, such as protected areas, collective territories and indigenous reserves [*resguardos*], is of much concern, which is addressed below.

Coca in Protected Areas, Collective Territories and Reserves

The expansion of illicit crops in protected areas in different parts of the world, including the United States, has been debated in the literature.[33] Colombia, the world's most important producer of cocaine, has also been identified as an environmental problem. According to data from the Integrated Illicit Crop Monitoring System,[34] between 29% and 30% of coca crops are located in special management zones: the National System of Protected Areas (SINAP), which include, for example, natural parks and nature reserves, managed at national and regional levels; community councils of black communities; indigenous reserves; and peasant reserve zones (see Maps 11.1 and 11.2). By 2018, the proportion of each of these territories with respect to the total coca planted in the country was less than 16%, and with respect to total deforestation in the country was less than 10%, approximately (see Figure 11.1). Community councils, indigenous reserves and

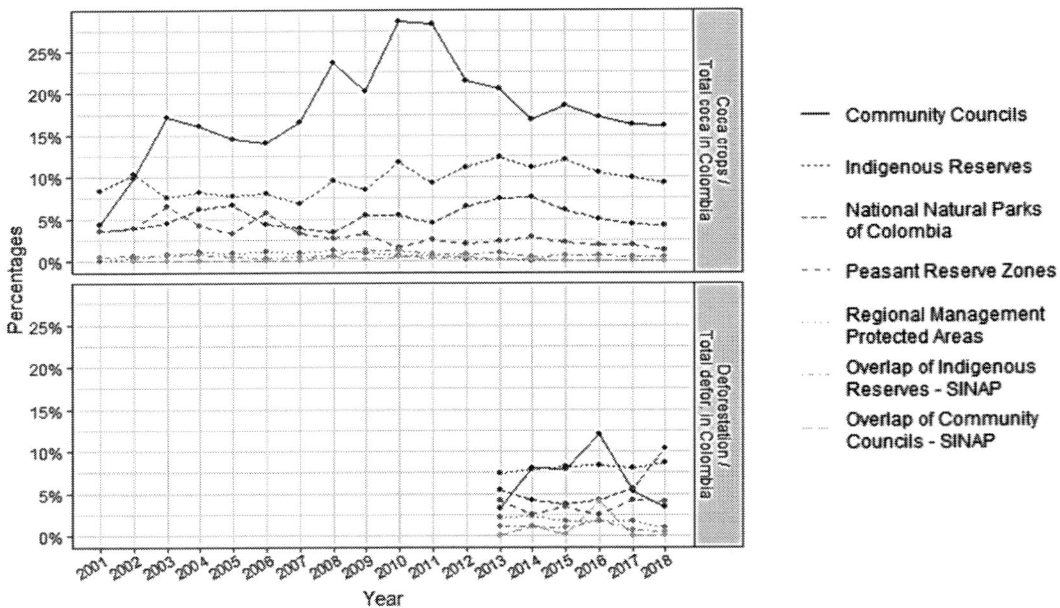

Figure 11.1 Time series of coca cultivation and deforestation in special management zones, in relative values.

Source: Authors based on data from the Forest and Carbon Monitoring System (SMBYC-IDEAM) and the Integrated Illicit Crop Monitoring System (SIMCI-UNODC).

national protected areas have played a key role in containing deforestation in general and, more specifically, in preventing deforestation from illicit crops. Vélez and co-authors showed that collective titling to community councils in the Pacific decreases deforestation significantly and represents an over 27% reduction in the deforestation rates that would have resulted without land titling.[35] Another study found that national protected areas, indigenous reserves and community councils reduced deforestation by 0.011, 0.016 and 0.024 ha/km^2/year respectively, equivalent to a reduction of 5.1%, 8.1% and 26.7%, in comparison to the control groups' means.[36] However, they report that national protected areas had a positive and significant effect on the presence of coca crops, while community councils and indigenous reserves significantly reduced illicit crops, even in remote areas. Hence, in contexts where State presence is weak, it seems that ethnic territories can limit the cultivation of illicit crops. Previous articles highlight the role of the community organisation that defines rules for the communal use of its resources and is able to resist or, at the least, set a ceiling on the expansion of illicit crops, as is the case for the community councils of black communities.[37]

Despite these findings, Figure 11.2 shows that black communities, indigenous reserves and national natural parks reported a strong growth on coca crops since 2013 (27,197.5, 15,719.4 and 6,966.7 hectares, respectively, for 2018[38]). However, with the exception of the indigenous reserves, these trends do not seem to be clearly related to the deforestation series calculated with data obtained from the Forest and Carbon Monitoring System (SMBYC-IDEAM) for these same territories.[39]

By disaggregating these series by department (see Figure 11.3), it is possible to more precisely explore the spatiotemporal differences that exist between these two variables in these areas of the country. In the case of community councils, Nariño's high concentration of coca shows a growth trend similar to that of the deforested area only up to 2016. In Chocó, by contrast, it is likely that deforestation is due to causes other than illicit crops (e.g. illegal mining). The indigenous communities in Nariño also concentrate a significant number of coca-cultivated hectares, yet their deforested areas seem to be spread among the departments of the Amazonian Region. On the other hand, the constant growth of deforestation in national natural parks is alarming. However, this is mostly concentrated in the department of Meta, and its values bear little relation to the patterns of coca cultivation. Finally, although there are only seven officially constituted peasant reserves in the country, special attention should be paid to deforestation in Guaviare and coca cultivation in Putumayo.

What Actions to Take and What Can Be Expected in a Regulated Market?

Although there are other direct and more important causes that may explain the country's recent deforestation,[40] the indirect effects of illicit crops and their recent expansion into special protection categories require environmental policy and drug policy to be aligned.[41] Otherwise, the force of illegal economies and the interfaces between both licit and illicit economies will continue to push the agricultural frontier, causing irreversible deforestation and environmental degradation.

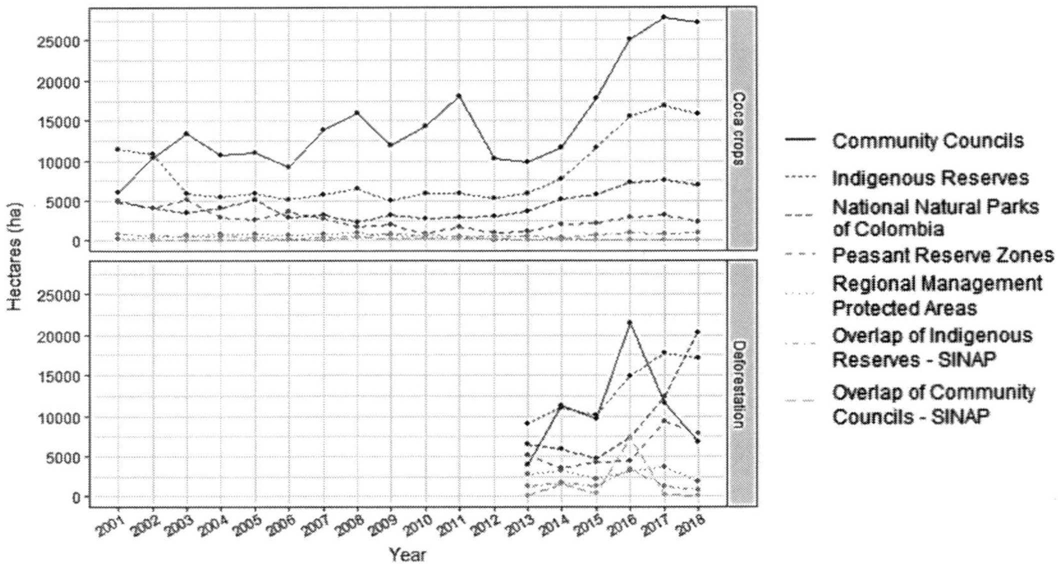

Figure 11.2 Time series of coca cultivation and deforestation in special management zones, in absolute values.

Source: Authors based on data from the Forest and Carbon Monitoring System (SMBYC-IDEAM) and the Integrated Illicit Crop Monitoring System (SIMCI-UNODC).

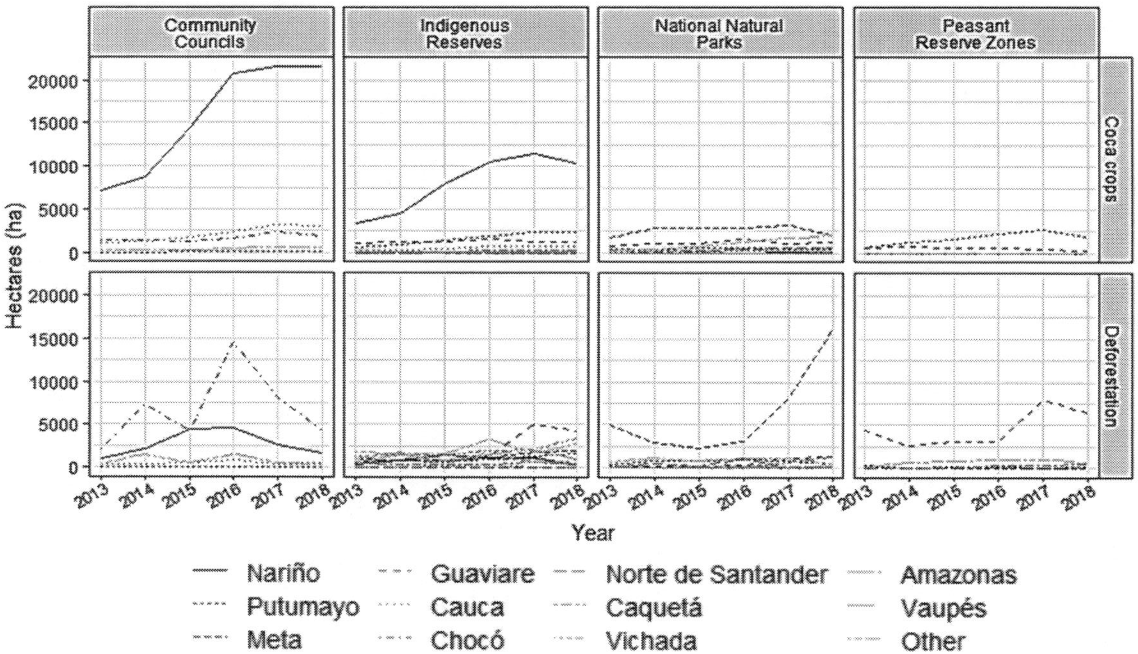

Figure 11.3 Time series of coca cultivation and deforestation in special management zones, in absolute values disaggregated by department.

Source: Authors based on data from the Forest and Carbon Monitoring System (SMBYC-IDEAM) and the Integrated Illicit Crop Monitoring System (SIMCI-UNODC).

Public policies aiming at reducing illicit crops in Colombia and beyond have assumed that the effectiveness of the so-called 'war on drugs' depends exclusively on the State's monitoring and strength (through forced eradication or aerial spraying) or by the implementation of alternative development programmes, causing in some cases further environmental problems. For example, as has been documented by Grillo and others in Peru, the implementation of alternative development programmes after forced eradication of coca crops has had both social and environmental impacts.[42] First, access to this programme has only been successful for the farmers who have the economic resources to handle the costs of crop replacement. Thus, marginalised growers, who have not been able to harvest other licit crops, lose the income for their livelihoods or keep investing on coca crops that will later be eradicated numerous times. Regarding environmental impacts, coca producers who do not benefit from the alternative development programme but are forced to eradicate, expand their crops to other territories. The impact of coca crops on deforestation in Peru is low, as only 2.3% of the deforestation in the country was caused by coca cultivations between 2001 and 2013. Instead, the major cause of deforestation in regions where this replacement crop programme has been implemented is due to licit crops, such as cacao, coffee and oil palm that have been promoted by the alternative development programme to reduce coca crops in the country.[43] This case portrays how 'drug policy, due to its historical disconnect from sustainable development and environmental policy, has often failed to rein in – if not actively facilitated and rewarded – poor environmental practices'.[44]

In contrast with the top-down drug regulations approach, the expansion of coca crops on special environmental management zones for the Colombian case, including collective ethnic lands, suggests a complementary path including sustainable and inclusive practices, by investing in the communities' organisational capacity to strengthen local leadership and community resistance.[45] Also, to promote sustainable practices, alternative development programmes should include an environmental differential approach where the focus is not substituting one product for another but valuing ecosystem services provision with a regional focus. The implementation of payments for environmental services (PES), for example, should be assessed as a complementary tool to the country's anti-drug policies.[46] PES, broadly understood as a voluntary and decentralised environmental policy instrument, has been implemented worldwide in more than 60 countries and 550 programmes.[47] It promotes forest conservation and the provision of ecosystem services by creating a new market in which buyers (global or local) of ecosystem services (e.g. carbon sequestration and storage, biodiversity protection, among others) pay landowners conditionally on conserving or providing ecosystem services.[48] Peasants dedicated to cultivating coca crops could be beneficiaries of these type of programmes when coca crops are cultivated in environmental strategic areas. Environmental requirements, thus, should be included on this new and more ambitious alternative development programmes.[49]

However, any effort to include environmental requirements under a prohibitionist framework would fall short. These programmes are not going to solve the problem of illicit crops, and the illegal nature of this market makes more difficult to include the environmental dimension in the cultivation process and other parts of the value chain. Thus, an obvious question is raised: Would a regulated market benefit the environment and in particular forest conservation?

At this point, any argument regarding the environmental impacts of a future cocaine-regulated market is speculative.[50] But lessons from the new regulated market of cannabis in the United States and other regions of the world might give us some ideas about the future that could be faced by a regulated coca and cocaine market.

In the case of cannabis, according to Zuleta and co-authors,[51] the main environmental concerns for illegal cannabis crops are their high-water requirements, the high-energy consumption of indoor crops, the use of pesticides and the deforestation promoted by illegal cultivation in areas of high environmental value. The latter two are also a concern for the coca crops. In the region of the Rif in Morocco, for example, where marijuana production is illegal, cannabis growers have implemented intensive practices that deteriorate the environment because of the pressures of the international market that enhances an industrial production of the plant.[52] Also, cannabis growers have been able to hoard water reservoirs to maintain the cultivation of hybrid species, which demand a higher provision of water. Thus, large-scale producers have been able to control every stage of the chain of cannabis cultivation, including the management of water sources. Furthermore, in Morocco, cannabis growers have disagreed on the debate in favour of legal medicinal and industrial use of cannabis, as this will diminish their power in the supply chain.[53]

A regulated market could address some of those issues.[54] Regulation, for example, could lead to a decline in illegal crops in protected areas or national forests as growers no longer need to move to places with less monitoring, as happened in the cannabis industry in California.[55] However, it is worth noticing that the net effect of a future regulated market, at least based on the cannabis case in the United States, would probably depend on tax levels and profit margins.[56] Of course, some illegal trading to avoid taxes and strict regulation might continue given that criminal structures are well established, so it would not be a perfect scenario.[57] But some improvements are expected. Under a legal regulation framework, for example, cannabis growers can also produce in greenhouses that consume up to 90% less energy than indoor crops and is more productive than outdoors.[58] However, as in any other agricultural industry, strong rules and a regulatory framework are necessary to include environmental practices as a requirement to access markets and acquire producing licenses. A legal market does not necessarily guarantee sustainable practices or reduced deforestation as has been the case with other agro-industrial activities around the world or with formalisation of illegal gold mining activities in the Peruvian Amazon.[59] In the cannabis industry, for example, a shift towards an intensive monoculture for exports could have new environmental threats and pressure over the land and water resources if it is not regulated correctly.[60] In 1996, when the medicinal use of marijuana was legalised in California, energy consumption increased and production processes were industrialised.[61] Thus, a new regulated drug market must include clear monitoring to enforce environmental regulations.[62]

In a new legal market, some special market and certification schemes that value even more strict social and environmental responsible practices (such as zero use of chemical pesticides) could also be developed to decrease environmental damage.[63] For example, in California, appellations or certified designation of originhave been assigned to local crops to avoid the commoditisation of marijuana and thus promote small-scale production, which can bring environmental benefits as well.[64] Thus, they increase the value of a strain in the market, by providing the rural grower a monopolistic power over the crop cultivated in a specific geographic area and/or by following strict quality and environmental regulations. It is hypothesised that this mechanism could regulate environmental problems of cannabis production. First, because as the plant is not commoditised, more strain diversity is desired in the market, and therefore, the crop produced in each area is the most adapted to each territory. Moreover, if environmental standards are part of the requirements to assign the appellation, then this designation of origin might act as a certification of sustainable practice. Finally, appellations could reduce indoor cultivation, as the effects of the outdoors environmental conditions of a specific geographic area are necessary to obtain the appellation.[65]

A future regulated market of coca crops in Colombia could have some of these features, if designed correctly. But it cannot be left to market forces. If regulated properly, for example, we can expect less cultivation in protected areas and a market that benefit small coca growers.[66] Moreover, we can expect less deforestation given that armed conflict and violence are expected to decrease in affected municipalities once the illegal market is eliminated. Given that violence and human rights violations[4] are correlated with deforestation, a regulated market would be a mechanism to indirectly reduce deforestation.

Transition to a regulated market will not be easy, and there are also some important questions regarding equitable access and inclusive development.[67] New legal markets might displace former producers. Back in the early 20th century, when cocaine had a legal market mainly for the medical industry, coca crops produced in Peru were displaced by extensive production in Java (the island now part of Indonesia) promoted by the Dutch Industry, 'an historical reminder that even today coca might escape the Andes for other tropical realms if pressure warrant'.[68] In the case of cannabis, due to the high price of the numerous and demanding licenses for legal cultivation in California, many rural growers were forced to return to the illegal market. In Colombia, the medical cannabis industry, made up of large companies is behaving similarly.[69]

This type of market and regulatory models can promote the concentration of the industry in the hands of large companies and corporations which would make more difficult to regulate production and commercialisation to protect health and environment, as happened also with the tobacco industry worldwide.[70] In California, cannabis producers have pressed the legislation to promote the accumulation of permits to cultivate, which enhances large-scale production and thus higher demand of natural resources.[71] Designing an industry that is socially inclusive and environmentally sound is a pending challenge in the cannabis regulation process and certainly could also be one of the challenges of a future coca-regulated market.[46] However, there are some experiences that would allow building a roadmap. For example, Zuleta and co-authors[72] mentioned that legal poppy production in Turkey remains in the hands of around 100,000 small growers with crops of 0.4 hectares on average,[73] and in Jamaica the alternative development programme currently in place is designed to provide technical and financial support to traditional cannabis growers in their transition to legality.[74]

Thus, it is not utopian to start thinking about a regulated cocaine market with social and environmental requirements. If some countries were to regulate consumption of cocaine, it would be necessary to start thinking about regulations to produce coca, with environmental and social prerequisites. With sustainable development lens, a new regulated market of cocaine needs to be thought to address consumption as a public health issue but also production as a rural development problem with an environmental focus.

Notes

* This chapter is based on María Alejandra Vélez and Camilo Erasso, '¿Los cultivos de coca, causan deforestación en Colombia?' (Center for the Study of Security and Drugs, 2020). The final section was not included in the Spanish version. I thank all the comments made by David Restrepo, Maria Juliana Rubiano, Lucas Marin Llanes and Beatriz Irene Ramos and the excellent research assistance by Maria Paula Gutierrez.

1 Daniel Brombacher, Juan Carlos Garzón & María Alejandra Vélez, 'Introduction Special Issue: Environmental Impacts of Illicit Economies' (2021) 3(1) *Journal of Illicit Economies and Development* 1.

2 Ibid.

3 In relation to cannabis, see, for example, Jennifer K Carah, et al, 'High Time for Conservation: Adding the Environment to the Debate on Marijuana Liberalization' (2015) 65 *BioScience* 822.; Mark Klassen and Brandon P. Anthony, 'The Effects of Recreational Cannabis Legalization on Forest Management and Conservation Efforts in U.S. National Forests in the Pacific Northwest' (2019) 162 *Ecological Economics* 39.; Martin Jelsma, et al, 'A Sustainable Future for Cannabis Farmers Alternative Development Opportunities in the Legal Cannabis Market' (Transnational Institute, 2021).

4 Dolors Armenteras, et al, 'National and Regional Determinants of Tropical Deforestation in Colombia'(2013) 13 *Regional Environmental Change* 1181.; Liliana M Dávalos, et al, 'Forests and Drugs: Coca-Driven Deforestation in Tropical Biodiversity Hotspots' (2011) 45 *Environmental Science and Technology* 1219.; Alexander Rincón-Ruiz, Unai Pascual & Suzette Flantua, 'Examining Spatially Varying Relationships between Coca Crops and Associated Factors in Colombia, Using Geographically Weight Regression' (2013) 37 *Applied Geography* 23.; Mounu Prem, Santiago Saavedra & Juan F Vargas, 'End-of-Conflict Deforestation: Evidence from Colombian's Peace Agreement' (2018) 129 *World Development* 104852.; Pablo Jose Negret, et al, 'Emerging Evidence That Armed Conflict and Coca Cultivation Influence Deforestation Patterns' (2019) 239 *Biological Conservation* 108176.; Liliana M Dávalos, et al, 'Forests, Coca, and Conflict: Grass Frontier Dynamics and Deforestation in the Amazon-Andes' (2021) 3(1) *Journal of Illicit Economies and Development* 74.

5 Beth Tellman, et al, 'Narcotrafficking and Land Control in Guatemala and Honduras' (2021) 3(1) *Journal of Illicit Economies and Development* 132.

6 Pavel Horký, et al, 'Methamphetamine Pollution Elicits Addiction in Wild Fish' (2021) 224(13) *Journal of Experimental Biology*.; Mafalda Pardal, Charlotte Colman & Tim Surmont, 'Synthetic Drug Production in Belgium – Environmental Harms as Collateral Damage?' (2021) 3(1) *Journal of Illicit Economies and Development* 36.

7 Chloe Carpentier, et al, 'Drug Market Trends: Cocaine, Amphetamine-Type Stimulants' (United Nations Office on Drugs and Crime, 2021).

8 If land located in other types of forest reserves, such as forest under the Ley 2nd framework are included in this figure, the percentage goes to up 48%.

9 Data from the National Police Anti-Narcotics Directorate [Dirección Antinarcóticos de la Policía Nacional], reported by El Tiempo (2019), indicate that the process required to transform coca into cocaine leads to 3.5 tons per hectare per year, of chemical substances derived from residue being dumped, affecting both soil and water.

10 José Julián González, et al, 'Caracterización de las principales causas y agentes de la deforestación a nivel nacional. Período 2005–2015' (Programa ONU-REDD, Organización de las Naciones Unidas para la Alimentación y la Agricultura and PNUD ONU Medio Ambiente, 2018).

11 Dávalos, et al, 'Forests, Coca, and Conflict: Grass Frontier Dynamics and Deforestation in the Amazon-Andes' (n 4).; Institute of Hydrology, Meteorology and Environmental Studies, 'Resultados del Monitoreo de Deforestación: Año 2020 y Primer Trimestre Año 2021' (Ministerio de Ambiente, 2021).

12 For the case of Bolivia, Bradley and Millington (2008) report lower forest cover losses' rates in presence of coca crops but an increase in those rates when legal substitutes for the illegal crops became dominant given policy interventions. The authors suggest two potential mechanisms to explain their results. First, labor force in coca substitutes could be less demanding and enable growers to allocate time to deforestation. Second, coca substitutes do not produce the same income nor economic stability, thus, growers look for alternative income sources.

13 AHC Van Bruggen, et al, 'Environmental and Health Effects of the Herbicide Glyphosate' (2018) 616–617 *Science of the Total Environment* 255.; María Juliana Rubiano, et al, '¿Reanudar la fumigación aérea de cultivos ilícitos en Colombia? Un resumen de la literatura científica. Comentario de Política #2' (Center for Studies on Security and Drugs, 2020).

14 A recent study does not find evidence of a balloon effect caused by aerial fumigation at a municipal level in Colombia. Authors report that spraying an additional hectare of coca implies a reduction of 0.08 hectares of new coca crops in the same municipality and a reduction of 0.03 hectares of coca crops in neighbouring fumigated municipalities. See Eleanora Davalos and Leonardo Fabio Morales, 'Is There a Balloon Effect? Coca Crops and Forced Eradication in Colombia' (Universidad EAFIT, 2019).

15 Liliana M Dávalos, Karina Sánchez & Dolors Armenteras, 'Deforestation and Coca Cultivation Rooted in Twentieth-Century Development Projects' (2016) 66 *BioScience* 974.; Alexander Rincón-Ruiz and Giorgos Kallis, 'Caught in the Middle, Colombia's War on Drugs and Its Effects on Forest and People' (2013) 46 *Geoforum* 60.; Rincón-Ruiz, et al, (n 4).

16 Adriana Camacho and Daniel Mejía, 'The Health Consequences of Aerial Spraying Illicit Crops: The Case of Colombia' (2017) 54 *Journal of Health Economics* 147.

17 Dávalos, et al (2021) (n 4).

18 González et al (n 10).

19 Institute of Hydrology, Meteorology and Environmental Studies, 'Resultados Monitoreo de la Deforestación 2018' (Ministerio de Ambiente, 2019).

20 Institute of Hydrology, Meteorology and Environmental Studies (n 11).

21 German Corporation for International Cooperation, 'Coca y deforestación: mensajes de acción para la planeación del desarrollo' (Cooperación Alemana, GIZ, Ministerio de Ambiente, IDEAM, UNODC, Instituto SINCHI, 2017).

22 González et al (n 11).

23 German Corporation for International Cooperation (n 21).

24 Coca data were provided by the Integrated Illicit Crop Monitoring System (SIMCI-UNODC) at a spatial resolution of 1 km. The original resolution of these data is 30 m, but it is confidential. Deforestation was obtained from the Forest and Carbon Monitoring System (SMBYC-IDEAM) at a resolution of 30 m and is defined as the conversion from forest to non-forest in one year with respect to the previous year. Deforestation data were aggregated to 1 km for comparison with coca data. This eliminates the possibility of calculating the exact number of areas deforested by coca cultivation as a direct cause of deforestation.

25 Armenteras et al (n 4).

26 Dávalos et al (2011) (n 4).

27 Rincón-Ruiz et al (n 4).

28 Dávalos et al (2011) (n 4).

29 Prem et al (n 4).

30 Negret et al (n 4).

31 Dávalos et al (2021) (n 4).

32 Dávalos et al (2011) (n 4).

33 Dávalos et al (2011) (n 4); José Bernal, Jerónimo Sudarsky & Catalina Riveros, 'Illicit Crop Cultivation in Colombia's National Natural Parks: Dynamics, Drivers, and Policy Responses' (2021) 3(1) *Journal of Illicit Economies and Development* 22.

34 SIMCI-UNODC, 'Informe de monitoreo de territorios afectados por cultivos ilícitos 2017. Bogotá: Sistema Integrado de Monitoreo de Cultivos Ilícitos' (United Nations Office on Drugs and Crime, 2018).

35 María Alejandra Vélez, et al, 'Is Collective Titling Enough to Protect Forests? Evidence from Afro-Descendant Communities in the Colombian Pacific Region' (2020) 128 *World Development* 104837.

36 Leonardo Bonilla-Mejía and Iván Higuera-Mendieta, 'Protected Areas under Weak Institutions: Evidence from Colombia' (2019) 122 *World Development* 585.

37 Iván D. Lobo and María Alejandra Vélez, 'From Strong Leadership to Active Community Engagement: Effective Resistance to Illicit Economies in Afro-Colombian Collective Territories' (2022) 102 *International Journal of Drug Policy* 103579. https://doi.org/10.1016/j.drugpo.2022.103579.

38 These figures are close to those reported by SIMCI-UNODC (2018) due to differences in the data grouping methodology and to the confidentiality of its more disaggregated spatial level (30 m pixel versus 1 km).

39 These data are annualised only as of 2012.

40 Dávalos et al (2021) (n 4).

41 Bernal et al (n 33); Héctor Fabio Santos Duarte, Antonia Schmidt & Sofia Wahl, 'Addressing Coca-Related Deforestation in Colombia: A Call for Aligning Drug and Environmental Policies for Sustainable Development' (2021) 3(1) *Journal of Illicit Economies and Development* 10.

42 Luciana Grillo, et al, 'Addressing Socio-Environmental Challenges and Unintended Consequences of Peruvian Drug Policy: An Analysis in Two Former Cocalero Valleys' (2021) 3(1) *Journal of Illicit Economies and Development* 97.

43 Ibid.

44 Jelsma et al (n 3).

45 Lobo and Veléz (n 37); María Alejandra Vélez, '¿Para qué glifosato? Aquí hay comunidades', *La Silla Vacía* (16 March 2019).

46 Duarte et al (n 41).

47 James Salzman, et al, 'The Global Status and Trends of Payments for Ecosystem Services' (2018) 1 *Nature Sustainability* 136.
48 Sven Wunder, 'When Payments for Environmental Services Will Work for Conservation' (2013) 6(4) *Conservation Letters* 230.
49 Lucas Marin, María Juliana Rubiano & María Alejandra Vélez, '6 ideas para los candidatos presidenciales sobre una política integral para la sustitución de cultivos de uso ilícito' (Center for Studies on Security and Drugs, 2021).
50 Susannah Schmurak, 'The Environmental Cost of Legalizing Marijuana', *Eartheasy* (4 October 2017).
51 Pablo Zuleta et al, 'Cannabis de uso adulto: análisis sobre el impacto económico y ambiental', *El Espectador* (30 August 2021).
52 Kenza Afsashi, 'The Rif and California: Environmental Violence in the Era of New Cannabis Markets' in Julia Buxton, Mary Chinery-Hesse & Khalid Tinasti (eds.), *Drug Policies and Development: Conflict and Coexistence* (Brill, 2020).
53 Marin et al (n 49).
54 Carah et al (n 3).
55 Jelsma et al (n 3).
56 Klassen and Anthony (n 3); Jeffrey Prestemon, et al, 'Cannabis Legalization by States Reduces Illegal Growing on US National Forests' (2019) 164 *Ecological Economics* 1.
57 Michael Vitiello, 'Legalizing Marihuana and Abating Environmental Harm: An Overblown Promise' (2016) 50 *UC Davis Law Review* 773.
58 Schmurak (n 50).
59 Nora Álvarez-Berríos, Jeeica L'Roe & Lisa Naughton-Treves, 'Does Formalizing Artisanal Gold Mining Mitigate Environmental Impacts? Deforestation Evidence from the Peruvian Amazon' (2021) 16 (6) *Environmental Research Letters* 064052.
60 Jelsma et al (n 3).
61 Evan Mills, 'The Carbon Footprint of Cannabis Production' (2012) 46 *Energy Policy* 58; Tony Silvaggio, 'Tony Silvaggio: Environmental Consequences of Prohibition' (Denver Open Media, 2018).
62 Vitiello (n 57).
63 Carah et al (n 3).
64 Ryan B Stoa, 'Marijuana Appellations: The Case for Cannabicultural Designations of Origin', (2017) 11 *Harvard Law and Policy Review* 513.
65 Ibid.
66 Jeffrey Prestemon and others, "Cannabis legalization by states reduces illegal growing on US national forests" (2019) 164 Ecological Economics <https://doi.org/10.1016/j.ecolecon.2019.106366> accessed 19 October 2021.
67 Jelsma et al (n 3).
68 Paul Gootenberg, *Andean Cocaine: The Making of a Global Drug* (The University of North California Press, 2008) 128.
69 Zuleta et al (n 51).
70 Zuleta et al (n 51); Jelsma et al (n 3).
71 Vitiello (n 57).
72 Zuleta et al (n 51).
73 Transform Drug Policy Foundation, 'Turkey's Opium Trade: Successfully Transitioning from Illicit Production to a Legally Regulated Market' (22 November 2018) <https://transformdrugs.org/blog/turkeys-opium-trade-successfully-transitioning-from-illicit-production-to-a-legally-regulated-market-2> accessed 1 March 2023.
74 JIS News, 'Gov't Assisting Transition of Traditional Ganja Growers to Legal Industry', *The Gleaner* (25 February 2020).

Part V

Reckoning with the Past

12 Consensus Breakdown and Recalcitrancy in the Drug Control System

Towards Disintegration or Re-Integration?

John Collins

Introduction

Since 2012, international drug control has undergone a period of significant structural, normative and institutional change. Governments now overtly ignore or reinterpret key legal and normative principles that had previously held firm. For example, the prohibition of non-medical/non-scientific cannabis production, supply and consumption is no longer followed in an increasing number of Member States. Meanwhile, the vast majority of States maintain overt adherence to the legal letter of the UN drug control treaties – even if implementation in practice is questionable. A significant amount of these States maintain an absolutist vision of prohibitionism, often characterised as the 'war on drugs'. In these countries, consumers still face severe penalties for minor infractions, and repression is the default approach to production and supply, with penalties up to and including the use of the death penalty in some countries. While some countries appear to have moved into a post-'war on drugs' approach, others maintain the core symmetrical enforcement of a severe war on drugs.

This chapter looks at the recent trends in international drug control and suggests a historical, political and policy framework for understanding these changes within the UN system context. It suggests that as the regime undergoes an internal evolution of policies, with some Member States maintaining a focus on prohibition and others pursuing new policies beyond prohibition, the system will effectively evolve to encapsulate both approaches.

The Significance of Disintegration

I have previously written about two, generally opposing, views on the significance and direction of fragmentation. The first is an 'integrationist' school, based on an 'orthodox' regime ontology which sees the regime's tenets as immutable and fixed absent formal legal reform. This subdivides into a reformist branch and conservative branch. Reformist integrationists tend to view the UN drug regime as moulded by US hegemony and thereby operates as a form of colonialism.[1] They extrapolate

DOI: 10.4324/9781003169765-18

this perspective to declining US hegemony and suggest this will now provoke a crisis of legitimacy within the system and thereby prohibition.[2] The conservative integrationist branch is similarly set in its perspective of the system's hard prohibition norms and legal underpinnings as fixed, immutable and clear. Proponent countries include China, Russia and many others. They advocate strict adherence to and coherence with these prohibitive approaches. Both reformist and conservative integrationists believe cannabis legalisation and other forms of normative and policy fragmentation represent a systemic risk to the regime. Reformists highlight these tensions to expedite collapse or reformation within the system. The conservatives wish to avoid it.[3]

Pluralists adopt a position of historical regulatory complexity pointing to repeated, often continuous, periods of dissensus in the system's history. For example, they look to the tumultuous negotiations around the 1961 *Single Convention on Narcotic Drugs*,[4] the bedrock treaty of the multilateral system, and the complex viewpoints held by Member States about what the system actually mandated.[5] Pluralists also tend to suggest a pragmatic utility of short-term divergences as a means to expand the global evidence base, provided core international legal and human rights norms are adhered to.[6] This chapter highlights that the evidence from the period 2012–2021, when the consensus seemingly 'fractured', shows just how malleable and politically resilient the system can prove, even with widespread division and disagreement on parts of its vision or political trajectories.[7]

The Origins of Drug Control

The international drug control system began at the turn of the 20th century. The system initially coalesced around a series of multilateral treaties under the auspices of the League of Nations treaties and later, after World War II, under the United Nations Commission on Narcotic Drugs (CND). The system has, from its outset, been wracked by inherent tensions, divided by national interests and weakened by staunchly competing visions and conflicting bureaucratic interests. Consensus came in fits and starts, with entire decades governed by dissensus and division. The years 1925–1930 was one such period, where the United States walked out of negotiations around the 1925 *International Opium Convention*[8] and became virtually estranged from the system. A brief period of consensus forged the 1931 Convention for Limiting the Manufacture and Regulating the Distribution of Narcotic Drugs,[9] which regulated the manufacture of controlled drugs around the world, establishing both the systems of estimates and scheduling. This consensus period also proved short-lived as States once again divided over key regulatory and prohibitive issues. In 1931, the United States had warned that:

> There is but one real method by which to suppress the evil of opium smoking in the Far East…[it] is complete statutory prohibition of the importation, manufacture, sale, possession or use of prepared opium, coupled with active enforcement of such prohibition.[10]

This continued disagreement between the United States and European States over the latter's governance of the colonial opium trade through a monopoly system led the US delegation to try walkout of the 1936 plenipotentiary conference. The US State Department ultimately refused to allow a repeat of the embarrassing walkout of 1925 where the drug warriors had, in their eyes, tarnished broader US foreign policy interests. However, the United States refused to sign the 1936 Convention for the Suppression of the Illicit Traffic in Dangerous,[11] which aimed at tackling the growing global illicit traffic.[12]

Over the period 1925–1939, the international drug control system was a highly fragmentary collection of national visions for drug control, which only managed to coalesce around some broad principles for international regulations. Underpinning it was a general view that multilateral control should not front-run the domestic controls of States, many of which already had imposed, or were moving towards, various forms of prohibitions on their domestic markets. Consensus international regulations, and prohibitions, therefore, became about creating a system of monitoring for the international trade, one that could provide early warning systems for accumulations of stocks and large-scale diversions of trade. Hard-line States, such as the United States, zealously drove a strict vision for the system, enforcing uniform prohibitions in all parts of the world on non-medical and non-scientific trade and consumption. European colonial powers, grappling with the complexities of widespread opium markets and the legacy of centuries of their own opium trading throughout Asia, were willing to pursue tighter regulations around the transnational trade, but ultimately bucked at the idea of an international control system that could dictate policies within their territories.[13]

Alongside this prohibition debate was the monumental task of trying to limit global opium production to medical and scientific needs. Even if Britain, for example, prohibited all non-medical opium consumption in Burma, how was it to be enforced if Persia or China continued to produce thousands of tons of opium which would follow circuitous routes into global illicit supplies and eventually their colonial domestic markets? Production control thereby became the lynchpin of international drug control from 1931 to 1961. It proved a painfully difficult diplomatic endeavour which saw rupture after rupture within drug diplomacy. For example, by the outbreak of World War II, the Turkish-Yugoslav Opium Combine, the loadstone of the licit global market for opium supplies, had effectively collapsed under the weight of market complexities and imbalances. In the decades following the war, US and UN drug officials struggled to construct a successor. UN efforts culminated in the 1950s when the head of the UN drug secretariat destroyed his career on the matter and severely damaged the Secretariat's relationship with the Commission on Narcotic Drugs by trying to advocate for an international opium monopoly.[14]

Given these complexities and divergences, national level reforms generally pre-dated international ones. Indeed, it was rare that international reforms did much more than reinforce or codify policies that had become the norm at national levels. When the system tried to push ahead beyond national level consensus or enact regulations that would materially impact one country's well-being vis-à-vis its trading partners, it risked getting stuck in disagreements, sometimes for decades. Within these interest-based constraints, debates on the optimal approach to drug demand and supply raged, but had little real impact on international regulations. National prerogatives remained first and foremost the drivers of international controls.[15] Moreover, the continued engagement with the system by most Member States demonstrated something else. Most, if not virtually all, agreed with the basic principle of an international regulatory system designed to limit the excesses of a laissez faire global trade. All were willing to subvert some level of national regulatory prerogative to that effort, provided it did not cross the aforementioned thresholds. There are almost no cases in the last century where a Member State was forced against its will to impose a domestic regulatory structure as a result of signing an international convention. Most wholeheartedly endorsed and adhered to the system. Some, particularly post-colonial states in the aftermath of World War II, went much, much further.

In cases where governments shifted policies drastically against their will, bilateral pressure proved key and was often just reinforcing domestic public and bureaucratic pressure. US bilateral pressure during World War II was one such case which profoundly reshaped European colonial policies and shifted the regulatory balance within the system. Amazingly it was the bluff and bluster, cowboy diplomacy policies of US Federal Bureau of Narcotics Chief Harry Anslinger, who used wartime confusion to feign a US government policy which did not exist – the end of colonial opium monopolies. Britain and the Netherlands fell for his gamble and announced a radical shift in policies in 1943, the end of the colonial opium monopoly system in most of their territories. France followed suit at the end of the war. Britain had come close to such a policy in 1925 due to domestic and internal government pressure, but governance and implementation concerns had continued to win out. The abstraction of the policy in World War II, when Britain and the Netherlands were discussing territories they had no effective control over tipped the scales towards a broad political announcement, that ended up being rolled back in practical implementation once hostilities ceased.[16]

However, the onset of decolonisation strongly reinvigorated the move towards prohibition. Post-colonial governments enthusiastically embraced the strictest visions of drug control. Regulated drug markets were associated with colonial abuses, revenue models and power structures. They were anathema to nationalist visions for how post-colonial countries would operate.[17] At the same time, producer States – particularly Iran, Turkey, Afghanistan and others – fought for market share in the lucrative post-war market. As recreational consumption in Asia appeared to be a diminishing market, States came to see adherence to the international system as a means towards a profitable outlet for their opium production and sought to demonstrate their willingness and capabilities to control and regulate their domestic production. Ultimately some, such as Afghanistan, would prove unable to exert any regulatory control of their domestic producer markets, licit or illicit. Similarly, Iran would choose simply to forgo a role in global opium production for a variety of political and regulatory reasons.[18] Within this challenging environment, actors such as the Soviet Union rebelled against any notion of international interference or monitoring of domestic production. This extended to boycotts of official production limitation meetings aimed at forging the basis for an international convention.[19]

Drugs and the United Nations

Despite these challenges and disagreements, the reinvigoration of multilateral drug control through the United Nations at the end of World War II proved relatively uncontested. The most disaffected parties were hard-line drug control advocates within the US government and civil society, who envisioned taking advantage of the period of disruption and driving through a radically stricter system. They failed on most counts, and a consensus period emerged from 1946 to 1948 as legal structures solidified and Member States readily agreed the 1948 Protocol on Synthetics.[20] Drugs similar to opium alkaloids were increasingly being derived synthetically from coal-tar and were thereby not covered by the existing 1931 Convention. Highlighting just how uncontroversial this manufacturing-focused treaty had been, Member States simply applied its principles to synthetic drugs via the Protocol.[21]

Beneath the seeming consensus, however, old disagreements simmered, ready to resurface. Hard-liners in the United States had not given up on their vision of the UN Commission on Narcotic Drugs as an arbiter on Member State behaviour and a venue where their diplomats could chastise and challenge seemingly delinquent governments. Harry Anslinger's efforts in this regard quickly fell flat, however, as the State Department neutered his ability to call out specific countries such as Mexico. He did succeed in generating enormous tensions around the People's Republic of China, creating a fictional narrative of a massive global opium conspiracy, much as he had done with Japan in the 1930s. The reality for mainland China in the 1950s was an incredibly aggressive domestic suppression campaign and a shift in the locus of production out of Yunnan Province and into the neighbouring states forming the Golden Triangle. Anslinger's motive was likely an attempt to piggyback on domestic anti-China sentiments to shore up his bureaucratic position. All he succeeded in doing was undermining consensus and US credibility within the Commission as even the US Federal Bureau of Investigation (FBI) Director, J. Edgar Hoover, privately acknowledged there was no validity to Anslinger's claims.[22]

As discussed, the main political focus for post-war drug control was dividing up the global licit market. In this zero-sum game, States competed for market share and global regulations that would play to their individual strengths. After tumultuous years of negotiations, including a period of open rupture between the Commission on Narcotic Drugs and its Secretariat, the United States and its ally at the time, France, drove through the 1953 Opium Protocol.[23] This treaty, bucking consensus and seemingly doomed, imposed strict production controls, including a permanently closed list of seven countries legally entitled to produce opium for the global market.

While the United States remained wedded to the 1953 Opium Protocol, Britain and European States sought to bury it through agreeing a superseding

Convention, the long-vaunted Single Convention that would unify all existing treaties. Following a series of contentious drafts, Member States finally agreed the UN Single Convention on Narcotic Drugs in 1961. A consensus treaty, which weakened or removed the key provisions which had doomed the 1953 Protocol, the Single Convention established a measure of production control and expanded the control regime in a number of key areas. Harry Anslinger, however, ensured that the United States initially rejected the Single Convention and instead redoubled efforts to ratify the 1953 Protocol. The battles to ratify came to a close in November 1964 when Kenya become the 40th country to accede to the Single Convention, thereby defeating Anslinger and effectively killing the 1953 Protocol.[24]

The United States eventually joined the Single Convention in 1967 after Anslinger had retired. States soon turned to a new Convention, aimed at barbiturates, tranquilizers and amphetamines, which lay beyond the legal scope of the Single Convention. In 1971, States readily agreed the Convention on Psychotropic Substances to cover these drugs.[25] Like the Single Convention, it operated through four 'schedules' that listed the various substances under international control under various categories. However, out of deference to western pharmaceutical interests, which opposed harsh restrictions on these drugs, the levels of control were considerably less than under the Single Convention.[26]

The 1961 and 1971 Conventions together provided the key regulatory foundations for the control system. Soon attention turned to enforcement. Contrary to widespread conceptions, Latin American governments were the key drivers of this new effort as they faced seemingly existential threats from illicit drug economies. North American and European governments were generally reticent to impose additional international obligations. However, in the face of persistent Latin American pressure they eventually acquiesced, viewing a consensus convention process as the key mechanism to water down more aggressive elements, such as calls to make drug trafficking a crime against humanity.[27] Negotiations soon produced 14 elements to be built into a new Convention against the Illicit Traffic in Narcotic Drugs and Psychotropic Substances, including asset seizure, extradition, control of precursor chemicals, intelligence sharing and all activities related to trafficking, including 'crop substitution'.[28]

The 1988 Convention enshrined two key innovations. First, it enabled control of precursor substances which were key to the manufacture of narcotic drugs and psychotropic substances and second, it targeted the financial gains and freedom of movement of drug traffickers.[29] More controversially, the Convention included a paragraph dealing with 'personal consumption contrary to the provisions of the 1961 Convention...or the 1971 Convention'.[30] Ultimately, while the 1988 Convention offered support for States advocating criminalisation of consumption, it simultaneously left interpretive flexibility for States to opt out.[31]

UN Drug Control since the 1990s

From 1988 to 2008, the system focused on implementation and coalesced around tackling a seemingly ever growing crime problem associated with illicit drug markets. The apparent consensus of the 1998 UN General Assembly Special Session (UNGASS) on the World Drug Problem operating under the banner, 'A drug free world – We can do it!', masked the beginnings of divergence. Supply-side policies were simply not working. Hard-line demand reduction policies showed little indication of success and had created their own universe of harms, including a substantial contribution to racially disproportionate mass incarceration and widespread human rights abuses. Harm reduction polices, those grounded in an agnostic view about drug use and targeted specifically at reducing the harms of drugs and drug policies to the individual, showed hugely more impressive results than the countervailing demand and supply reduction policies.[32] More recently, discussions have focused on expanding the concept of harm reduction further towards the supply side, with an aim to reduce the impacts of markets rather than the seemingly unobtainable goal of market reduction.[33]

Throughout the 1990s, while consensus remained hard-line in its international manifestation, local and national level policies in some countries were shifting. This would have enormous implications for the system in the 2000s as it was forced to evolve around these. Governments like Switzerland appeared to be system outliers and had to spend significant political capital forging coalitions with like-minded governments to change the normative underpinnings of multilateral drug control.[34]

Pressures on the post-1988 consensus ultimately began to build around 2007–2008, and the dam ultimately broke around 2012. In the United States, President Barack Obama had openly criticised the drug war and his administration opened the door to a regional dialogue on alternatives. The Organization of American State (OAS) stepped into the discussion, producing the report *Scenarios for the Drug Problem in the Americas, 2013–2025*.[35] The social justice dimensions of the Obama administration's critique were magnified by local level financial crises exacerbated by the 2007–2008 financial crisis as states and localities looked to reduce expenditure on incarceration and began to eye cannabis as a potential new tax revenue source.

With the legalisation of cannabis in Uruguay and the US states of Colorado and Washington, the UN drug control system appeared to face an existential moment. Some long-time reform advocates anticipated collapse or at least an inescapable legal crisis for the treaty regime.[36] Instead Member States worked around it. The US State Department argued for treaty flexibility and the reality that 'some countries will have very strict drug approaches; other countries will legalize entire categories of drugs'.[37] This 'Brownfield doctrine',[38] likely had an equally strategic as legal intent. It opened the legalisation door for Latin American governments recognising that few, if any, would walk through.[39] With the exception of cannabis, none did.

Reformers looked to a discordant UNGASS in 2016 as a means towards radical system reform. What they got instead was a broadening of the system and a recognition that the legal complexities around cannabis legalisation would be simply overlooked for the present.[40] More than 100 years after the conclusion of the first multilateral drug treaty, the system was in the midst of yet another period of change and dissensus. Yet a new consensus seemed to be forming and new coalitions of policy focus. While some grumbled about cannabis legalisation, Member States chose largely to look elsewhere and focus on the areas of consensus remaining, specifically around preserving the regulatory core of the system and further its implementation with regard to key issues such as access to medicine and aligning it further with other UN missions and mandates on sustainable development, human rights and gender.

Fragmentation or Integration?

Debates around what has come to be known as the 'fragmentation' of international law[41] have become increasingly influential in recent years, including in the context of drug control.[42] The discussion emerged in response to the 'manifold'[43] growth of international legal regimes, institutions and instruments since World War II. As new regimes and systems created new rules and obligations, as well as differing governing exigencies and incentives, it is argued that there is an 'increasing likelihood that two or more rules or principles of international law will be applicable' on any given issue, and therefore an increasing likelihood of normative or regime conflict.[44]

There is often an assumption among scholars 'that international law is likely to continue down a path of increasing fragmentation'.[45] However, others see the integrationist possibilities of these processes: that international outcomes are a by-product of two competing forces: 'international legal fragmentation and international legal integration'.[46] Megiddo, for example, provides a compelling portrayal of these 'integrationist forces' of fragmentation. Specifically, the author focuses on the possibility that diverging international regimes, and the contradicting normative obligations placed on States, could be overcome as States work to 'build bridges' between regimes and seek to promote new forms of integration through 'proactive, creative' approaches to legal conflicts which sustain international law while protecting their domestic agendas. The author specifically avoids analysing 'the coherence between international law and domestic law', something of particular relevance to drug control debates, although suggests these efforts 'may sometimes also render the domestic law on a particular issue more in line with the governing norms of international law'.[47]

Megiddo's thesis offers an interesting lens through which to understand the (latest) breakdown in the global drug control consensus and examine scenarios as States seek to overcome differences of implementation, normative visions and broader geopolitical goals within the context of the global drug control system. As with the broader literature on legal fragmentation, which suggests that 'inconsistent guidance received from different international legal regimes places States in an impossible conflict, having to breach the binding norms of one regime to abide by another',[48] the international drug control regime has experienced similar tensions. For example, the conflicts between the often draconian policies espoused by some within the drug control system, on the one hand, and human rights norms, on the other, have become the subject of intense scrutiny.[49] Further, the complexities of the relationship between the UN Agenda for Sustainable Development and the goals of global drug control have been another area of discussion and debate.[50] Moreover, the divergence between national drug control policies and those required by the drug treaties have offered perhaps even more fertile ground for discussion, debate and diplomatic wrangling. These tensions have received heavy coverage within the civil society grey literature and became the subject of academic debate among integrationist and pluralist schools of thought as States deviated from the traditional implementation norms of the system.

Conclusion: The Future of Drug Multilateralism

International drug diplomacy has been a constant process of change, evolution and oscillations between periods of dissensus and consensus over the last century. When interests and other factors sufficiently aligned, forward regulatory movement occurred, bringing the contemporary treaty system into existence and advancing it step by step. But major divisions remained throughout. The visceral disagreements over the colonial opium monopolies in the 1920s and 1930s were a pointed example. They were resolved through bilateral pressures, but also a variety of systemic political economy and geopolitical shifts which changed the policy arithmetic for Member States. So too, the arithmetic has now changed in other key areas.

In more recent times, Latin American governments have shown an increased unwillingness to tow a singular line in fighting what they see as a US-driven 'war on drugs'. Conversely, the reform debates within those countries have exposed continuing popularity and political-economic constituencies tied to the continuation of prohibitionist policies. The oscillations of Colombia's policies over the last decade are a good indicator of this complexity. Elsewhere I have written of Colombia's relationship with the UN drug control system as an example of outward policy displacement, utilising the UN system to deflect the drug reform debate from domestic constituencies where reform arguments may receive a more sceptical reception, into an international institutional structure which must reckon with the challenges and problems associated with drug war policies.[51] What this example shows is that policies are not unidirectional. There is a circularity and dialectic between national and international.

The emergence of a more functional, fragmented and complex drug control system indicates an inherent willingness and ability to adapt around international changes. The collapse of the International Opium Monopoly project in the 1950s did not provoke an existential crisis within the system. Member States would simply spend another decade forging a broad consensus on an acceptable production limitation framework that became enshrined in the 1961 Single Convention. After almost four decades of debate, disagreement and wrangling the system codified a relatively open-ended system for production control. Meanwhile, the only treaty that arguably lacked international legitimacy and consensus buy-in, the 1953 Protocol, was ultimately doomed. Again, this shows the system as having functional Member State support. States knew what they were agreeing and they knew what they were unwilling to tolerate.

A real challenge to a further progressive shift within the system comes from history and State capacity. Many States have a historical memory of drugs which makes them unwilling or unable to see the issue in purely evidence-based terms. This suggests that a policy widening will maintain even long after we have evidence of better practice. Reformist narratives, which seek to construct drug prohibition as a colonial endeavour, need to come to terms with the complexity of this issue. For China, opium is a symbol of western intervention and national humiliation. It is almost inconceivable for the national psyche to accept a normalisation of drug markets, despite the ongoing or future willingness to envision this among other countries. Other southeast Asian governments with histories of abusive colonial economic systems view drugs as a remnant of these systems.[52] Consensus is not always possible where such national conceptions and antipathies exist.

Moreover, in areas of extreme instability and fragility, drug policy critics need to be wary of over-ascribing conflict and crime determinacy solely to prohibition. Prohibition and regulation are not necessarily the beginning nor the end of conflicts and instability but exist within their wider milieu in contexts where State capacity to regulate or indeed prohibit drugs is virtually non-existent and far from a priority. Nevertheless, continued use of multilateral and bilateral mechanisms, alongside local initiatives, remains key in fostering the transfer of best-practice evidence-based policies. The success of domestic harm reduction policies in the 1980s and 1990s ultimately did lead to a tidal shift in global drug policies, but there remains a long way to go, evidenced by the continued controversy around using the term 'harm reduction' in official language at the Commission on Narcotic Drugs.

In practical terms, the division over cannabis legalisation daily recedes further into an abstract academic discussion over the tensions between national and international law. I have long maintained that cannabis legalisation can and will be made to co-exist with the system's overall coherence, and that Member States have demonstrated an almost universal resolve to maintain the core regulatory structure of the system – something domestic cannabis reforms do not challenge. Events since the UNGASS in 2016 have only reinforced this viewpoint. There remains no international constituency within the UN drug control system for reforming the conventions, and there is overt hostility among even the most progressive governments to the idea. Integrationist reformist hopes that inelegant legal accommodations or overwrought intra-UN tensions can provide a wedge to drive through systemic reforms are not only misplaced in their reading of contemporary trends, they also ignore the history of the system's painful, evolutionary and complex development.

Within the drug control system there remain two strands. One focused on regulation, one on prohibition. Each was an essential feature of the other, as in all regulatory systems. To prohibit an activity or commodity, the State must first regulate it. To regulate it the State must, by definition, prohibit some aspect of it. The regulatory logic within the system originated with European States seeking to make accommodations with local drug producing and consuming settings in areas of weak or limited governance. The prohibition logic held that effective suppression of the non-medical/scientific consumption market at the outset would squeeze out illicit supplies, leaving a relatively minor role for prohibition and police enforcement.

The prohibitionist logic, particularly after the 1960s, became unquestionably ascendant until 2012. With the breakdown in the prohibition consensus, and a diversification of national approaches to drug policy, Member States were faced with a question of where to take the system. Instead of a systemic rethink or comprehensive strategic shift, a clear process of policy widening and interpretive flexibility was chosen and the system continued on. The survival of the system, as with previous and repeated periods of dissensus and disagreement, showed a continued functionalist logic around managing the cross-border flows of 'dangerous drugs' and preventing regulatory arbitrage by organised criminal actors. In other words, the increasing widening and diversification of domestic drug policy among States appeared to drive re-integration and continued evolution at the international level.

As with other areas of international legal tension and conflict, States in the drug control system have worked assiduously to square their international commitments with their domestic agendas, without prejudicing the latter. While these efforts have sometimes been rejected or criticised as shallow and hypocritical, the political outcomes remain. States have avoided conflict where possible and sought new routes towards international cooperation as a means to bridge a widening divide between the letter of international law and their own domestic policy choices. As such, we may likely see a process whereby continued consensus breakdown and recalcitrancy in the system serve simply to re-integrate it in a new and more malleable form.

Notes

1 John Collins, *Legalising the Drug Wars: A Regulatory History of UN Drug Control* (Cambridge University Press, 2021).

2 See, for example, David R Bewley-Taylor, *International Drug Control: Consensus Fractured* (Cambridge University Press, 2012).

3 Collins, *Legalising the Drug Wars* (n 1).

4 Single Convention on Narcotic Drugs, 1961 (30 March 1961) 520 UNTS 151.

5 Collins, *Legalising the Drug Wars* (n 1).

6 John Collins, 'Evaluating Trends and Stakeholders in the International Drug Control Regime Complex' (2021) 90 *International Journal of Drug Policy* 103060.; Vanda Felbab-Brown and Bradley S Porter, 'Global Consensus and Dissensus on Drug Policy', *Brookings* (4 April 2016) <www.brookings.edu/blog/order-from-chaos/2016/04/04/global-consensus-and-dissensus-on-drug-policy/> accessed 10 March 2023.

7 Collins, 'Evaluating Trends and Stakeholders in the International Drug Control Regime Complex' (n 6).

8 International Opium Convention (adopted 19 February 1925) 81 LNTS 319.

9 Convention for Limiting the Manufacture and Regulating the Distribution of Narcotic Drugs (adopted 13 July 1931) 139 LNTS 303.

10 Quoted in Collins, *Legalising the Drug Wars* (n 1) 53.

11 Convention of 1936 for the Suppression of the Illicit Traffic in Dangerous Drugs (adopted 26 June 1936) 198 LNTS 301.

12 'U.S. Remains Aloof on Narcotics Pact; Refuses to Sign "Retrograde" Convention Accepted by Other Nations at Geneva', *The New York Times* (27 June 1936).
13 John Collins, 'Breaking the Monopoly System: American Influence on the British Decision to Prohibit Opium Smoking and End Its Asian Monopolies, 1939–1945', *International History Review* 39, no. 5 (February 2017): 770–790.
14 John Collins, 'A Brief History of Cannabis and the Drug Conventions', *AJIL Unbound*, October 2020.
15 Collins, *Legalising the Drug Wars* (n 1).
16 John Collins, 'Breaking the Monopoly System: American Influence on the British Decision to Prohibit Opium Smoking and End Its Asian Monopolies, 1939–1945', 39 *International History Review* 770.
17 Collins, 'A Brief History of Cannabis and the Drug Conventions' (n 14).
18 Collins, *Legalising the Drug Wars* (n 1).
19 Ibid.
20 United Nations, 'Protocol Bringing under International Control Drugs Outside of the Scope of the 1931 Convention for Limiting the Manufacture and Regulating the Distribution of Narcotic Drugs', 1948.
21 Quoted in: Collins, *Legalising the Drug Wars* (n 1) 211.
22 Collins, *Legalising the Drug Wars* (n 1).
23 Protocol for Limiting and Regulating the Cultivation of the Poppy Plant, the Production of, International and Wholesale Trade in, and Use of Opium (23 June 1953) 456 UNTS 3.
24 William B McAllister, *Drug Diplomacy in the Twentieth Century: An International History* (New York: Routledge, 2000).
25 1971 Convention on Psychotropic Substances (21 February 1971) 1019 UNTS 14956.
26 Collins, *Legalising the Drug Wars* (n 1).
27 United Nations, *Commentary on the United Nations Convention against Illicit Traffic in Narcotic Drugs and Psychotropic Substances 1988* (United Nations, 1998).
28 UN Convention against the Illicit Traffic in Narcotic Drugs and Psychotropic Substances (20 December 1988) 1582 UNTS 95.
29 UN Office on Drugs and Crime, 'A Century of International Drug Control' (United Nations, 2008) 8.
30 Convention against the Illicit Traffic in Narcotic Drugs and Psychotropic Substances (n 28) art 3.
31 Collins, *Legalising the Drug Wars* (n 1).
32 Joanne Csete, 'Costs and Benefits of Drug-Related Health Services' in John Collins (ed.), *Ending the Drug Wars: Report of the LSE Expert Group on the Economics of Drug Policy* (LSE IDEAS, 2014).
33 Mark Shaw, 'What Could an Asymmetrical Strategy against Organised Crime Look Like? A Lesson from the Drug Policy Debate' (2019) 1 *Journal of Illicit Economies and Development* 99.
34 Joanne Csete and Peter J Grob, 'Switzerland, HIV and the Power of Pragmatism: Lessons for Drug Policy Development' (2012) 23 *International Journal of Drug Policy* 82.
35 Organization of American States, 'Scenarios for the Drug Problem in the Americas, 2013–2025' (OAS, 2012).
36 Martin Jelsma and David Bewley-Taylor, 'UNGASS 2016: A Broken or B-r-o-a-d Consensus?', *Transnational Institute* (5 July 2016) <www.tni.org/en/publication/ungass-2016-a-broken-or-b-r-o-a-d-consensus> accessed 10 March 2023.
37 William R Brownfield, 'Trends in Global Drug Policy' (9 October 2014) <http://fpc.state.gov/232813.htm> accessed 10 March 2023.

38 John Collins, 'The State Department's Move to a More Flexible Diplomatic Policy on Drugs Is a Rational Approach to a Difficult Question', *LSE Blog* (1 December 2014) <http://blogs.lse.ac.uk/usappblog/2014/12/01/the-u-s-new-more-flexible-diplomatic-doctrine-on-drugs-is-a-rational-approach-to-a-difficult-question/> accessed 10 March 2023.

39 Collins, 'Evaluating Trends and Stakeholders in the International Drug Control Regime Complex' (n 6).

40 Ibid.

41 International Law Commission, 'Fragmentation of International Law: Difficulties Arising from the Diversification and Expansion of International Law – Report of the Study Group of the International Law Commission' (13 April 2006) UN Doc No A/CN.4/L.682, 208, para 414 (Fragmentation Report).

42 See, for example, Richard Lines, *Human Rights and Drug Control in International Law* (Cambridge University Press, 2017).

43 International Law Commission (n 41) 10, para 7.

44 Lines (n 42).

45 Tamar Megiddo, 'Beyond Fragmentation: On International Law's Integrationist Forces' (2019) 44 *Yale Journal of International Law* 115, 116.

46 Ibid, 116.

47 Megiddo (n 45) 116.

48 Megiddo (n 45) 116.

49 Damon Barrett, 'Refections on Human Rights and International Drug Control' in John Collins (ed.), *Governing the Global Drug Wars* (LSE, 2012).; Lines (n 42).

50 M L Dispanadda Diskul, John Collins & Daniel Brombacher, 'Drugs and Development in the Urban Setting – Expanding Development-Oriented Interventions beyond Illicit Drug Crop Cultivation' (2021) 2 *Journal of Illicit Economies and Development* 80.; Daniel Brombacher and Sarah David, 'From Alternative Development to Development-Oriented Drug Policies' in Julia Buxton, Mary Chinery-Hesse & Khalid Tinasti (eds.), *Drug Policies and Development* (Brill, 2020).

51 John Collins and Karen Torres Alarcón, 'Colombia, the Drug Wars and the Politics of Drug Policy Displacement – from La Violencia to UNGASS 2016' (2021) 3 *Journal of Illicit Economies and Development* 190.

52 See Chapter 3, 'Debunking the Three Myths about Reforming Asian Drug Policies'.

13 The Last Drug Warrior in the West

UK Drug Policy and Shifting Material Interests from the Nineteenth to the Twenty-First Century

Kojo Koram

Introduction

While drug policy over the course of the twentieth and early twenty-first century has often been discussed as primarily a purely moral issue, it has always been also tied to concrete material interests. The trajectory that the United Kingdom has plotted through the drugs market over the past few centuries speaks to this fact perhaps better than anywhere else. The arch of British drug policy has paralleled its transition from a globe-spanning empire with healthy drug production monopolies in multiple colonies to a territorial bound and bordered island nation. In this essay I will trace the British government's shifting relationship to the concept of international drug prohibition and explore what might be the future of drug policy in this one-time global hegemon as it faces down the prospect of transformative constitutional restructuring. In doing so, I will show how drug policy reform connects to underlying political and economic interests that shift over the course of history, not just in Britain but across the world.

'Drugs' Are Not Natural

In the contemporary moment, we have been educated to assume that the approach to a set of psychoactive substances that we have come to call 'drugs' – including opium, cocaine and cannabis derivates – is so rational as to almost be natural. The historical contingency of the recent global campaign to prohibit and eradicate the use and trade of drugs is masked by how all-encompassing it has been. It projects today's attitudes towards intoxicating substances into the past and pretends they have always been the norm. Yet the works of Derrida, Baudrillard and Taussig have all gone to great lengths to illustrate how 'drugs' do not exist in nature but are instead discursively produced through an historically specific human (mis)relation with particular psychoactive substances that emerged over the course of the late nineteenth-century and the early- to mid-twentieth century. As Derrida argues,

> There are no drugs 'in nature'. There may be natural poisons and indeed naturally lethal poisons, but they are not as such 'drugs'. As with addiction, the

DOI: 10.4324/9781003169765-19

> concept of drugs supposes an instituted and institutional definition: a history is required and a culture, conventions, evaluations, norms, an entire network of intertwined discourses.[1]

The historian Roy Porter reiterates the recency of the discursive production of our contemporary notion of drugs by reminding us that

> If you'd talked about the 'drugs problem' two hundred years ago, no one would have known what you meant. There was no notion then of 'drugs', in the sense of a small group of substances scientifically believed to be harmful because addictive or personality destroying…The term 'drugs' as a shorthand for a bunch of assorted narcotics is in fact a twentieth-century coinage.[2]

Prior to the emergence of prohibition, intoxication was glamourised within certain European artistic and literary circles, as seen in the works of Samuel Coleridge, Thomas De Quincey and Charles Baudelaire.[3] The attraction of drug use in this era was perhaps best captured by Thomas De Quincey's 1822 memoir *Confessions of an English Opium Eater*, which popularised an image of privileged drug dependence.[4] It should be remembered that drugs like opium, cannabis and cocaine did not spread through the world by happenstance, and many regionally popular psychoactive substances that British imperialists encountered – popular traditional drugs such as qat, peyote or kava – never became global commodities in the way the drugs now referred to in drug policy studies as 'the big three' did.[5] This is because there was a concerted effort by British imperialists to cultivate the supply of the 'big three' substances – particularly opium – due to their popularity with British consumers.

Paralleling the increasing supply was a growing demand for such intoxicants within the British market. David Courtwright credits the increased demand for drugs like opium to the growing ability for the wealth of places like Britain to satisfy the basic needs of its population, leaving them free to give increasing focus to matters of pleasure and adventure. Courtwright explains that 'drug commerce […] flourished in a world in which the hungry psyche was replacing the hungry belly'.[6] This was particularly true for the bourgeois class of British society, who, with new-found wealth and a detachment from the narrow behavioural norms of old aristocratic society, encouraged experimentation with new substances and states of mind. In addition to being something to spend their new-found wealth on, drugs were also a great source of wealth for British imperialists.

The Imperial Drugs Trade

In Britain in the 18th and 19th centuries, substances such as opium and cocaine were sources of great wealth for the companies that were driving the expansion of Britain into the largest empire the world has ever known, in terms of territory, population and wealth. As Courtwright identifies 'European expansion in the sixteenth, seventeenth, and eighteenth centuries turned psychoactive drugs, including spirituous alcohol and tobacco, into global products'.[7] Companies that are now mainstays of mainstream capitalism such as the P&O Shipping Company (now P&O ferries), the Hong Kong and Shanghai Banking Corporation (HSBC) and Jardine, Matheson & Co (Jardine Matheson Holdings) built up their initial wealth through profiting from the opium trade.

The apex of Britain's imperial drugs trade probably arrived with the opium wars of 1839–1842 and 1856–1860, when Britain was actually fighting against the prohibition of drugs. Despite having been able to extend its imperial authority over much of Asia, the British Empire entered the nineteenth century still being thwarted by the Qing Dynasty of China. China was then considered the wealthiest kingdom in the world, home to luxury products like tea, silk and porcelain. Britain was locked into a trade deficit with China as the extensive demand for Chinese tea in Britain was not counterbalanced with an equivalent demand for British goods from a highly protectionist and insular China. The largest of Britain's colonial company-States, the East India Company, was carrying these losses as the British government had granted it a colonial monopoly on trade with China. Therefore, it was imperative that the company found a product that would cultivate mass demand in China. The product would prove to be the opium that the East India Company was already producing in industrial quantities in the Bengal region of India.

When the Chinese emperor prohibited the trade of opium in his territory in order to protect against incursions by British colonial companies, the British government declared war in order to protect the interests of this opium traders, sending a Royal Navy fleet to engage in gunboat diplomacy in order to force China to open its borders to the opium trade. The opium wars involved world-changing events such as the burning of the Summer Palace, the signing of the Treaty of Nanking and the transfer of Hong Kong into the hands of British sovereignty. Furthermore, it extended the commercial colonial drugs trade to its point of greatest relevance, adding the Chinese opium trade to cannabis cultivation farms in its colonies of India and Jamaica and coca leaf cultivation in Sri Lanka and British Guyana.[8]

The commercialised drugs trade and the taxes accrued from it were a fiscal cornerstone for the European empires,[9] and the material benefits to Britain influenced the moral position these drugs occupied within the broader national consciousness. In the late nineteenth century, the profits the British Empire and its imperial rivals acquired from the international trade in drugs overrode any concerns regarding the morality of their use. As late as 1895, the British government published a report by the Royal Commission on Opium, which had been tasked with investigating opium and potential problems from its use and trade, which concluded that there was 'no evidences of extensive moral or physical degradation' resulting from the use of opium in its colonial jewel of India.[10]

While there was a rise in evangelical Christian temperance movements in Britain over the course of the nineteenth century, which advocated against the use of not just alcohol but also intoxicants such as opium, the mainstream perspective, especially within the corridors of power, was that these drugs were simply commodities that could be mined from the colonies and traded for profit. Contrasting with the way prohibition would be understood in the twentieth-century drug war, nineteenth-century English liberalism 'had no difficulty construing the Opium Wars as a crusade for free trade and for liberty', suggesting that the moral imperative lay with those who wanted to trade the drug while the prohibitionists were characterised as an instance of an uncivilised violation of free capitalist exchange.[11]

In his seminal text unpacking liberalism as a political philosophy, *On Liberty*, canonical English political theorist John Stuart Mill critiques the idea of China attempting to legally prohibit the trade of opium into their country for being 'interferences [that] are objectionable, not as infringements on the liberty of the producer or seller, but on that of the buyer'.[12] Mill's position on opium would be the argument that one would presume if taking liberalism's claims at face value, as it claims to protect the individual liberty to engage in activities that do not harm any members of the community other than one's own self. However, the rise of American liberalism coming to supersede British liberalism as the hegemonic political system of the early decades of the twentieth century, and the greater influence of evangelical puritanism within the American political tradition, facilitated a retreat from the classical liberal presumption of freedom of the drugs trade towards a new era of drug prohibition.

The Winds of Change

Drug prohibition has been described as the 'first significant foray by the United States onto the stage of global diplomacy' pre-figuring, and in many ways providing the template for, the American vision of internationalism that it would promote over the rest of the 'American Century'.[13] With the United States driving the first international drug control initiatives, the Shanghai Opium Commission in 1909 and the *International Opium Convention* of 1912[14] (the first multilateral legal treaty prohibiting drugs), Britain and its imperial drug monopolies needed to adjust to a new geopolitical reality. The development of international drug prohibition was partly stunted during the interwar years by the fractured nature of the League of Nations. Despite the League putting in place many of the building blocks the international drug control machinery, the fact that the United States as the driving nation failed to become a member because of its own internal divisions weakened the effectiveness of these actions.

A number of new drug control treaties were adopted through the League of Nations, but none had the comprehensive authority required to enforce international drug prohibition. The establishment of the United Nations following the Second World War provided prohibitionists with the ideal forum through which far-reaching legislation on drugs could be produced. The treaties that had been established through the League had been limited in their effectiveness, meaning American prohibitionists would require a more ambitious legislative framework if the United Nations was to succeed where the League failed. The first major drug treaty to be adopted during this new period of the American leadership was the '1953 Opium Protocol'.[15] The Opium Protocol Conference met in May 1953 in New York. The US location (rather than Geneva) only amplified the influence that US representative Harry Anslinger, as the President of the Conference, and his 'inner circle' of hard-line prohibitionists enjoyed over the process. In the face of opposition – even from some of America's major international allies – the draconian negotiating attitude taken up by 'the inner circle' at this conference ensured that 'the 1953 Opium Protocol contained the most stringent drug-control provisions yet embodied in international law'.[16] Its provisions extended the import and export controls from opium trade to opium poppy cultivation, a development that was a breakthrough for the American prohibitionists, who had been agitating for cultivation limitations in previous agreements.[17] The 1953 Opium Protocol was taken as a personal victory for Anslinger.[18]

However, the aggressive restrictions driven into the treaty by Anslinger and his acolytes alienated other major allies, particularly the United Kingdom.[19] Britain still benefited from its imperial drug monopolies in the mid-twentieth century and recognised the impact the controls might have upon them. Britain used its fading geopolitical weight to lobby against the 1953 Opium Protocol and ensure that this aggressive treaty of drug prohibition would be killed in its crib. As a result, although the 1953 Opium Protocol was adopted, it did not receive a sufficient number of ratifications to come into force for the remainder of the decade. Traditional imperial powers Britain and the Netherlands, both with large drug trades, would not ratify the treaty, claiming its provisions were overly draconian and infringed on sovereignty.[20]

However, the territorial scope of Britain was going through a drastic shift at the same time as these arguments over drug prohibition were playing out. It was in 1960, when British Prime Minister Harold Macmillan gave the 'Winds of Change' speech that is now widely taken as the moment where the British government finally accepted the inevitability of the decolonisation of its once grand empire. In the speech, Macmillan announced that 'the wind of change is blowing right through Africa. This rapid emergence of the countries of Africa gives the continent a new importance in the world'.[21] While the 1960s in Britain is often associated with swinging London, once we expand the lens to encompass the entirety of Britain's territorial terrain, the 1960s could be better understood as the decade of decolonisation. From Nigeria in 1960, to Jamaica in 1962, to Kenya in 1963 to Malta, Malawi and Rwanda in 1964, the 1960s saw the redrawing of the map of Britain as little red marks left the empire one by one. The winds of change would blow apart much of the rest of the empire in a few short years, and 1960s began with Britain's closet ally, the United States, openly saying that 'Great Britain has lost an empire and has not yet found a role'.[22]

Britain was in a drastically different geopolitical position to the one it had been at the start of the twentieth century when the long, antagonistic drafting process for the *United Nations Single Convention on Narcotic Drugs*, still the bedrock of the global system of drug prohibition, came to its conclusion in 1961. Drug policy historian John Collins has stressed the importance of a struggle between Britain and the United States in informing the orientation of post-war drug prohibition. For Collins, it is the interplay between the emerging hegemony of America and the declining hegemony of the British Empire with 'the US favouring immediate and strict prohibition and the UK favouring incrementalism and various forms of regulation, [that] would determine not just their own relationship, but also the shape of the international drug control system going forward'.[23]

Collins's studies lend themselves to the argument that, once the chaos of war and the growth of decolonisation had disrupted Britain's connections to her imperial drug monopolies, it was more amenable to taking a role supporting its main ally in cohering various global interests into a consensus around prohibition, 'deploying a mixture of sticks and carrots, which only a joint Anglo-American effort could effectively wield'.[24] While accepting that US prohibitionists, led by Anslinger, initially drove this partnership, Collins reads the British response as ultimately determining the ground for the international drug laws. After helping to drive the hostility and ultimate failure of the 1953 Opium Protocol, Britain's much more conciliatory approach to the Single Convention helped to get this first major building block of the current international system of universal drug prohibition over the line. With the architecture of the new international prohibitionist mechanism falling heaviest upon countries where the organic raw materials of drugs like opium and cannabis were being produced, the transition of a number of these countries from being colonial dependencies of the British Empire to being independent sovereign territories in their own right may have helped encourage the growing openness of United Kingdom to international legislation.

The Single Convention requires States Parties to enact domestic legislation in order to give its provisions necessary effect. In the United Kingdom, the obligations of the Single Convention were realised through the *Misuse of Drugs Act 1971*,[25] which classified and criminalised drugs in a manner similar to the Single Convention. Prior to the *Misuse of Drugs Act*, the United Kingdom had a relatively loose collection controls against psychoactive substances entrenched within actual legislation. However, the changing international climate invited a changing domestic legislative approach.

The *Misuse of Drugs Act* was drafted during the same era as a wave new immigration legislation was passed through Parliament, redrawing the boundaries of British citizenship. Prior to this era of new citizenship legislation, subjects of the Crown from the colonies and from the metropole were not formally defined within different citizenship categories. A subject of the Crown from Jamaica was legally as British as a subject of the Crown from Leeds, and Britain drew heavily on this global collection of imperial subjects to win both World Wars, with soldiers from Kenya to South Africa and airmen from Canada to the West Indies, all coming to the motherland's aid. The Windrush generation of post-war 'immigrants' from the colonies was only possible because these imperial subjects already possessed the same citizenship status as the rest of Britain, resulting in them not needing entrance papers, a factor in the 'Windrush scandal' that would strike 70 years later.[26]

However, with decolonisation being forced upon Britain after the Second World War, successive governments made the restructure of Britain's citizenship categories a priority, changing the geographic and racial component of what it meant to be British. In 1962, the *Commonwealth Immigration Act* was passed, bringing to an end the automatic right of people from the British colonies and commonwealth to settle in the United Kingdom.[27] Though this piece of legislation now rendered all commonwealth citizens subject to possible immigration control, the main targets for these controls were not the white colonial subjects coming from Canada or Rhodesia. Conservative Home Secretary Rab Butler is reported to have said at the time that the Act's 'great merit' was that it looked like it would apply to all parts of the commonwealth when in practice, its 'restrictive effect is intended to, and would in fact, operate on coloured people almost exclusively'.[28] In 1968, the Labour Party continued the trend of excluding colonial subjects from access to Britain by updating the 1962 Act with the *Commonwealth Immigrants Act 1968*, which tightened controls further in fear of tens of thousands of Kenyan Asians moving to Britain.[29] Finally, in the same year that the *Misuse of Drugs Act* was passed, the *1971 Immigration Act* created the new citizenship concept of the 'right to abode', the right to enter and live in the United Kingdom.[30] This 'right to abode' made access dependent on the ability to prove 'British ancestry', greatly advantaging white British subjects from both the mainland and the colonies who would be more likely to have had a parent or grandparent born in Britain.[31]

The Last Drug Warrior in the West

In its new mode of a territorially bounded, nationally restrictive island State, the once-expansive Great Britain is now one of the Western countries most tightly wedded to an international drug prohibition regime to which it was so resistant to in the days of empire. In 2021, the *Misuse of Drugs Act* marked its 50th anniversary and the UK government celebrated by announcing a new drug strategy that doubles down on the prohibitionist, draconian language it finally adopted half a century earlier. But while the *Misuse of Drugs Act* was in alignment with the shifting international context of its age, by its 50th anniversary the United Kingdom's continuing attachment to a 'War on Drugs' rhetoric looks increasingly out of step with the rest of the Western world.

Laws are now changing with incredible speed. In December 2013, Uruguay became the first nation since the passing of the Single Convention to legalise the production, distribution and possession of recreational cannabis. Canada followed with full national cannabis legalisation in 2018. A host of states in the United States, from California to Alaska to Colorado to New York, have legalised the recreational trade in cannabis over the past decade. In 2021, Malta, Luxembourg and Germany announced plans to legalise cannabis. In recent years, we have also seen the decriminalisation of possession for personal use of all drugs in Portugal and the US state of Oregon, meaning that personal possession of cocaine, heroin and other drugs prohibited by the Single Convention is no longer a crime in these states. Meanwhile, successive British governments remain highly resistant to any form of substantive drug policy reform.

Despite governmental intransigence, the British public is increasingly aware of the failure of the country's prohibitionist policies, and we are hearing calls for the need of a drug policy overhaul from an array of political perspectives. Prior to the new German government agreement to implement drug policy reform, only 34% of German citizens were supportive of the legalisation of cannabis.[32] By contrast, the UK already has considerably higher support for cannabis legalisation. A 2021 poll that showed that 52% of adults support the complete legalisation of all forms of cannabis use, with only 32% opposing.[33]

Leaving aside the issue of legalisation, the British government has shown itself even unwilling to support less far-reaching drug policy and harm reduction reforms. The 50th anniversary of the *Misuse of Drugs Act* came in the midst of an explosion in drug-related deaths across the United Kingdom, a trend that was particularly acute in Scotland, where the United Kingdom's northernmost country was christened the 'drug death capital of the world'.[34] The ability to address this issue is complicated by the bizarre constitutional set-up of the British State, a part nation state, part transnational trade agreement, part zombified corpse of imperial bureaucracy. While the devolved government of Scotland wished to open safe drug consumption rooms to help address the crisis, this effort was derailed by the UK government in Westminster.

In 1998, partly in a bid to halt the growing calls from Scotland for independence, the UK government agreed to the comprised constitutional arrangement of devolved government for Scotland, Wales and Northern Ireland. Through devolution, Scotland gained its own parliament at Holyrood in Edinburgh that would take responsibility for a number of domestic affairs away from the central UK Parliament. The Scottish government enjoys the power to legislative over issues like agriculture, healthcare, education policy and alcohol licensing. However, powers over drug policy are not devolved and remain the preserve of the old imperial 'mother of parliaments' at Westminster. In early 2022, the Scottish Parliament voted to recognise 'that safer consumption facilities are an important public health measure' and committed to exploring how these facilities could be delivered to the drug users of Scotland.[35] A confrontation between Holyrood and Westminster over drug policy now appears inevitable, with this conflict likely to spill over into a wider debate over the constitutional structure of a union that is now devoid of the empire that anchored it together in the first place.

Over the course of this article, I have sought to illustrate how drug policy can reflect shifting material and political interests rather than the purely moralistic or scientific language it is often couched within, by tracing the changing drug policy of the United Kingdom alongside its geographic transformation from an expanding empire to an insular nation state. The past century has seen huge shifts in Britain's approach to the transnational trade of drugs. Our understanding of drugs is not produced by nature but is dependent on contingent historical, political or financial interests. Understanding this perhaps opens a door towards understanding the contemporary deep resistance of Westminster towards exploring the type of progressive drug policies that are being explored in other jurisdictions at the current moment and that are likely to increase in future.

At the moment, Westminster's priority is to maintain a fragmenting union, and 'War on Drugs' rhetoric can be useful for unifying a divided nation against a symbolic enemy, in addition providing a weakening State with further draconian powers to demand compliance.[36] With the imperial drug monopolies now a memory, perhaps Westminster sees allowing drug policy reform across any of the four nations would take away its authority while providing it with little gain in return. If the United Kingdom were to embrace progressive drug policy reform in future, it is likely to coincide with a substantial reframing of the UK State to finally exercise the post-imperial anxieties of fragmentation with drug policy reformers having to convince politicians that it is in their moral, as well as religious interests to let go the prohibitionist 'War on Drugs' approach.

Notes

1 Ibid.
2 Roy Porter, 'The History of the "Drugs Problem"' (1996) 24 *Criminal Justice Matters* 3, 3.
3 For artistic engagements with opium use see Thomas De Quincey, *Confessions of an English Opium-Eater* (Penguin Classics, 2003).; Samuel Taylor Coleridge, 'Kubla Khan; or, A Vision in a Dream: A Fragment' in *The Complete Poems of Samuel Taylor Coleridge* (Penguin Classics, 1997).; Charles Baudelaire, *Artificial Paradises (Les Paradis Artificiels)* (Kensington Publishing, 1998). For further reading on this trend, see Alethea Hayter, *Opium and the Romantic Imagination* (Faber and Faber, 2009).
4 De Quincey (n 4) 3. 'The Immediate Occasion of This Practice Was the Lowness of Wages, Which at That Time Would Not Allow Them to Indulge in Ale or Spirits, and Wages Rising, It May Be Thought That This Practice Would Cease'.
5 David T Courtwright, *Forces of Habit: Drugs and the Making of the Modern World* (Harvard University Press, 2002) 3.
6 Ibid., p.4.
7 David T Courtwright, 'A Short History of Drug Policy or Why We Make War on Some Drugs but Not on Others' in John Collins (ed.), *Governing the Global Drug Wars* (LSE, 2012).
8 See Richard J Grace, *Opium and Empire: The Lives and Careers of William Jardine and James Matheson* (McGill-Queen's University Press, 2014).
9 Courtwright (n 6) 5.
10 *Final Report of the Royal Commission on Opium Great Britain* (1895) Sessional Papers of the House of Commons, XLII, 124.
11 Domenico Losurdo, *Liberalism: A Counter-History*, trans Gregory Elliott (Verso, 2011) 151.
12 John Stuart Mill, *On Liberty and The Subjection of Women* (Penguin Classics, 2006) 125.
13 Julia Buxton, 'The Historical Foundations of Narcotics Control' in Philip Keefer and Norman Loayza (eds.), *Innocent Bystanders: Developing Countries and the War on Drugs* (Palgrave Macmillan, 2010) 62.
14 International Opium Convention (signed 23 January 1912) 1922 LNTS 189.
15 Protocol for Limiting and Regulating the Cultivation of the Poppy Plant, the Production of International and Wholesale Trade in, and use of Opium (23 June 1953).
16 William McAllister, *Drug Diplomacy in the Twentieth Century* (Routledge, 2000) 204–209.
17 Julia Buxton, *The Political Economy of Narcotics: Production, Consumption and Global Markets* (Zed Books, 2006) 55.
18 McAllister (n 17).
19 John Collins, *Legalizing the Drug Wars: A Regulatory History of UN Drug Control* (Cambridge, 2021).

20 McAllister (n 17).
21 Colin Baker, "Macmillan's 'Wind of Change' Tour, 1960" (1998) 38/1 *South African Historical Journal* 171, 181.
22 Dean Acheson, former United States Secretary of State, 'Britain's Role in the World', *The Guardian* (6 December 1962).
23 John Collins, *Regulations and Prohibitions: Anglo-American Relations and International Drug Control, 1939–1964* (PhD dissertation, London School of Economics, 2015) 75.
24 Ibid, 160.
25 Misuse of Drugs Act, 1971.
26 For more on the Windrush Scandal, read Amelia Gentleman, *The Windrush Betrayal: Exposing the Hostile Environment* (Faber, 2019).
27 *Commonwealth Immigrants Act, 1962,* 10 & 11 Eliz. 2. c. 21.
28 David Olusoga, 'Windrush: Archived Documents Show the Long Betrayal', *The Guardian* (16 June 2019).
29 *Commonwealth Immigrants Act 1968,* c. 9.
30 1971 Immigration Act, c. 77.
31 Nadine El-Enany, *(B)ordering Britain: Race, Law and Empire* (Manchester University Press, 2020).
32 'Two Thirds of Germans are against Cannabis Legalization, Survey Shows', *The Local* (13 November 2017).
33 YouGov, 'Generally Speaking, to What Extent Would You Support or Oppose the Legalisation of Cannabis in the UK?' (6 April 2021) <https://yougov.co.uk/topics/politics/survey-results/daily/2021/04/06/fcf4a/3?utm_source=twitter&utm_medium=daily_questions&utm_campaign=question_3> accessed 8 June 2022.
34 Martin Powell, 'Scotland Is Drug Death Capital of the World, Here's How We Can Shed That Title', *The National* (15 December 2020).
35 Emer M O'Toole, 'MSPs Vote to Explore How Safe Drug Consumption Rooms Can Be Established', *The National* (13 January 2022).
36 See Nils Christie and Kettill Bruun, *Den Gode Fiende: Narkotikapolitikk i Norden* (Universitets-forlaget, 1985).

Index

Note: Endnotes are indicated by the page number followed by "n" and the note number e.g., 122n31 refers to note 31 on page 122.

Made in the USA
Columbia, SC
19 June 2024

30e4fcc8-3c45-4b06-9fc4-82e7f36168bcR02